Garfield
SOUPED UP

BY JIM DAVIS

Ballantine Books Trade Paperbacks • New York

A Ballantine Books Trade Paperback Original

Copyright © 2014 by PAWS, Inc. All Rights Reserved.
"GARFIELD" and the GARFIELD characters are trademarks of PAWS, Inc.

Published in the United States by Ballantine Books, an imprint of The Random House Publishing Group,
a division of Random House LLC, a Penguin Random House Company, New York.

BALLANTINE and colophon are registered trademarks of Random House LLC.

ISBN 978-0-345-52598-7
eBook ISBN 978-0-345-54563-3

Printed in the United States of America

www.ballantinebooks.com

9 8 7 6 5 4 3 2 1

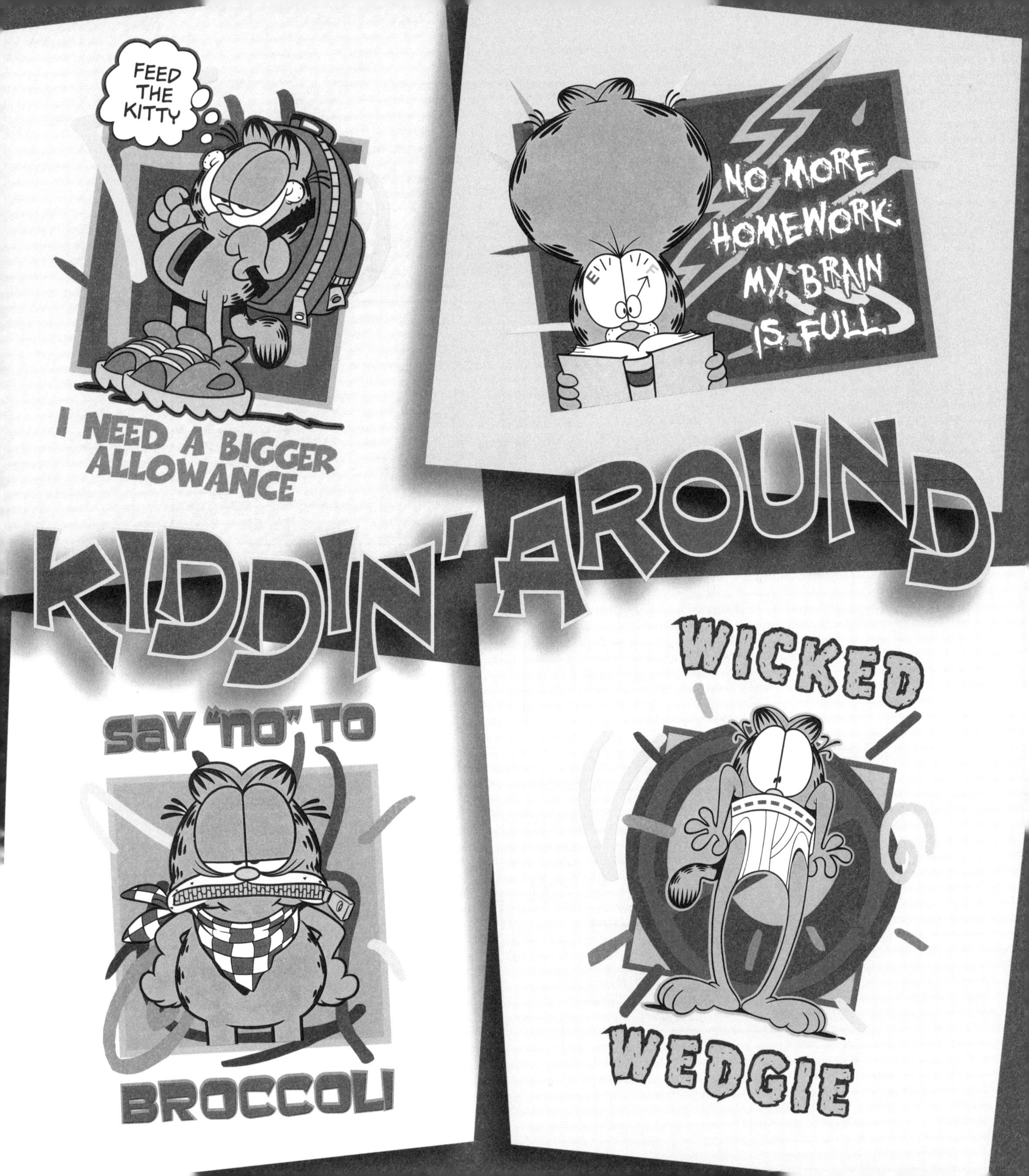
KIDDIN' AROUND
FEED THE KITTY
I NEED A BIGGER ALLOWANCE
NO MORE HOMEWORK. MY BRAIN IS FULL.
E
F
say "no" TO
BROCCOLI
WICKED
WEDGIE

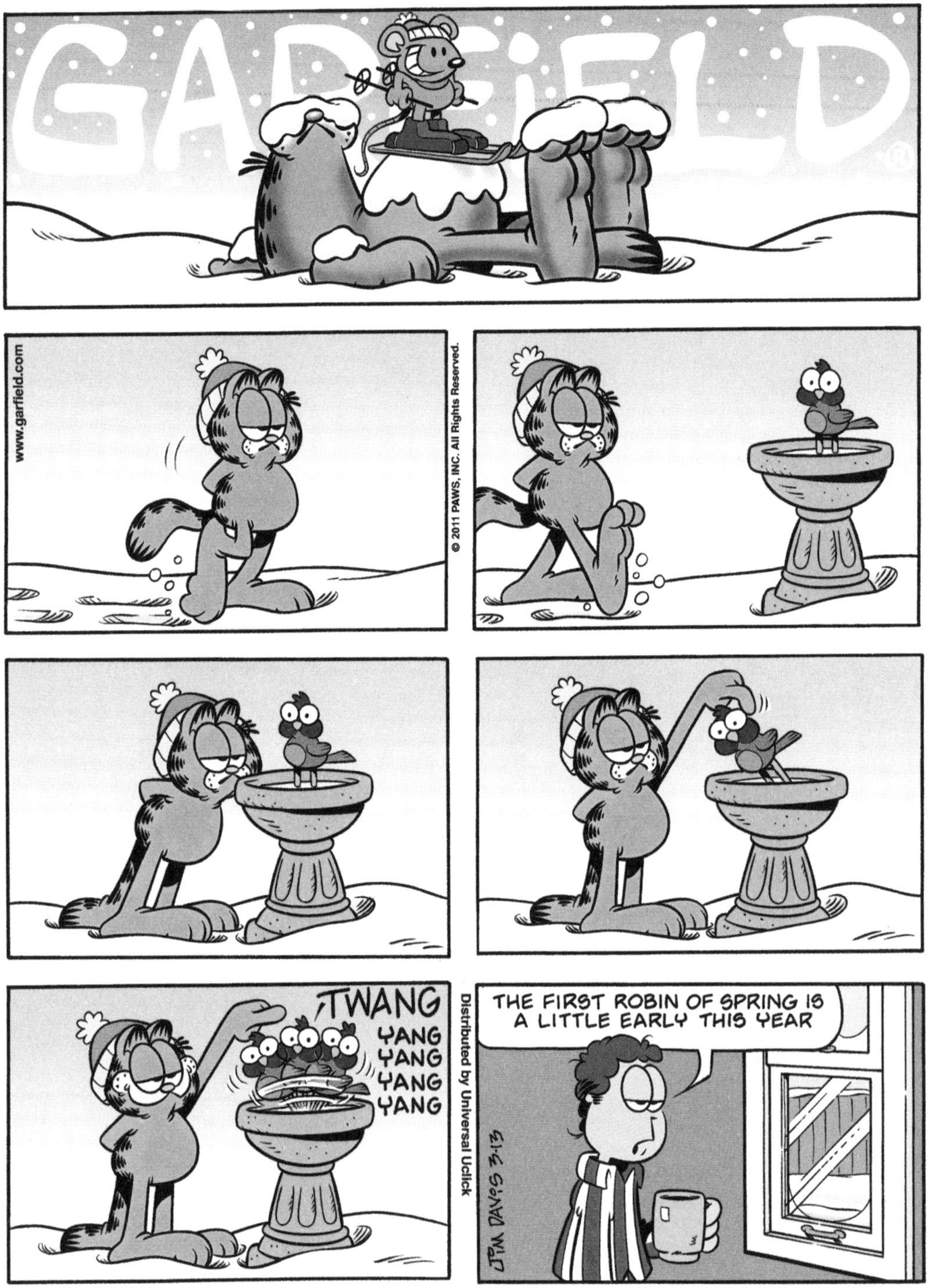
GARFIELD
www.garfield.com
© 2011 PAWS, INC. All Rights Reserved.
TWANG
YANG
YANG
YANG
YANG
Distributed by Universal Uclick
JPM DAVPS 3-13
THE FIRST ROBIN OF SPRING IS A LITTLE EARLY THIS YEAR

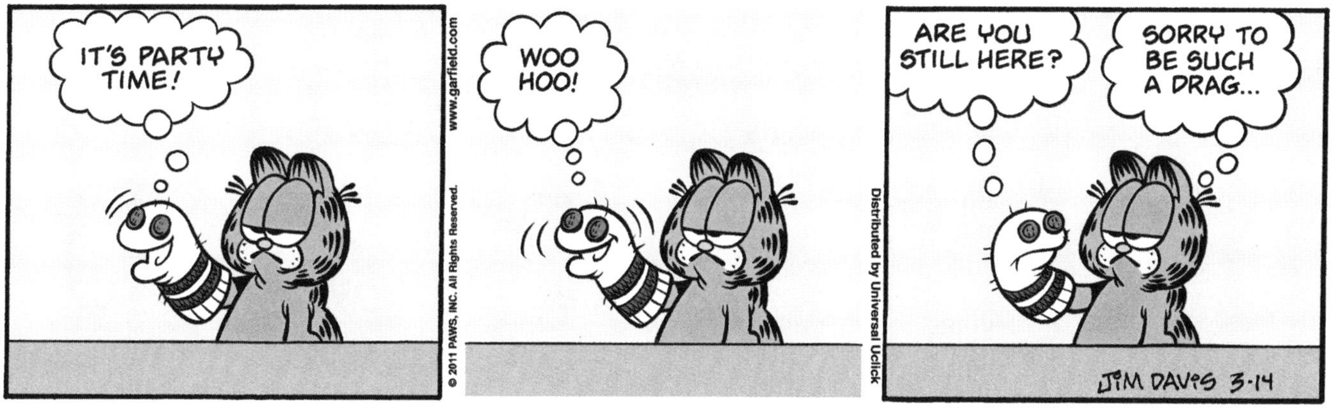
IT'S PARTY TIME!
© 2011 PAWS, INC. All Rights Reserved. www.garfield.com
WOO HOO!
Distributed by Universal Uclick
ARE YOU STILL HERE?
SORRY TO BE SUCH A DRAG...
JIM DAVIS 3-14

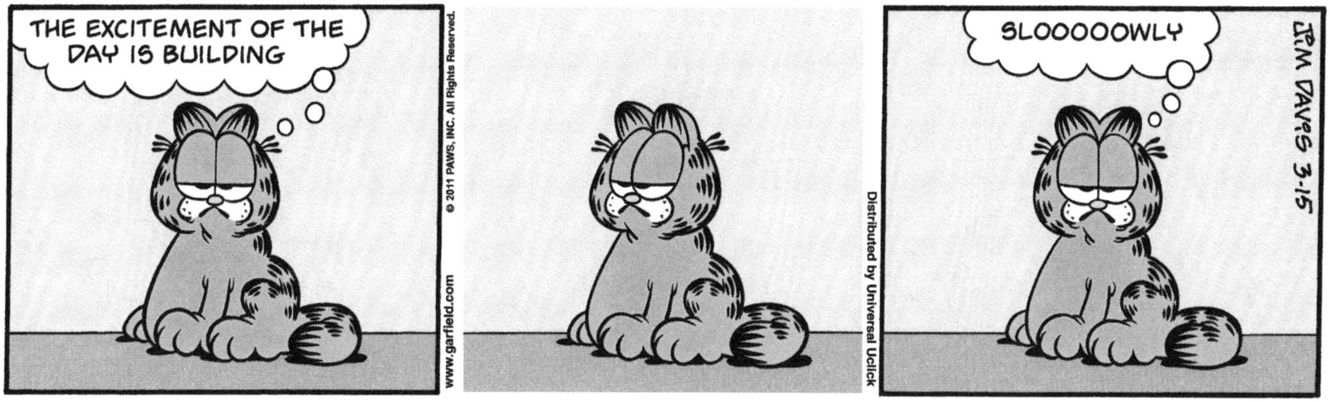
THE EXCITEMENT OF THE DAY IS BUILDING
© 2011 PAWS, INC. All Rights Reserved. www.garfield.com
Distributed by Universal Uclick
SLOOOOOWLY
JIM DAVIS 3-15

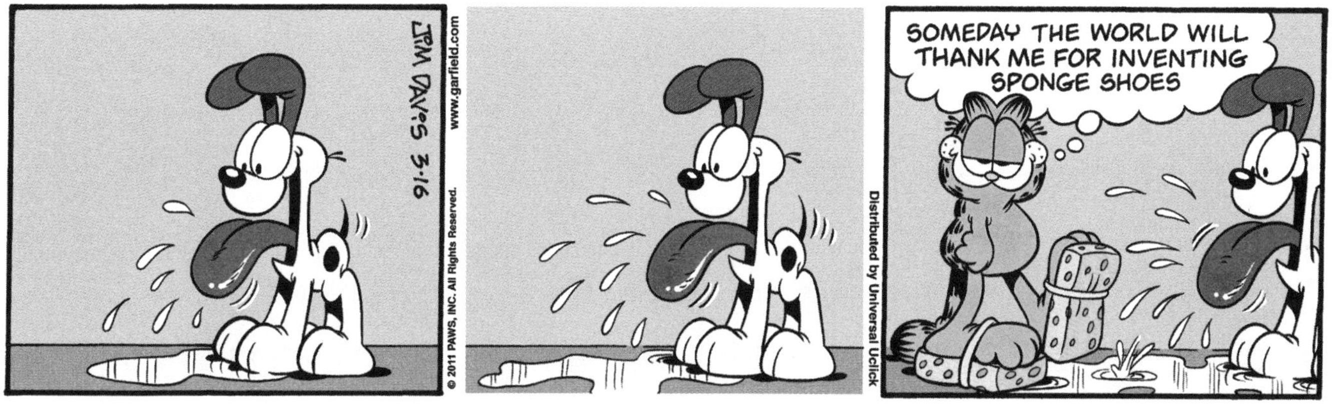
JIM DAVIS 3-16
© 2011 PAWS, INC. All Rights Reserved. www.garfield.com
Distributed by Universal Uclick
SOMEDAY THE WORLD WILL THANK ME FOR INVENTING SPONGE SHOES

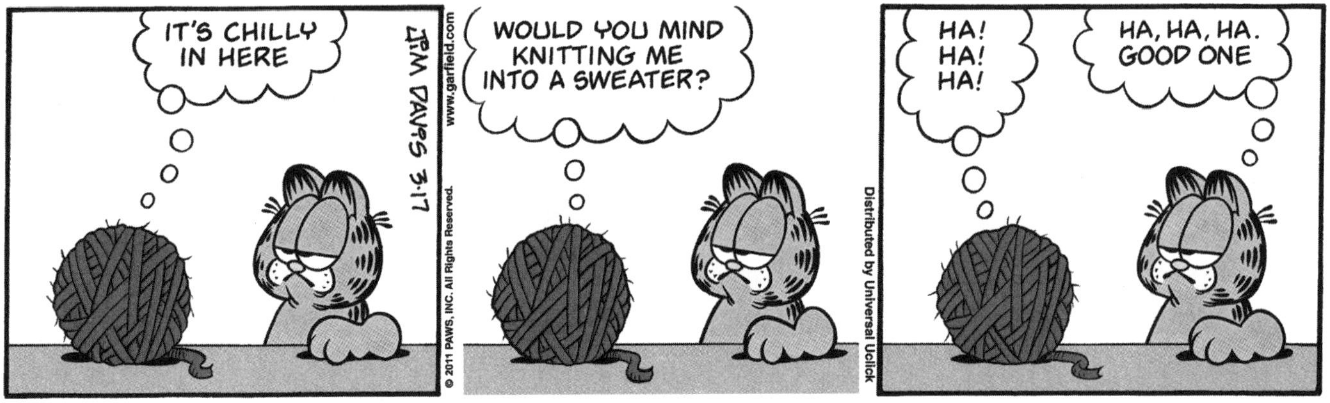
IT'S CHILLY IN HERE
JIM DAVIS 3-17
WOULD YOU MIND KNITTING ME INTO A SWEATER?
HA! HA! HA!
HA, HA, HA. GOOD ONE
© 2011 PAWS, INC. All Rights Reserved. www.garfield.com
Distributed by Universal Uclick

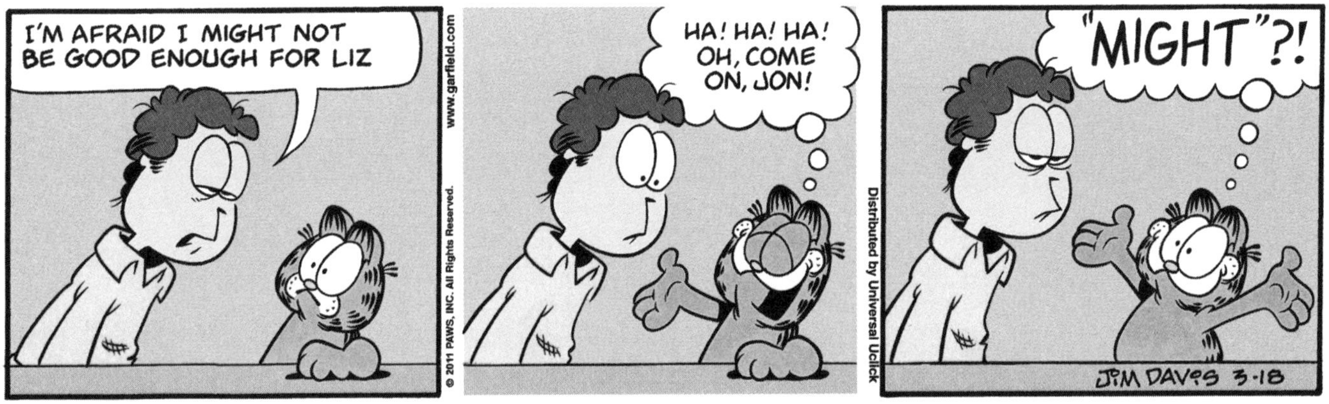
I'M AFRAID I MIGHT NOT BE GOOD ENOUGH FOR LIZ
HA! HA! HA! OH, COME ON, JON!
"MIGHT"?!
JIM DAVIS 3-18
© 2011 PAWS, INC. All Rights Reserved. www.garfield.com
Distributed by Universal Uclick

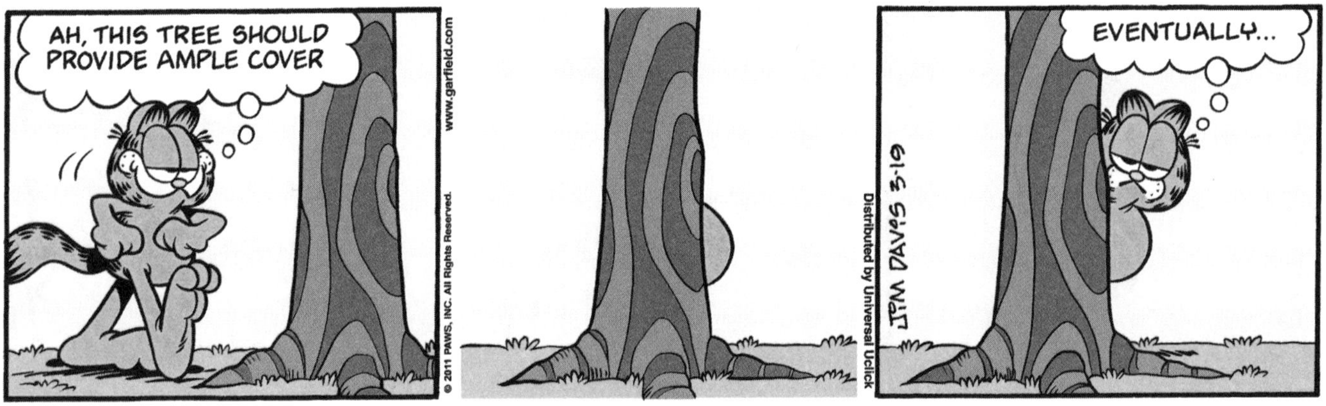
AH, THIS TREE SHOULD PROVIDE AMPLE COVER
EVENTUALLY...
JIM DAVIS 3-19
© 2011 PAWS, INC. All Rights Reserved. www.garfield.com
Distributed by Universal Uclick

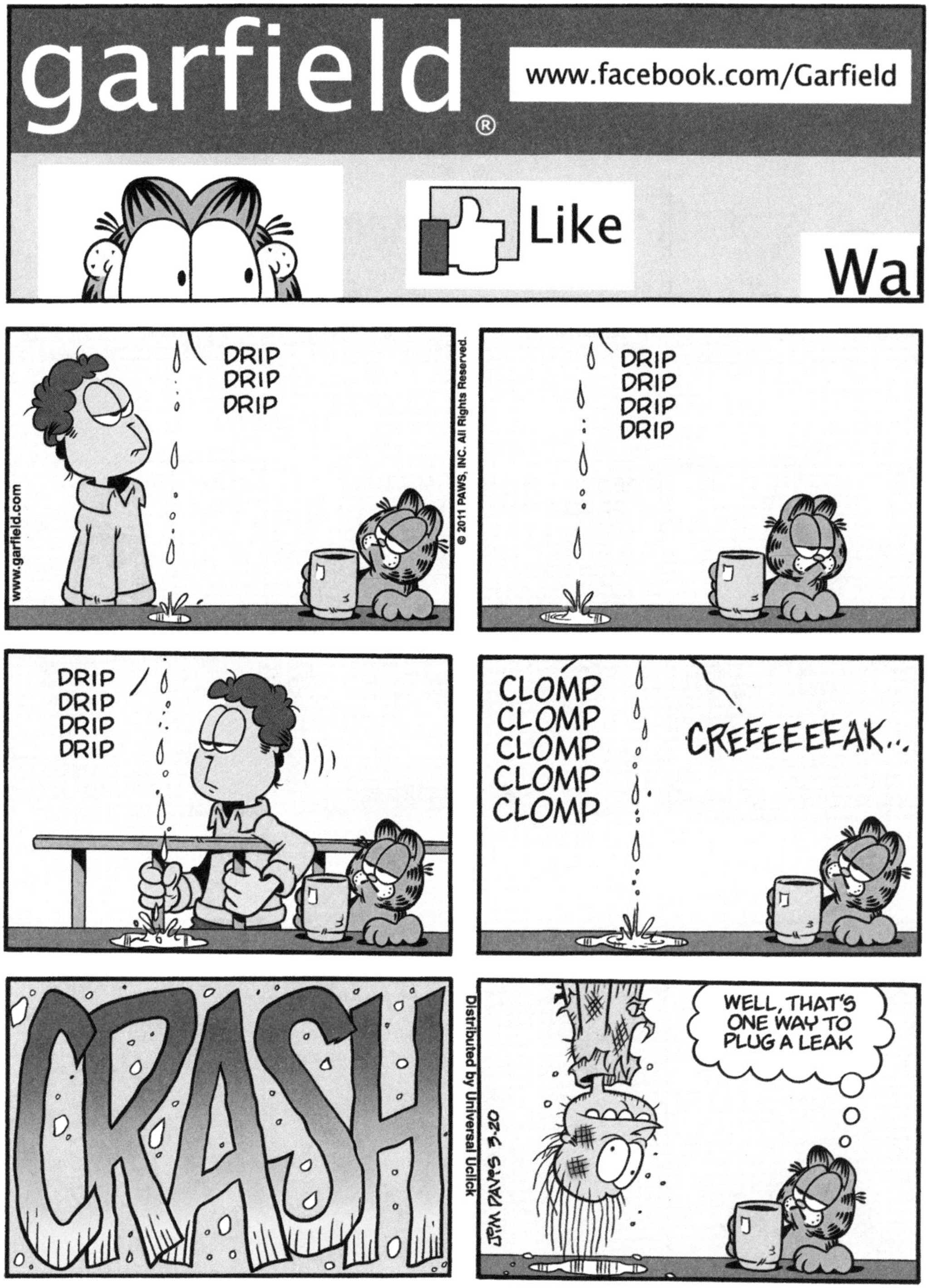
garfield®
www.facebook.com/Garfield
Like
Wal
www.garfield.com
© 2011 PAWS, INC. All Rights Reserved.
DRIP DRIP DRIP
DRIP DRIP DRIP DRIP
DRIP DRIP DRIP DRIP
CLOMP CLOMP CLOMP CLOMP CLOMP CLOMP
CREEEEEEAK...
CRASH
Distributed by Universal Uclick
JIM DAVIS 3-20
WELL, THAT'S ONE WAY TO PLUG A LEAK

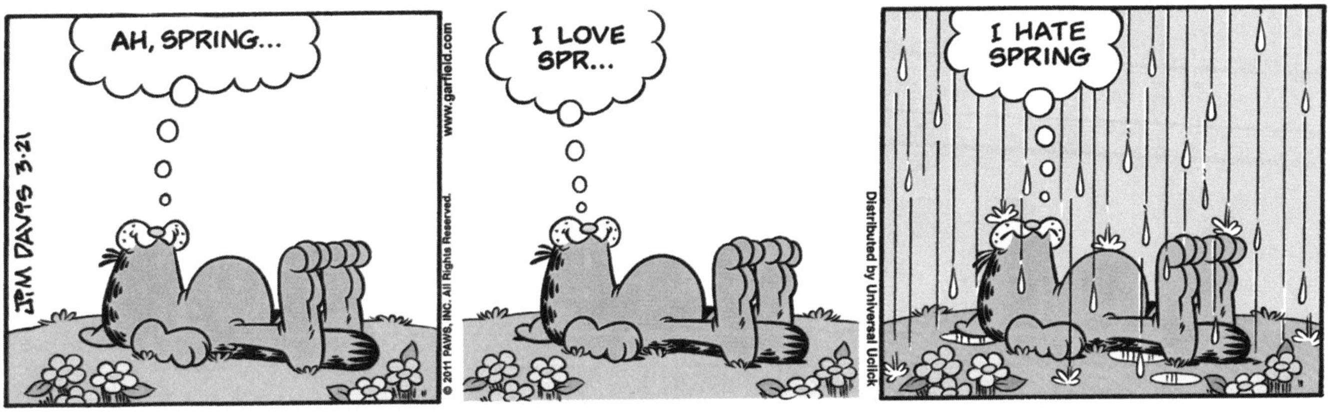
AH, SPRING...
JIM DAVIS 3·21
© 2011 PAWS, INC. All Rights Reserved. www.garfield.com
I LOVE SPR...
Distributed by Universal Uclick
I HATE SPRING

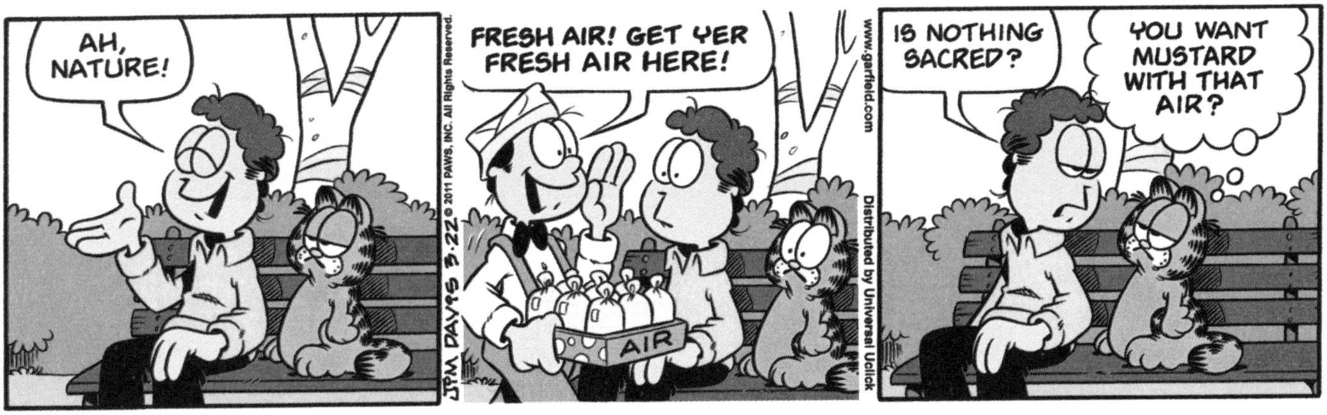
AH, NATURE!
JIM DAVIS 3·22 © 2011 PAWS, INC. All Rights Reserved.
FRESH AIR! GET YER FRESH AIR HERE!
AIR
www.garfield.com
Distributed by Universal Uclick
IS NOTHING SACRED?
YOU WANT MUSTARD WITH THAT AIR?

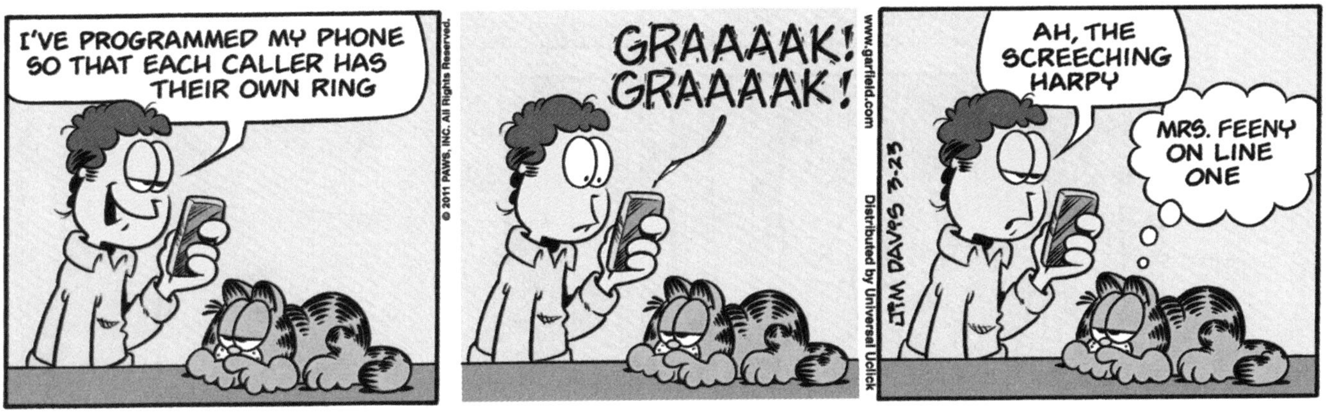
I'VE PROGRAMMED MY PHONE SO THAT EACH CALLER HAS THEIR OWN RING
© 2011 PAWS, INC. All Rights Reserved.
GRAAAAK! GRAAAAK!
www.garfield.com
JIM DAVIS 3-23
Distributed by Universal Uclick
AH, THE SCREECHING HARPY
MRS. FEENY ON LINE ONE

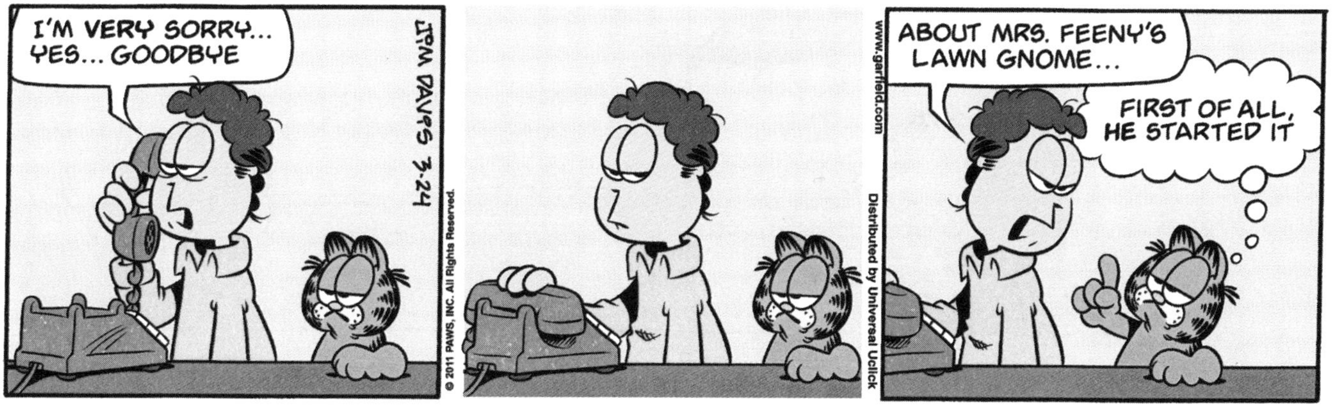
I'M VERY SORRY... YES... GOODBYE
JIM DAVIS 3-24
© 2011 PAWS, INC. All Rights Reserved.
www.garfield.com
Distributed by Universal Uclick
ABOUT MRS. FEENY'S LAWN GNOME...
FIRST OF ALL, HE STARTED IT

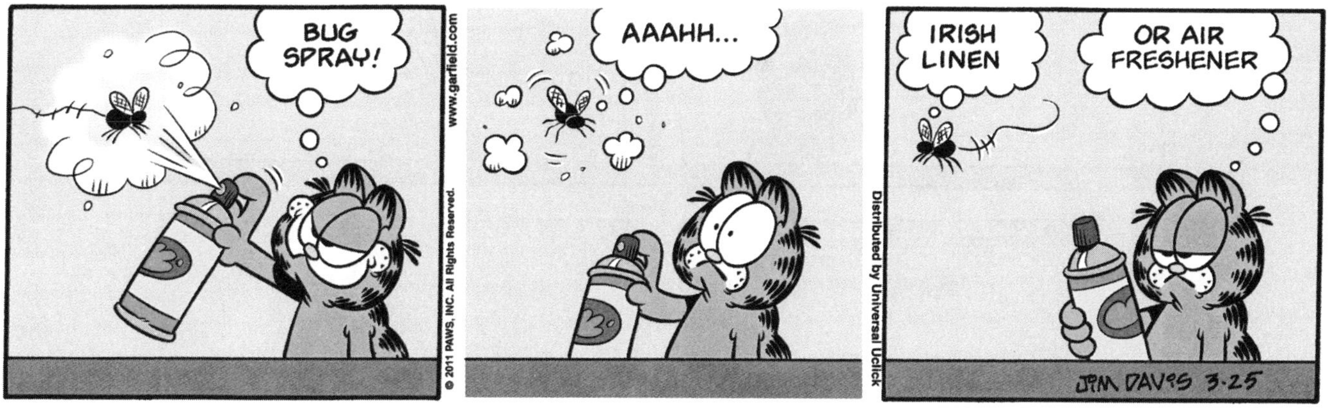
BUG SPRAY!
www.garfield.com
© 2011 PAWS, INC. All Rights Reserved.
AAAHH...
Distributed by Universal Uclick
IRISH LINEN
OR AIR FRESHENER
JIM DAVIS 3-25

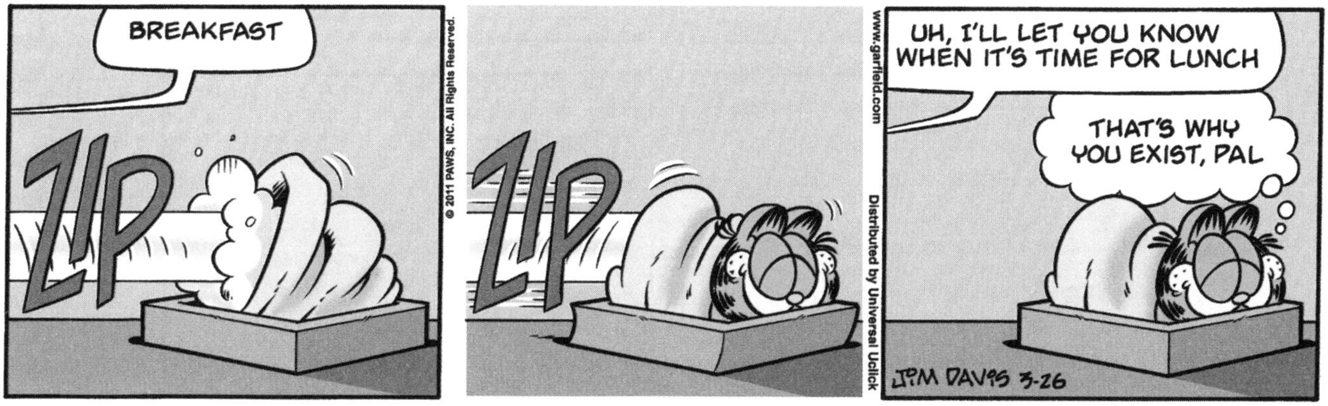
BREAKFAST
ZIP
© 2011 PAWS, INC. All Rights Reserved.
ZIP
www.garfield.com
Distributed by Universal Uclick
UH, I'LL LET YOU KNOW WHEN IT'S TIME FOR LUNCH
THAT'S WHY YOU EXIST, PAL
JIM DAVIS 3-26

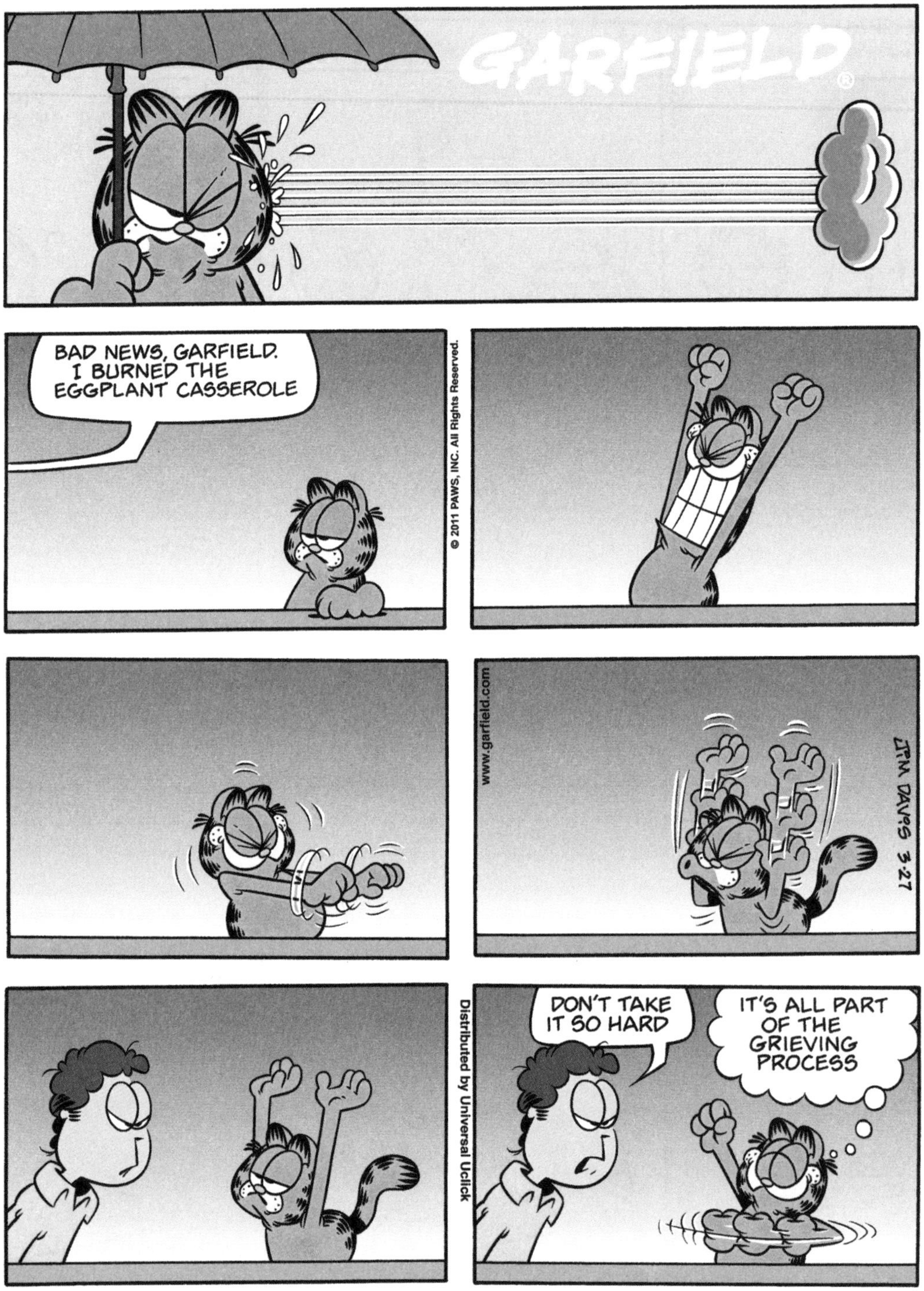
GARFIELD®
BAD NEWS, GARFIELD. I BURNED THE EGGPLANT CASSEROLE
© 2011 PAWS, INC. All Rights Reserved.
www.garfield.com
JIM DAVIS 3-27
Distributed by Universal Uclick
DON'T TAKE IT SO HARD
IT'S ALL PART OF THE GRIEVING PROCESS

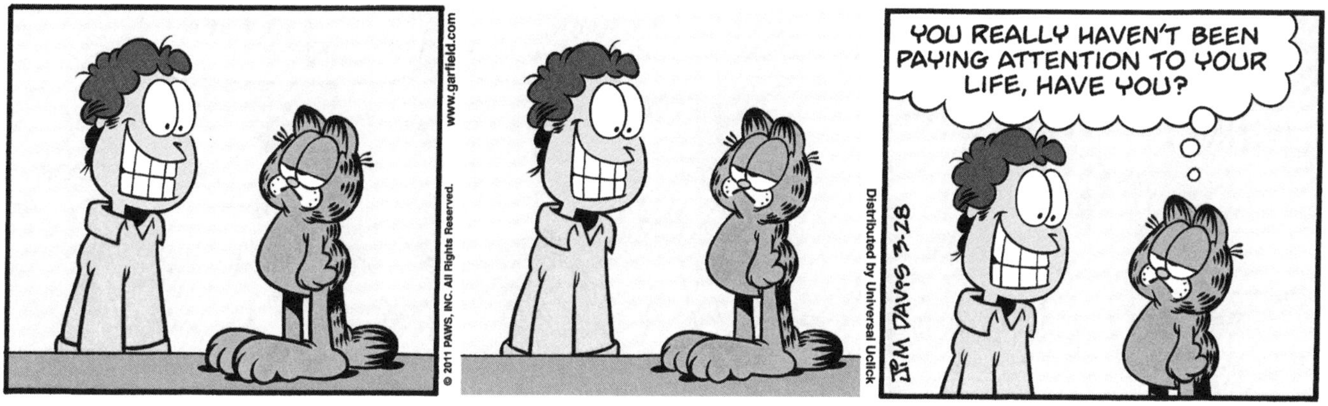
YOU REALLY HAVEN'T BEEN PAYING ATTENTION TO YOUR LIFE, HAVE YOU?
© 2011 PAWS, INC. All Rights Reserved. www.garfield.com
Distributed by Universal Uclick
JIM DAVIS 3-28

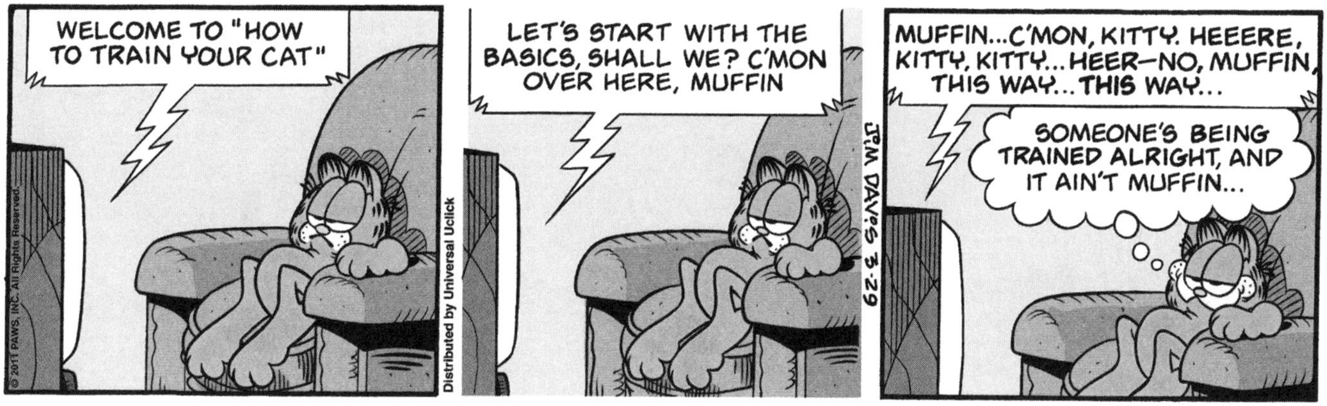
WELCOME TO "HOW TO TRAIN YOUR CAT"
LET'S START WITH THE BASICS, SHALL WE? C'MON OVER HERE, MUFFIN
MUFFIN...C'MON, KITTY. HEEERE, KITTY, KITTY...HEER–NO, MUFFIN, THIS WAY...THIS WAY...
SOMEONE'S BEING TRAINED ALRIGHT, AND IT AIN'T MUFFIN...
© 2011 PAWS, INC. All Rights Reserved.
Distributed by Universal Uclick
JIM DAVIS 3-29

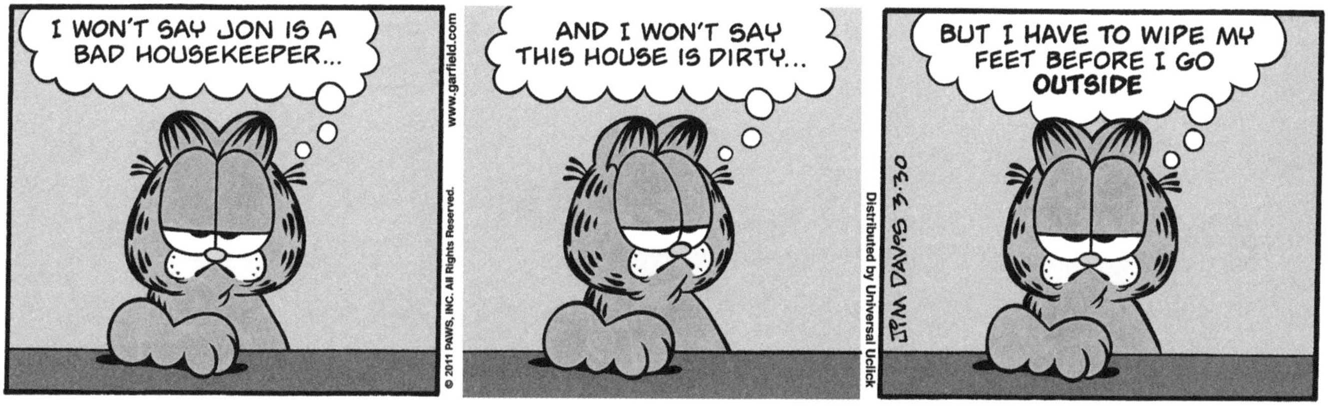
I WON'T SAY JON IS A BAD HOUSEKEEPER...
AND I WON'T SAY THIS HOUSE IS DIRTY...
BUT I HAVE TO WIPE MY FEET BEFORE I GO OUTSIDE
© 2011 PAWS, INC. All Rights Reserved. www.garfield.com
Distributed by Universal Uclick
JIM DAVIS 3-30

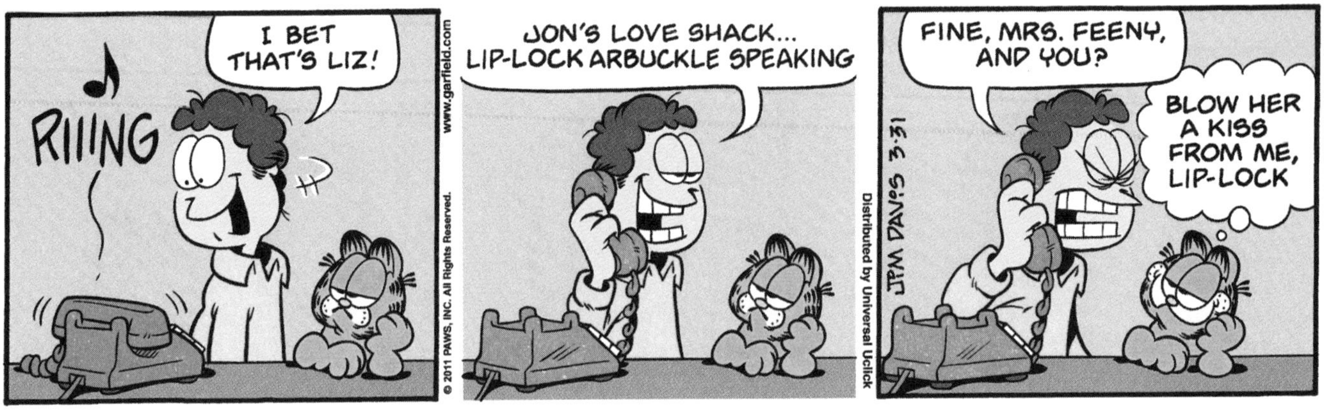
RIIING
I BET THAT'S LIZ!
JON'S LOVE SHACK... LIP-LOCK ARBUCKLE SPEAKING
FINE, MRS. FEENY, AND YOU?
BLOW HER A KISS FROM ME, LIP-LOCK
© 2011 PAWS, INC. All Rights Reserved. www.garfield.com
Distributed by Universal Uclick
JPM DAVPS 3·31

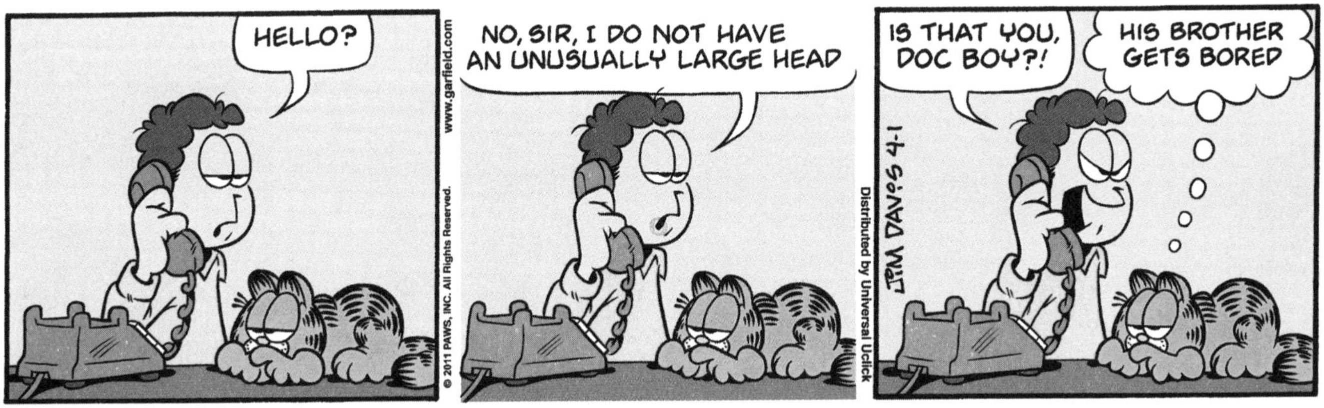
HELLO?
NO, SIR, I DO NOT HAVE AN UNUSUALLY LARGE HEAD
IS THAT YOU, DOC BOY?!
HIS BROTHER GETS BORED
© 2011 PAWS, INC. All Rights Reserved. www.garfield.com
Distributed by Universal Uclick
JPM DAVPS 4·1

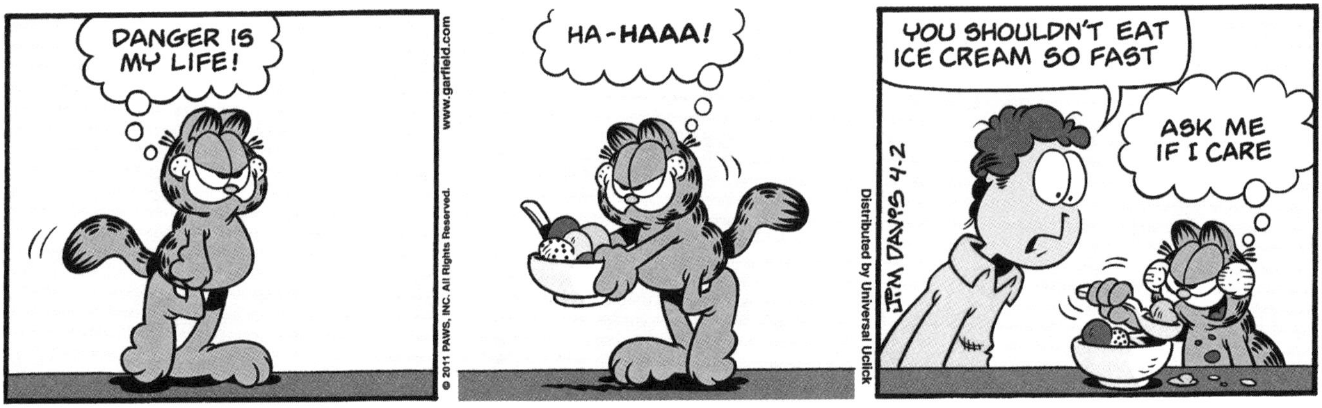
DANGER IS MY LIFE!
HA-HAAA!
YOU SHOULDN'T EAT ICE CREAM SO FAST
ASK ME IF I CARE
© 2011 PAWS, INC. All Rights Reserved. www.garfield.com
Distributed by Universal Uclick
JPM DAVPS 4·2

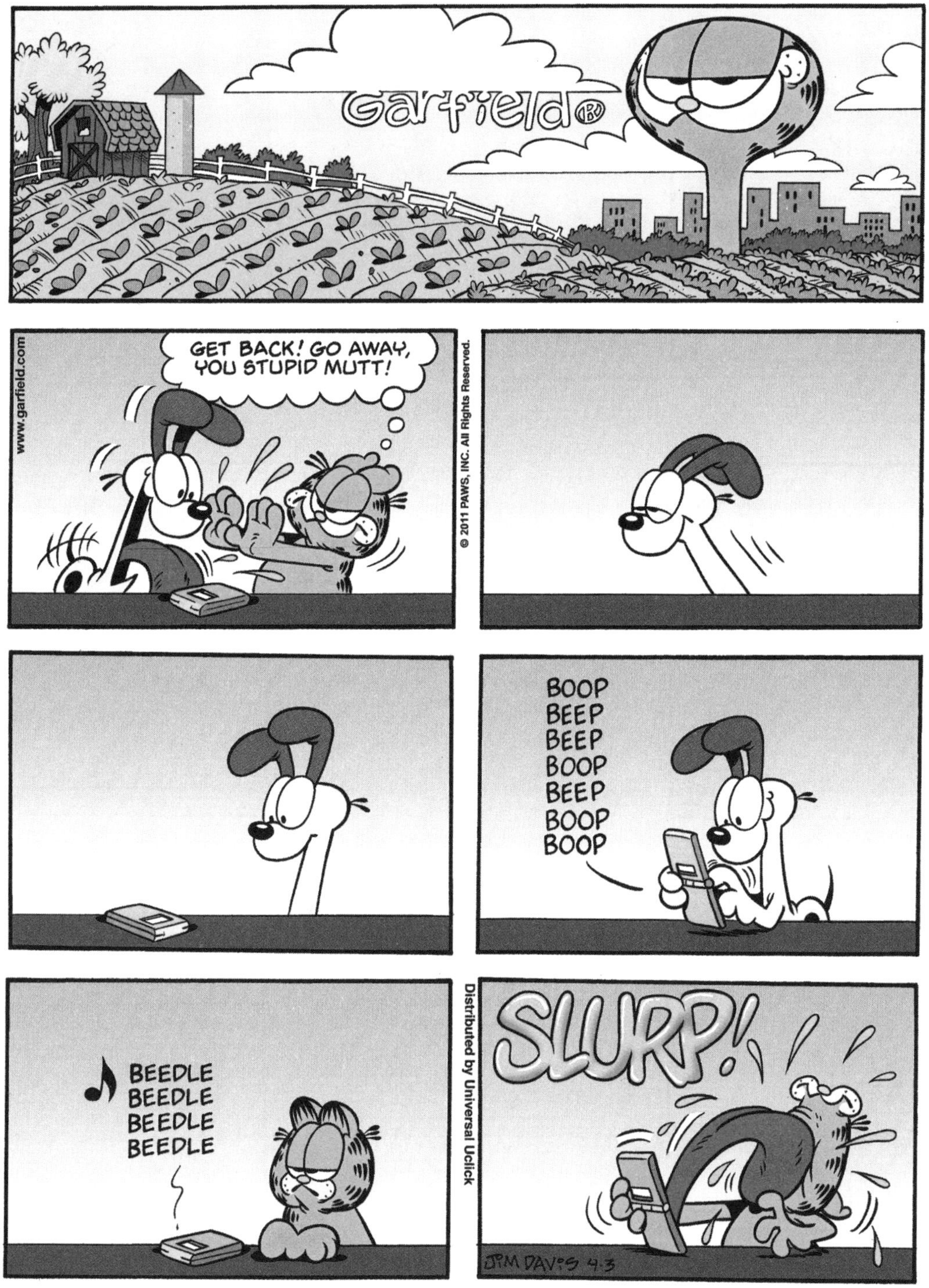
GARFIELD®
www.garfield.com
GET BACK! GO AWAY, YOU STUPID MUTT!
© 2011 PAWS, INC. All Rights Reserved.
BOOP
BEEP
BEEP
BOOP
BEEP
BOOP
BOOP
BEEDLE
BEEDLE
BEEDLE
BEEDLE
Distributed by Universal Uclick
SLURP!
JIM DAVIS 4-3

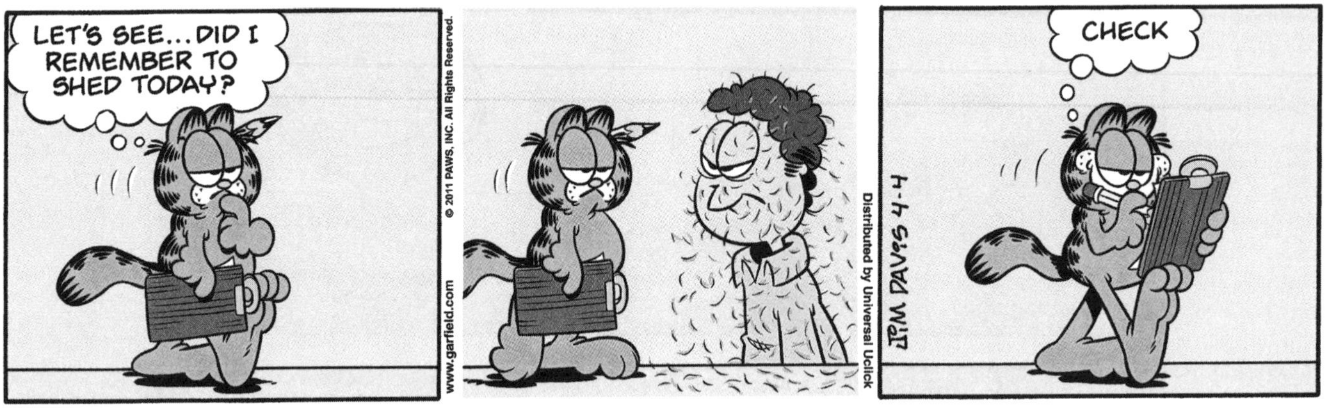
LET'S SEE... DID I REMEMBER TO SHED TODAY?
© 2011 PAWS, INC. All Rights Reserved.
www.garfield.com
Distributed by Universal Uclick
JPM DAVIS 4-4
CHECK

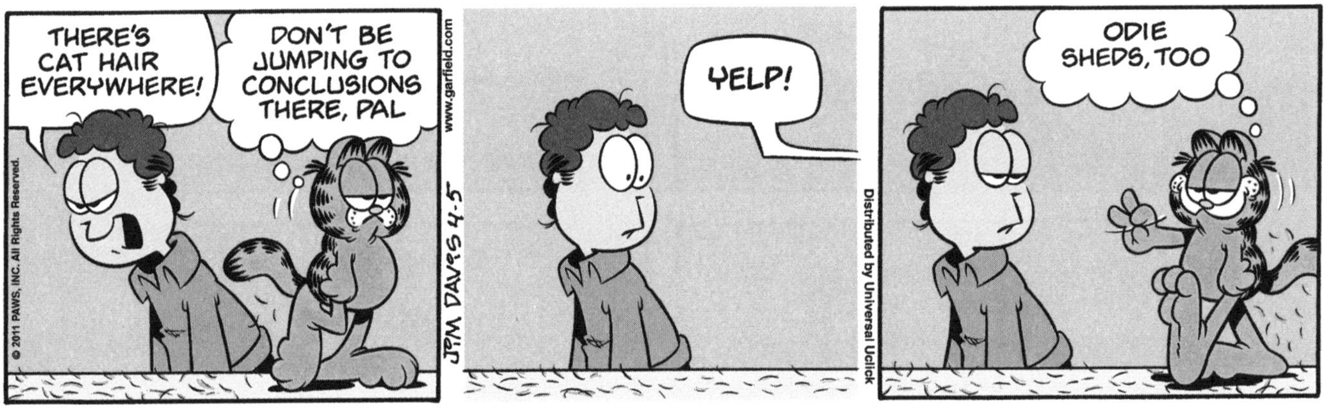
THERE'S CAT HAIR EVERYWHERE!
DON'T BE JUMPING TO CONCLUSIONS THERE, PAL
© 2011 PAWS, INC. All Rights Reserved.
www.garfield.com
JPM DAVIS 4-5
YELP!
Distributed by Universal Uclick
ODIE SHEDS, TOO

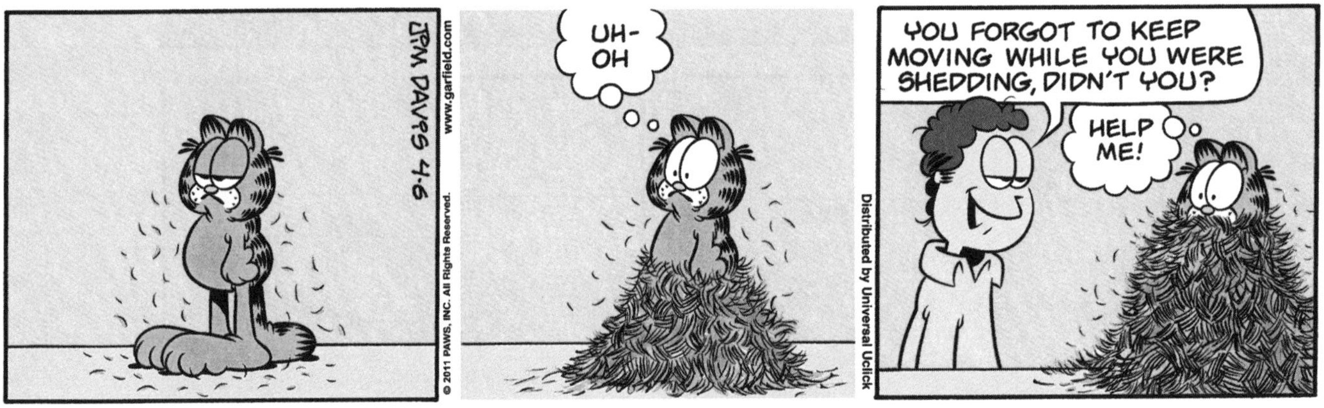
JPM DAVIS 4-6
www.garfield.com
© 2011 PAWS, INC. All Rights Reserved.
UH-OH
Distributed by Universal Uclick
YOU FORGOT TO KEEP MOVING WHILE YOU WERE SHEDDING, DIDN'T YOU?
HELP ME!

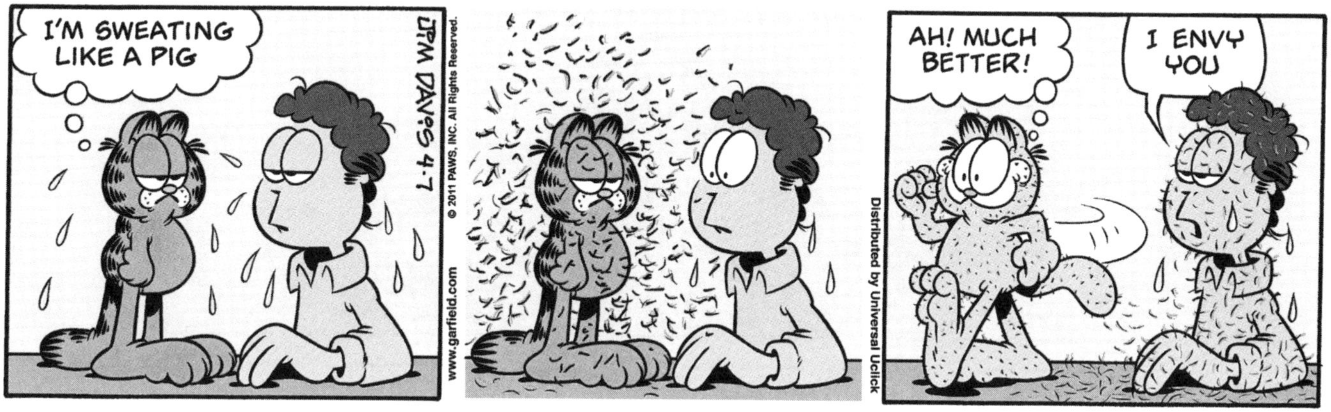
I'M SWEATING LIKE A PIG
JIM DAVIS 4-7
© 2011 PAWS, INC. All Rights Reserved.
www.garfield.com
AH! MUCH BETTER!
I ENVY YOU
Distributed by Universal Uclick

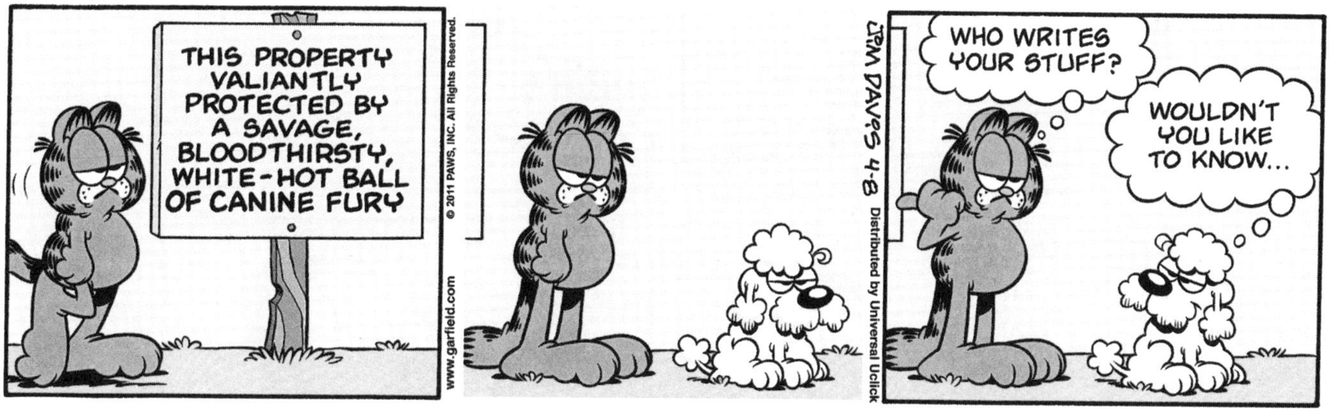
THIS PROPERTY VALIANTLY PROTECTED BY A SAVAGE, BLOODTHIRSTY, WHITE-HOT BALL OF CANINE FURY
© 2011 PAWS, INC. All Rights Reserved.
www.garfield.com
JIM DAVIS 4-8
WHO WRITES YOUR STUFF?
WOULDN'T YOU LIKE TO KNOW...
Distributed by Universal Uclick

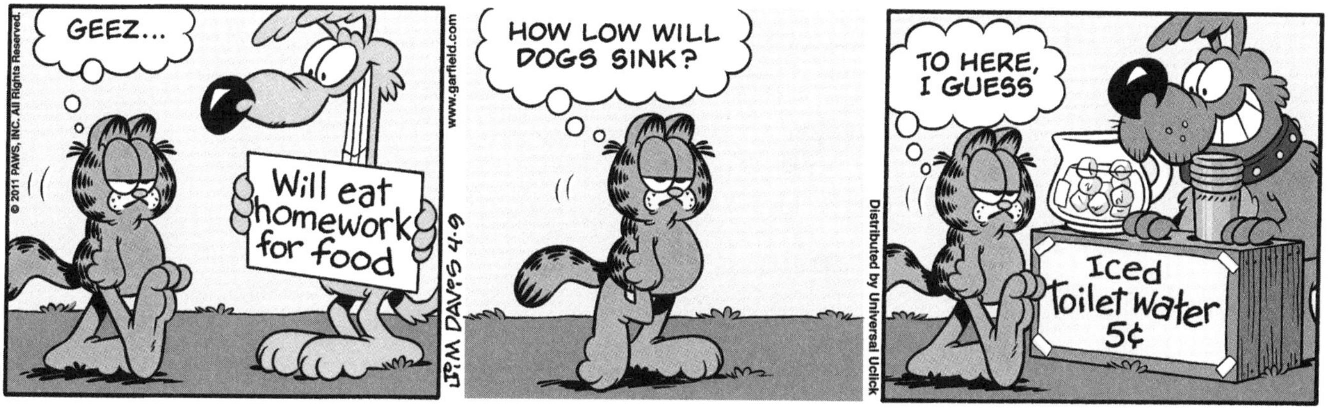
© 2011 PAWS, INC. All Rights Reserved.
GEEZ...
Will eat homework for food
www.garfield.com
JIM DAVIS 4-9
HOW LOW WILL DOGS SINK?
Distributed by Universal Uclick
TO HERE, I GUESS
Iced Toilet water 5¢

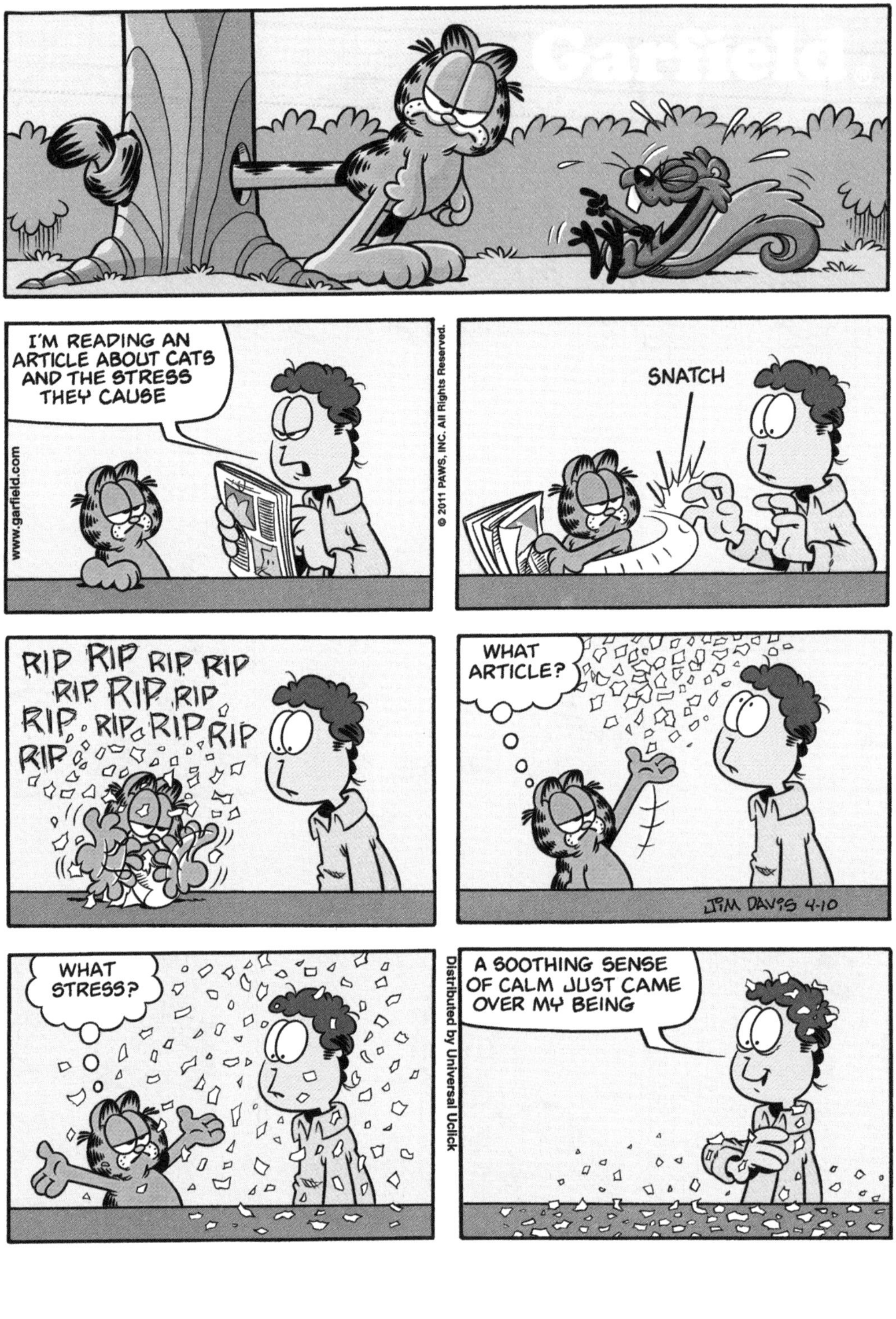
Garfield
I'M READING AN ARTICLE ABOUT CATS AND THE STRESS THEY CAUSE
SNATCH
RIP RIP RIP RIP RIP RIP RIP RIP RIP RIP RIP RIP
WHAT ARTICLE?
JIM DAVIS 4-10
WHAT STRESS?
A SOOTHING SENSE OF CALM JUST CAME OVER MY BEING

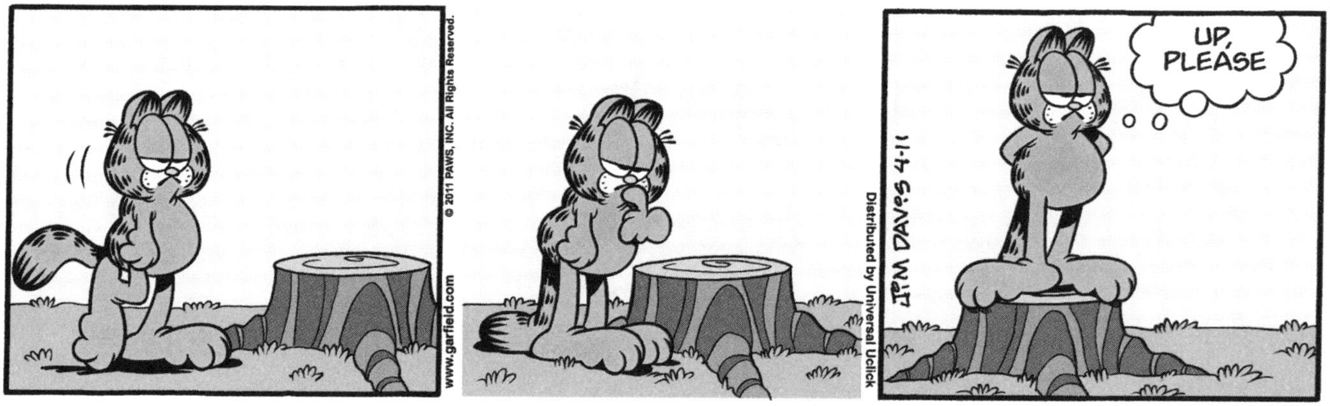
© 2011 PAWS, INC. All Rights Reserved.
www.garfield.com
Distributed by Universal Uclick
JIM DAVIS 4-11
UP, PLEASE

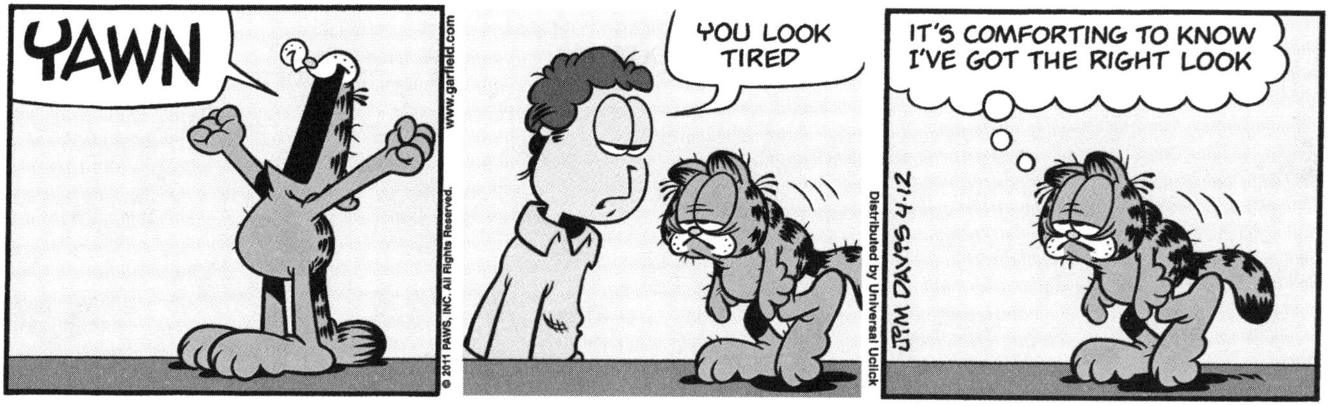
YAWN
© 2011 PAWS, INC. All Rights Reserved.
www.garfield.com
YOU LOOK TIRED
Distributed by Universal Uclick
JIM DAVIS 4-12
IT'S COMFORTING TO KNOW I'VE GOT THE RIGHT LOOK

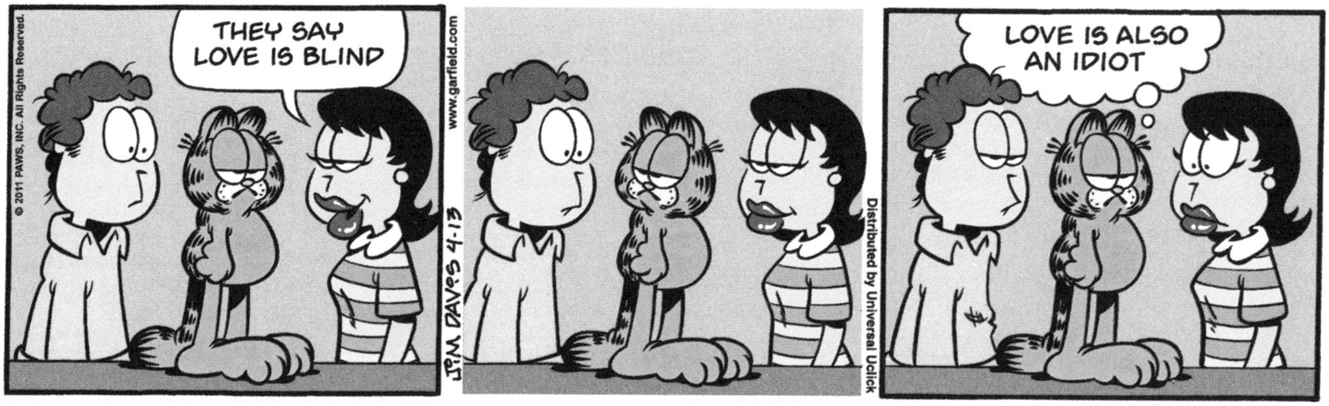
© 2011 PAWS, INC. All Rights Reserved.
THEY SAY LOVE IS BLIND
www.garfield.com
JIM DAVIS 4-13
Distributed by Universal Uclick
LOVE IS ALSO AN IDIOT

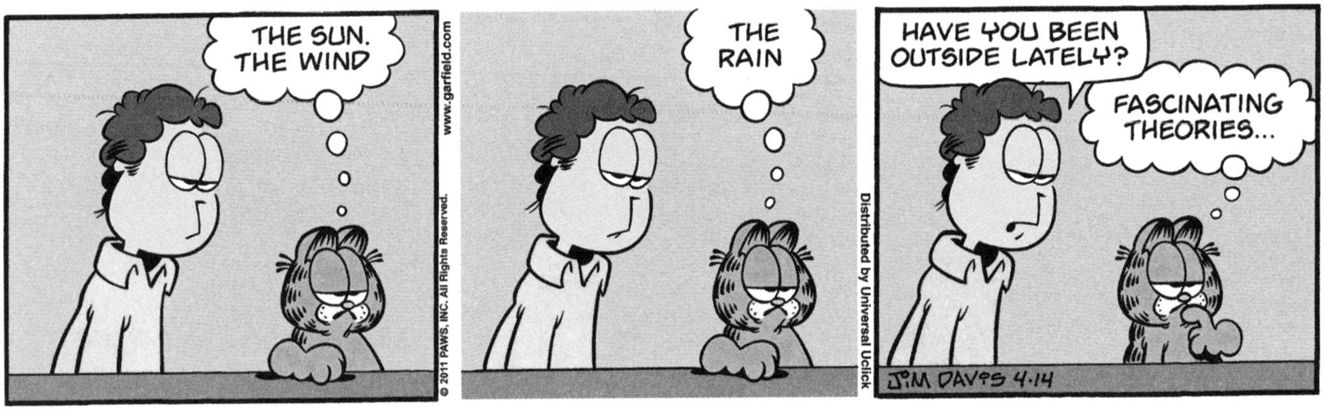
THE SUN. THE WIND
THE RAIN
HAVE YOU BEEN OUTSIDE LATELY?
FASCINATING THEORIES...
www.garfield.com
© 2011 PAWS, INC. All Rights Reserved.
Distributed by Universal Uclick
JIM DAVIS 4·14

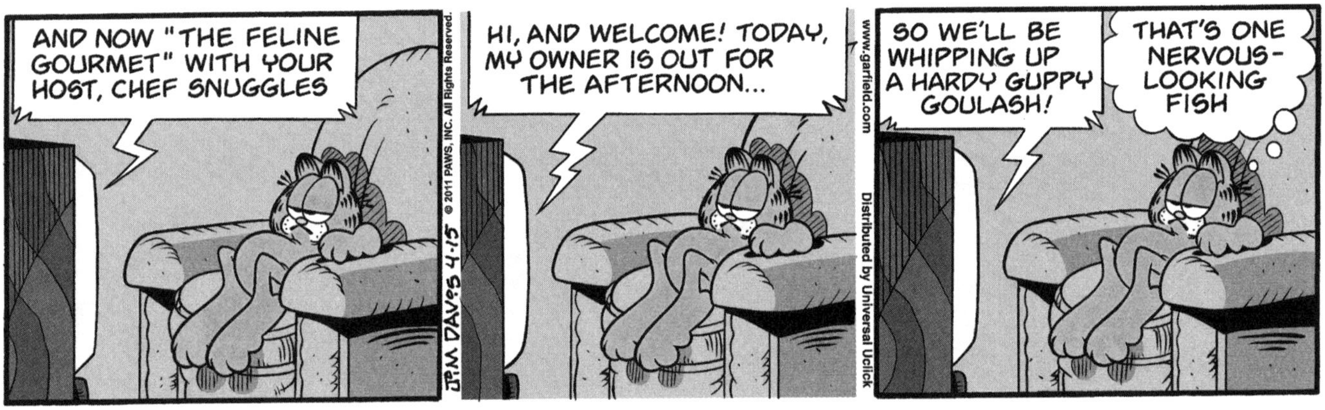
AND NOW "THE FELINE GOURMET" WITH YOUR HOST, CHEF SNUGGLES
HI, AND WELCOME! TODAY, MY OWNER IS OUT FOR THE AFTERNOON...
SO WE'LL BE WHIPPING UP A HARDY GUPPY GOULASH!
THAT'S ONE NERVOUS-LOOKING FISH
© 2011 PAWS, INC. All Rights Reserved.
www.garfield.com
Distributed by Universal Uclick
JIM DAVIS 4·15

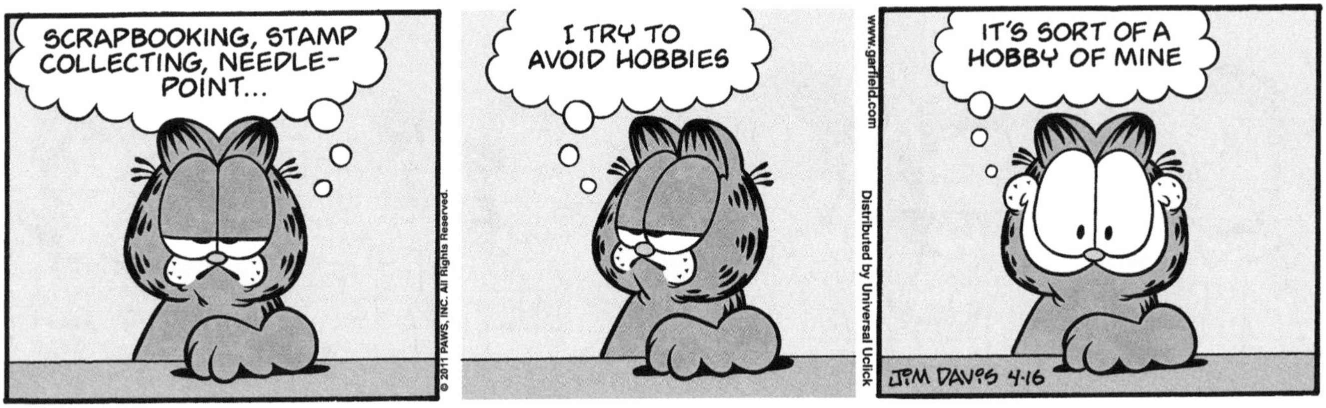
SCRAPBOOKING, STAMP COLLECTING, NEEDLE-POINT...
I TRY TO AVOID HOBBIES
IT'S SORT OF A HOBBY OF MINE
© 2011 PAWS, INC. All Rights Reserved.
www.garfield.com
Distributed by Universal Uclick
JIM DAVIS 4·16

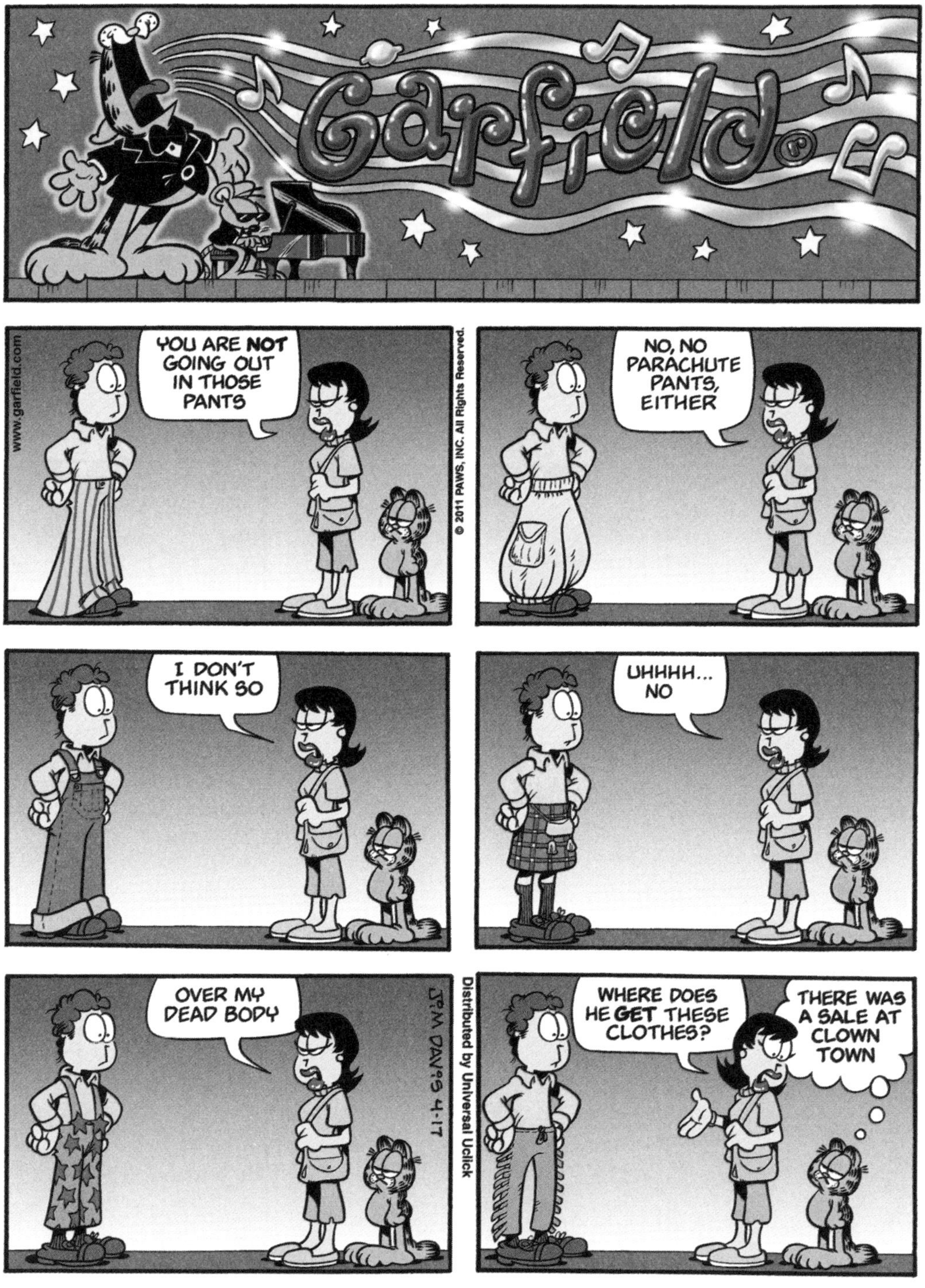
Garfield®
www.garfield.com
© 2011 PAWS, INC. All Rights Reserved.
YOU ARE NOT GOING OUT IN THOSE PANTS
NO, NO PARACHUTE PANTS, EITHER
I DON'T THINK SO
UHHHH... NO
OVER MY DEAD BODY
JPM DAVPS 4-17
Distributed by Universal Uclick
WHERE DOES HE GET THESE CLOTHES?
THERE WAS A SALE AT CLOWN TOWN

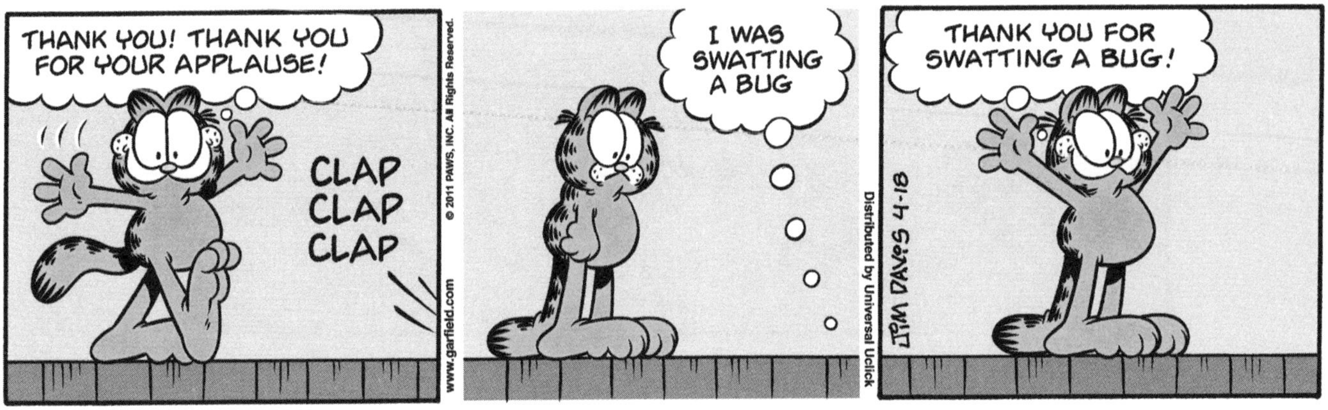
THANK YOU! THANK YOU FOR YOUR APPLAUSE!
CLAP CLAP CLAP
© 2011 PAWS, INC. All Rights Reserved. www.garfield.com
I WAS SWATTING A BUG
Distributed by Universal Uclick
JPM DAVIS 4-18
THANK YOU FOR SWATTING A BUG!

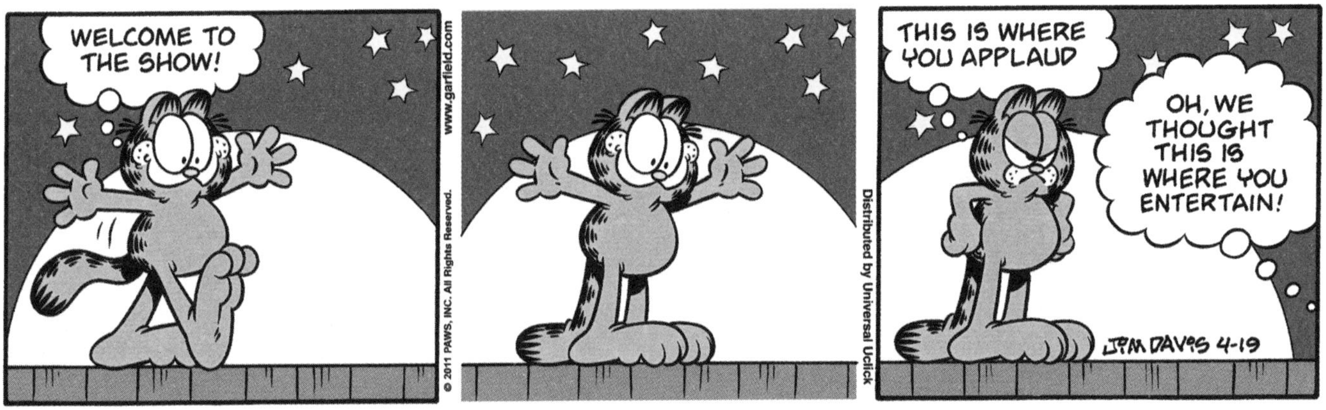
WELCOME TO THE SHOW!
© 2011 PAWS, INC. All Rights Reserved. www.garfield.com
Distributed by Universal Uclick
THIS IS WHERE YOU APPLAUD
OH, WE THOUGHT THIS IS WHERE YOU ENTERTAIN!
JPM DAVIS 4-19

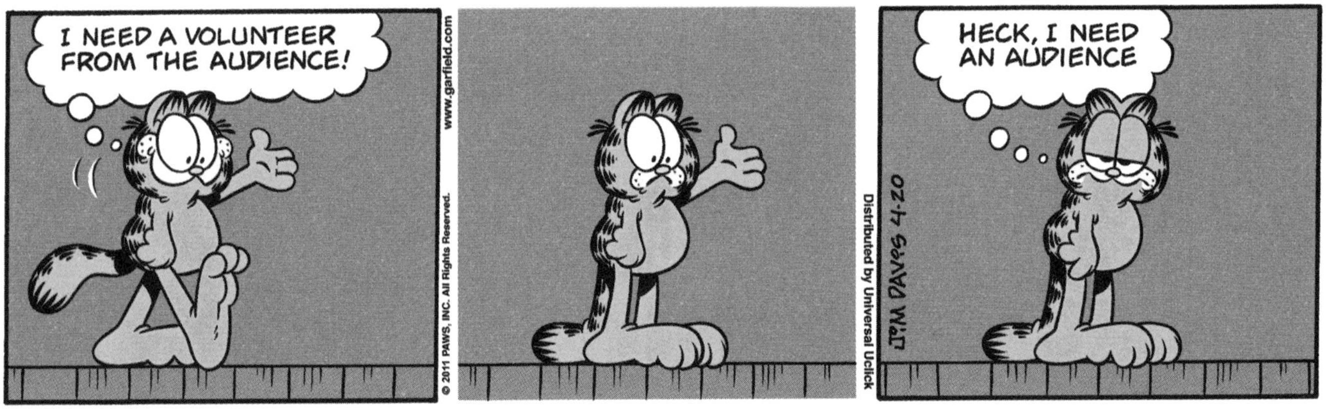
I NEED A VOLUNTEER FROM THE AUDIENCE!
© 2011 PAWS, INC. All Rights Reserved. www.garfield.com
Distributed by Universal Uclick
JPM DAVIS 4-20
HECK, I NEED AN AUDIENCE

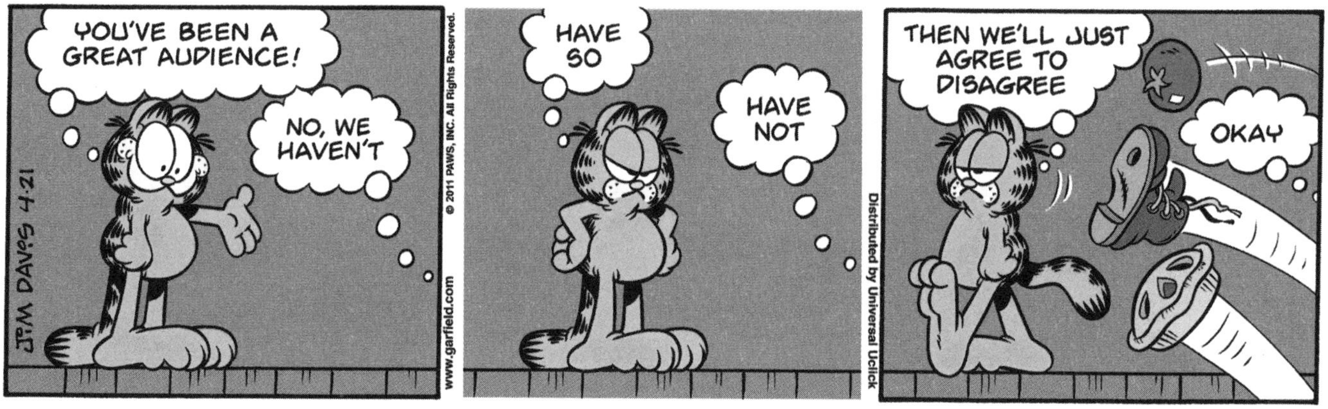
YOU'VE BEEN A GREAT AUDIENCE!
NO, WE HAVEN'T
JIM DAVIS 4·21
© 2011 PAWS, INC. All Rights Reserved.
www.garfield.com
HAVE SO
HAVE NOT
Distributed by Universal Uclick
THEN WE'LL JUST AGREE TO DISAGREE
OKAY

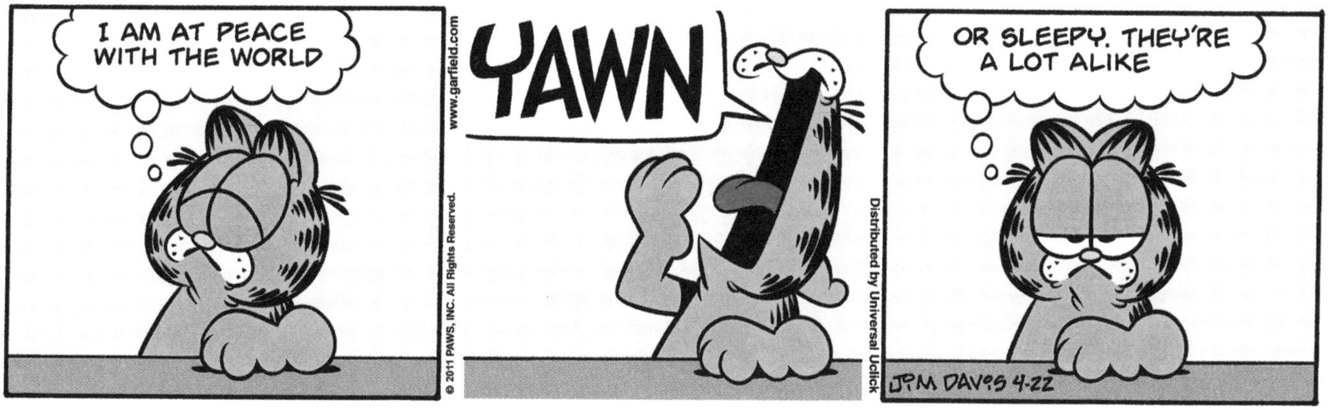
I AM AT PEACE WITH THE WORLD
www.garfield.com
© 2011 PAWS, INC. All Rights Reserved.
YAWN
Distributed by Universal Uclick
OR SLEEPY. THEY'RE A LOT ALIKE
JIM DAVIS 4-22

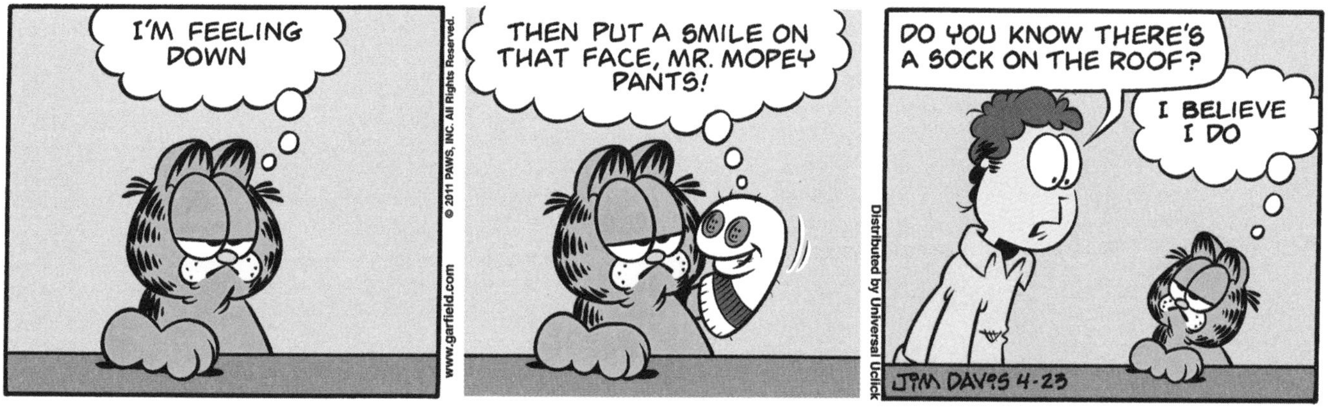
I'M FEELING DOWN
© 2011 PAWS, INC. All Rights Reserved.
www.garfield.com
THEN PUT A SMILE ON THAT FACE, MR. MOPEY PANTS!
Distributed by Universal Uclick
DO YOU KNOW THERE'S A SOCK ON THE ROOF?
I BELIEVE I DO
JIM DAVIS 4-23

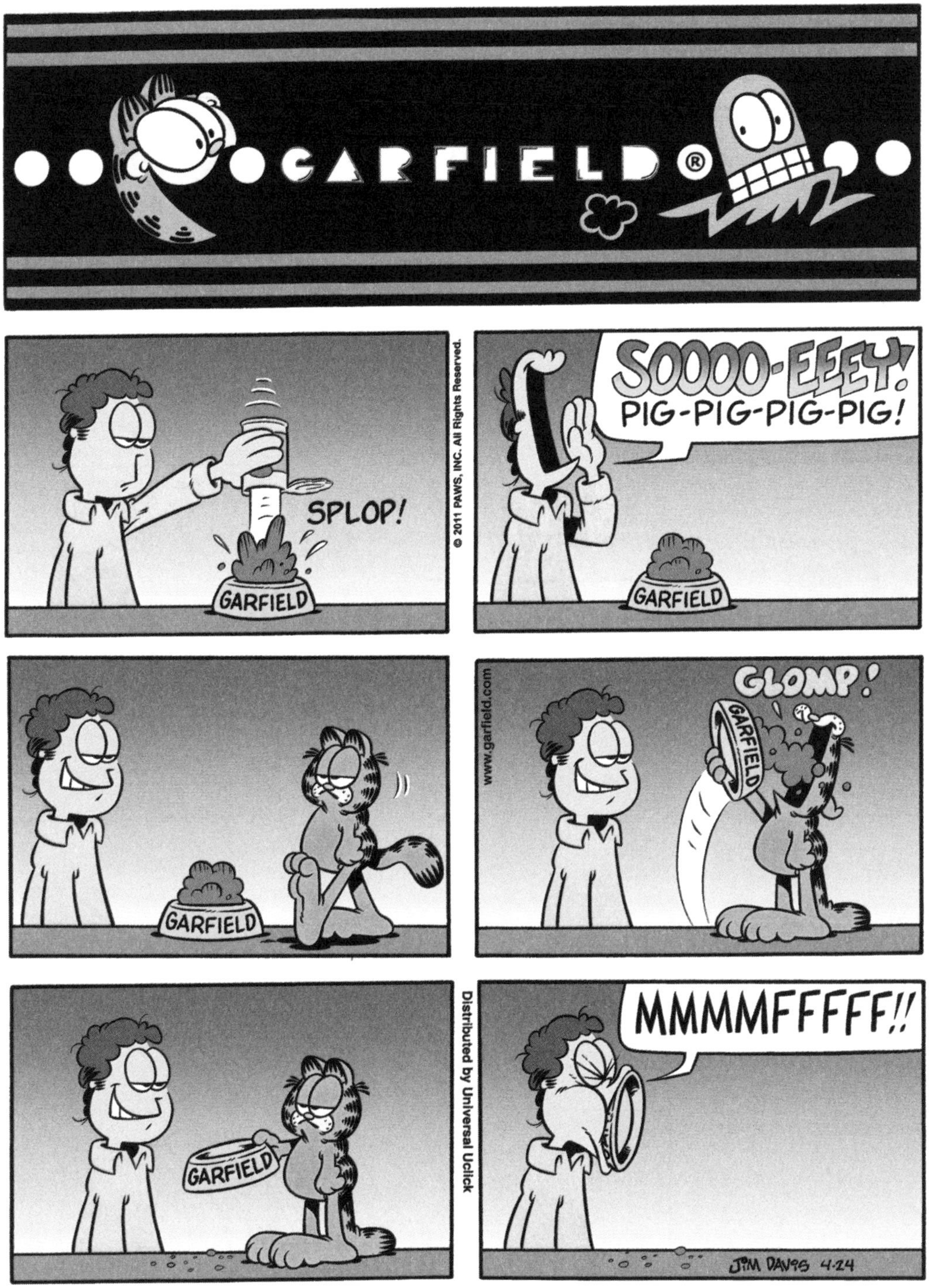
GARFIELD®
SPLOP!
GARFIELD
© 2011 PAWS, INC. All Rights Reserved.
SOOOO-EEEY!
PIG-PIG-PIG-PIG!
GARFIELD
GARFIELD
www.garfield.com
GLOMP!
GARFIELD
GARFIELD
Distributed by Universal Uclick
MMMMFFFFF!!
JIM DAVIS 4-24

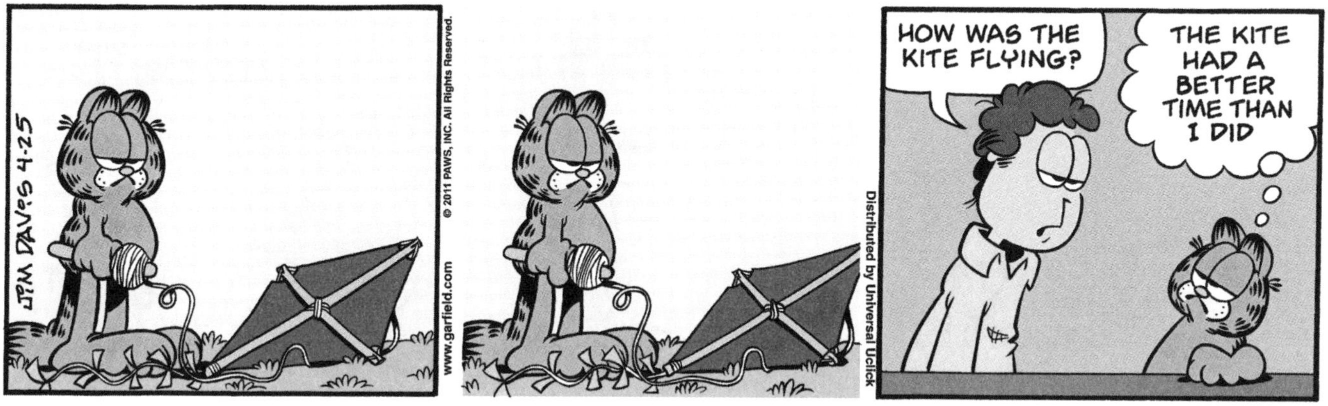
JIM DAVIS 4-25
© 2011 PAWS, INC. All Rights Reserved.
www.garfield.com
Distributed by Universal Uclick
HOW WAS THE KITE FLYING?
THE KITE HAD A BETTER TIME THAN I DID

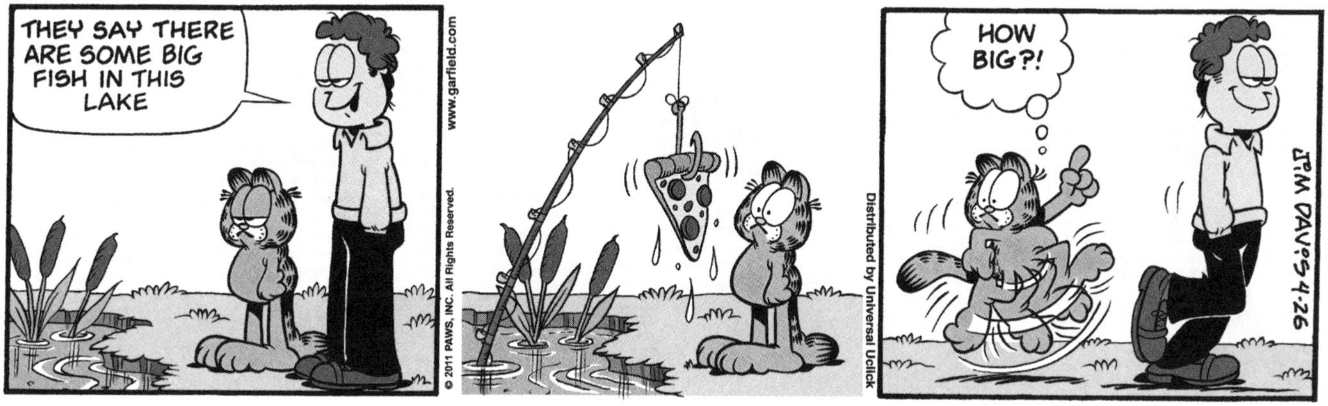
THEY SAY THERE ARE SOME BIG FISH IN THIS LAKE
www.garfield.com
© 2011 PAWS, INC. All Rights Reserved.
Distributed by Universal Uclick
HOW BIG?!
JIM DAVIS 4-26

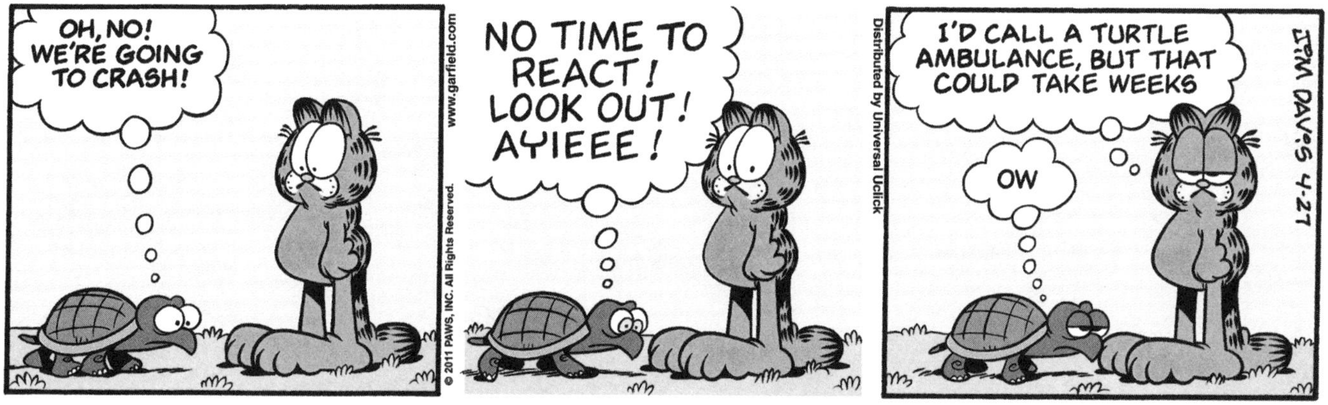
OH, NO! WE'RE GOING TO CRASH!
www.garfield.com
© 2011 PAWS, INC. All Rights Reserved.
NO TIME TO REACT! LOOK OUT! AYIEEE!
Distributed by Universal Uclick
I'D CALL A TURTLE AMBULANCE, BUT THAT COULD TAKE WEEKS
OW
JIM DAVIS 4-27

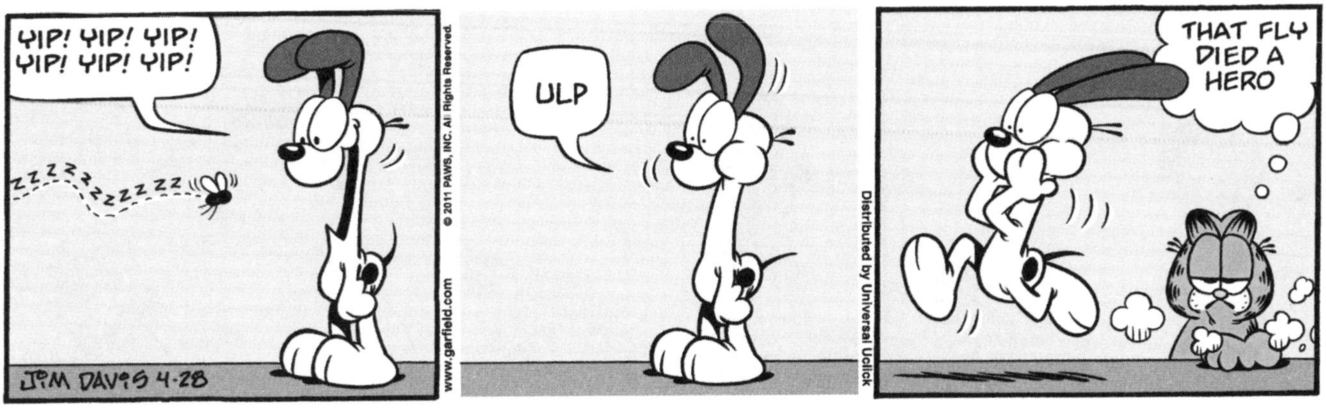
YIP! YIP! YIP! YIP! YIP! YIP!
ZZZZZZZZZZZZ
JIM DAVIS 4-28
© 2011 PAWS, INC. All Rights Reserved.
www.garfield.com
ULP
Distributed by Universal Uclick
THAT FLY DIED A HERO

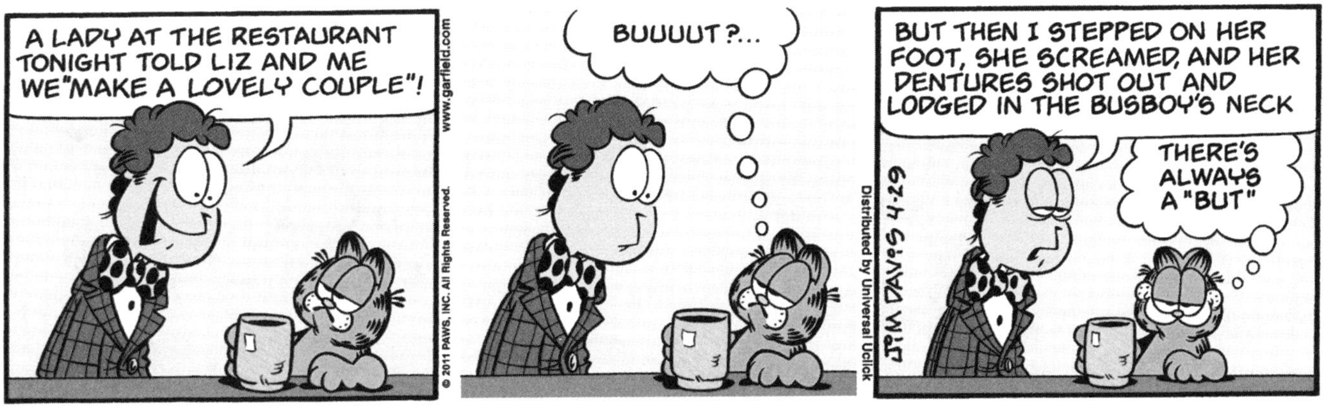
A LADY AT THE RESTAURANT TONIGHT TOLD LIZ AND ME WE "MAKE A LOVELY COUPLE"!
www.garfield.com
© 2011 PAWS, INC. All Rights Reserved.
BUUUUT?...
Distributed by Universal Uclick
JIM DAVIS 4-29
BUT THEN I STEPPED ON HER FOOT, SHE SCREAMED, AND HER DENTURES SHOT OUT AND LODGED IN THE BUSBOY'S NECK
THERE'S ALWAYS A "BUT"

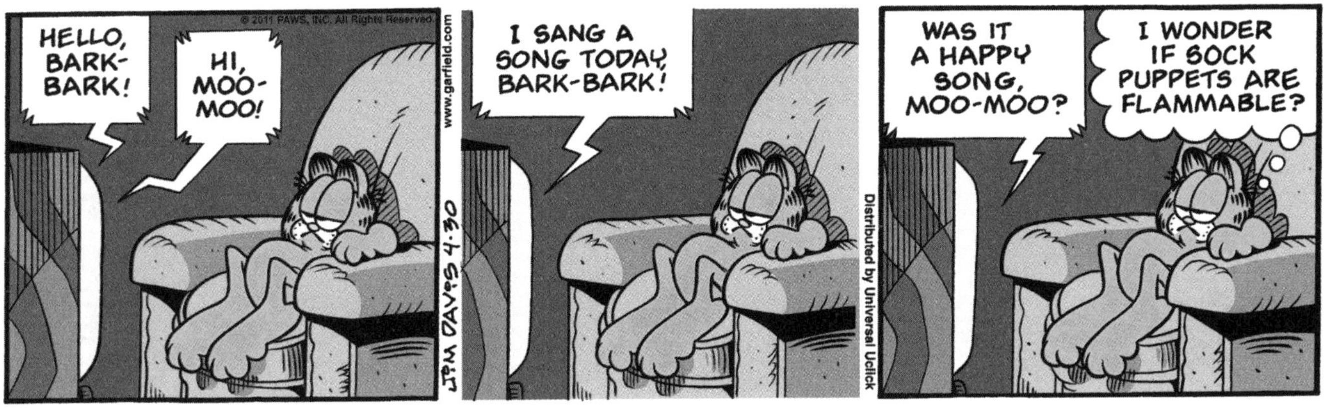
© 2011 PAWS, INC. All Rights Reserved.
HELLO, BARK-BARK!
HI, MOO-MOO!
www.garfield.com
JIM DAVIS 4-30
I SANG A SONG TODAY, BARK-BARK!
Distributed by Universal Uclick
WAS IT A HAPPY SONG, MOO-MOO?
I WONDER IF SOCK PUPPETS ARE FLAMMABLE?

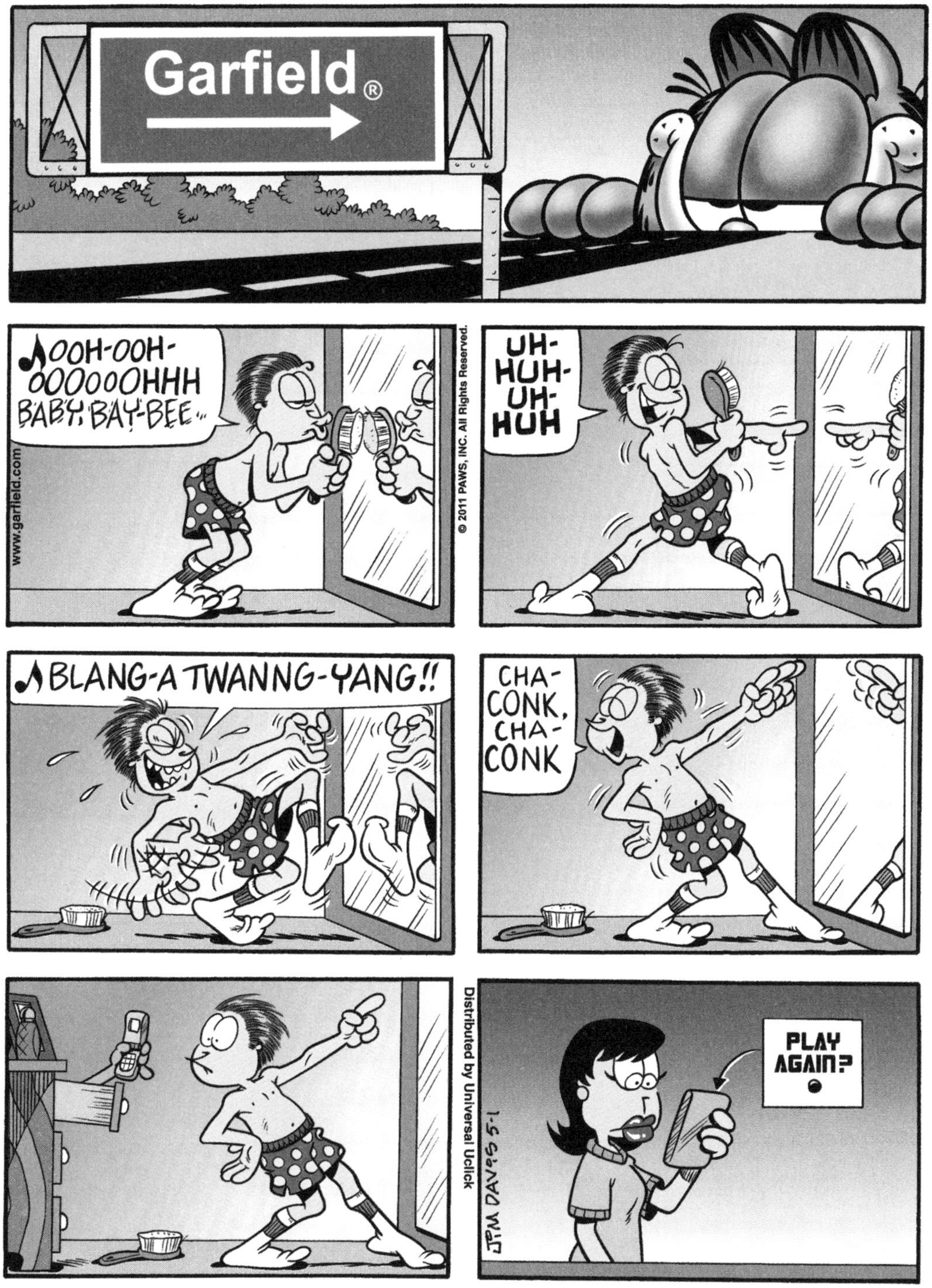
Garfield®
www.garfield.com
© 2011 PAWS, INC. All Rights Reserved.
♪OOH-OOH-OOOOOOHHH BABY, BAY-BEE...
UH-HUH-UH-HUH
♪BLANG-A TWANNG-YANG!!
CHA-CONK, CHA-CONK
Distributed by Universal Uclick
JPM DAVIS 5-1
PLAY AGAIN?

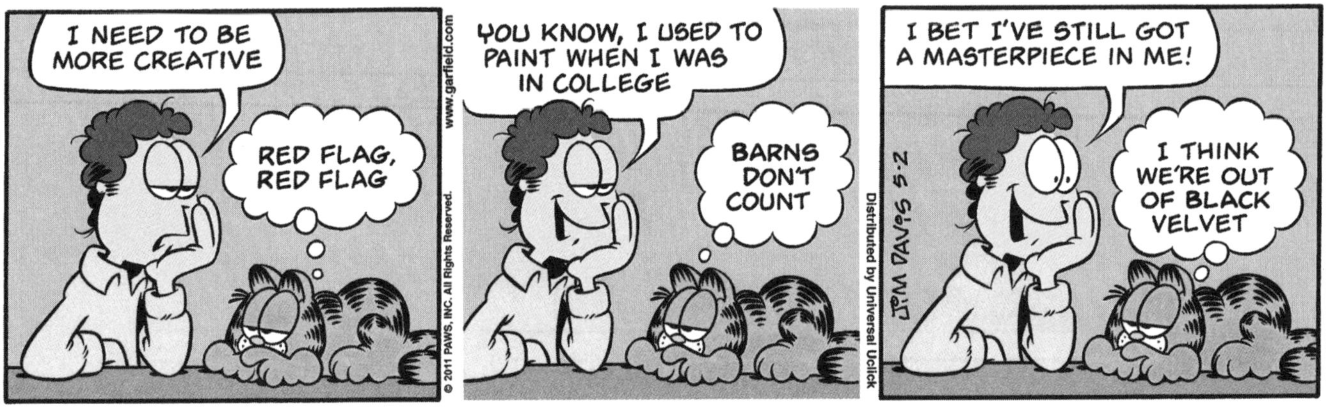
I NEED TO BE MORE CREATIVE
RED FLAG, RED FLAG
YOU KNOW, I USED TO PAINT WHEN I WAS IN COLLEGE
BARNS DON'T COUNT
I BET I'VE STILL GOT A MASTERPIECE IN ME!
I THINK WE'RE OUT OF BLACK VELVET
© 2011 PAWS, INC. All Rights Reserved. www.garfield.com
Distributed by Universal Uclick
JPM DAVIS 5-2

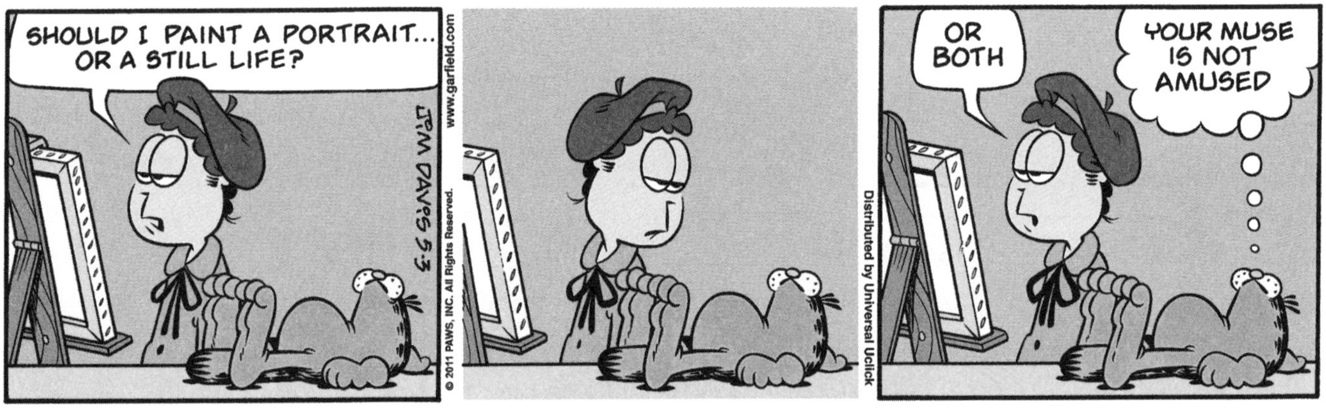
SHOULD I PAINT A PORTRAIT... OR A STILL LIFE?
OR BOTH
YOUR MUSE IS NOT AMUSED
© 2011 PAWS, INC. All Rights Reserved. www.garfield.com
Distributed by Universal Uclick
JPM DAVIS 5-3

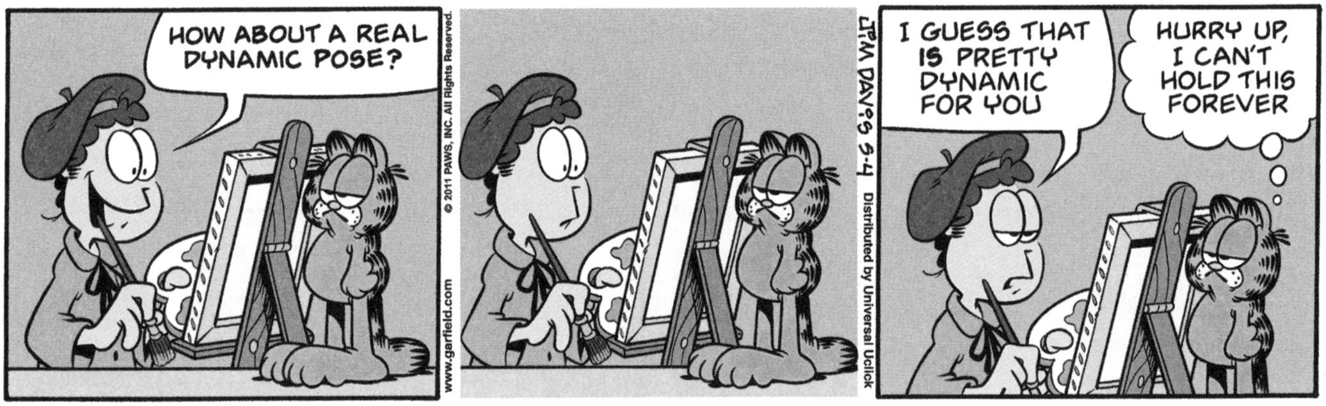
HOW ABOUT A REAL DYNAMIC POSE?
I GUESS THAT IS PRETTY DYNAMIC FOR YOU
HURRY UP, I CAN'T HOLD THIS FOREVER
© 2011 PAWS, INC. All Rights Reserved. www.garfield.com
Distributed by Universal Uclick
JPM DAVIS 5-4

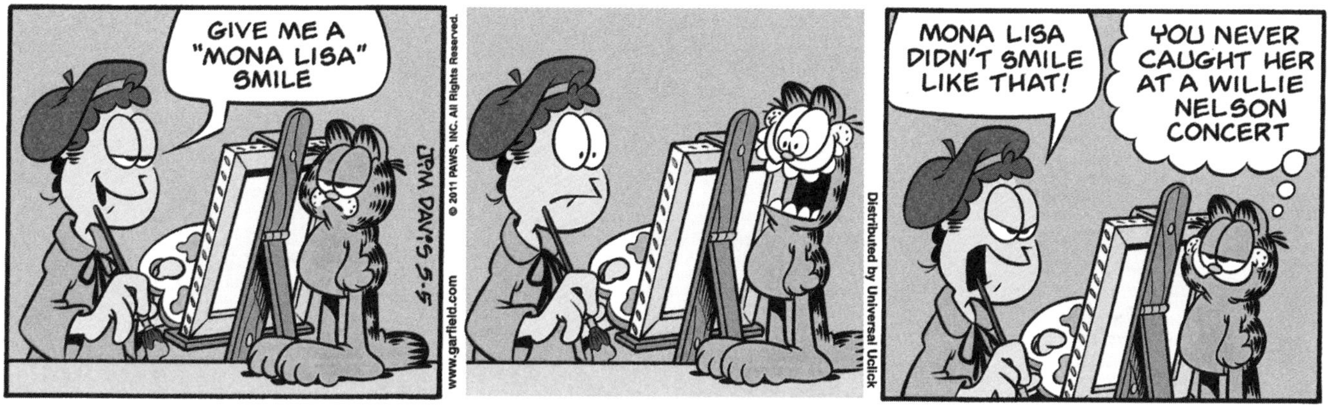
GIVE ME A "MONA LISA" SMILE
JIM DAVIS 5-5
© 2011 PAWS, INC. All Rights Reserved.
www.garfield.com
Distributed by Universal Uclick
MONA LISA DIDN'T SMILE LIKE THAT!
YOU NEVER CAUGHT HER AT A WILLIE NELSON CONCERT

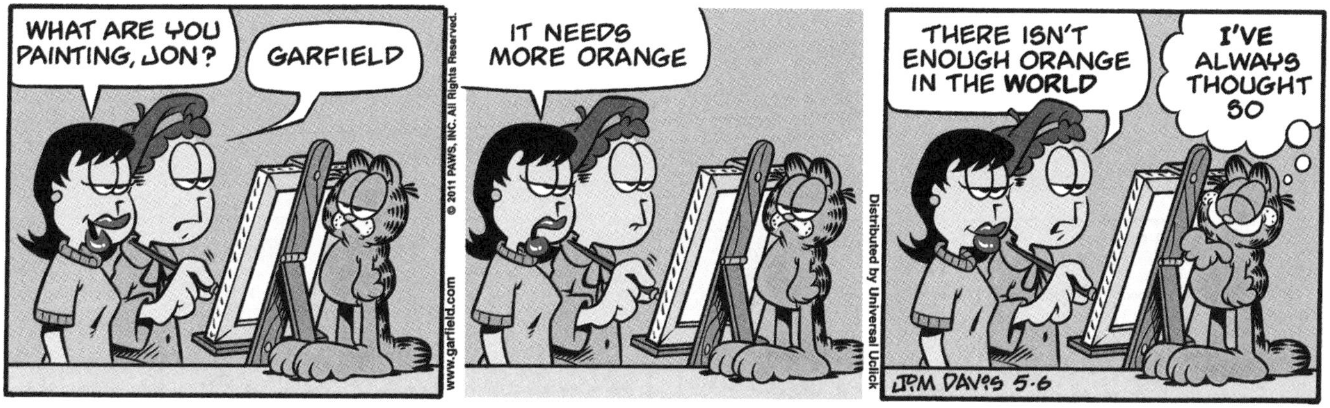
WHAT ARE YOU PAINTING, JON?
GARFIELD
© 2011 PAWS, INC. All Rights Reserved.
www.garfield.com
IT NEEDS MORE ORANGE
Distributed by Universal Uclick
THERE ISN'T ENOUGH ORANGE IN THE **WORLD**
I'VE ALWAYS THOUGHT SO
JIM DAVIS 5-6

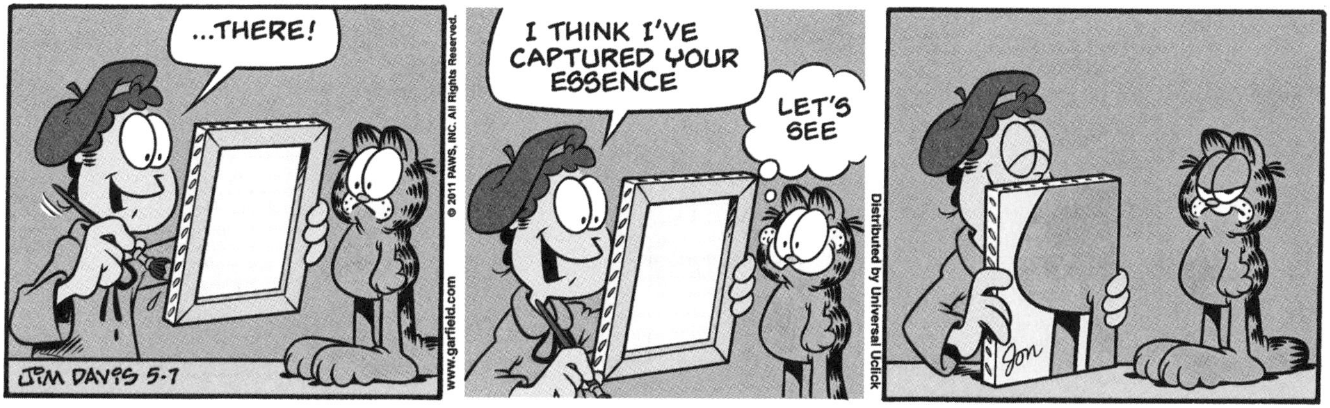
...THERE!
JIM DAVIS 5-7
© 2011 PAWS, INC. All Rights Reserved.
www.garfield.com
I THINK I'VE CAPTURED YOUR ESSENCE
LET'S SEE
Distributed by Universal Uclick
Jon

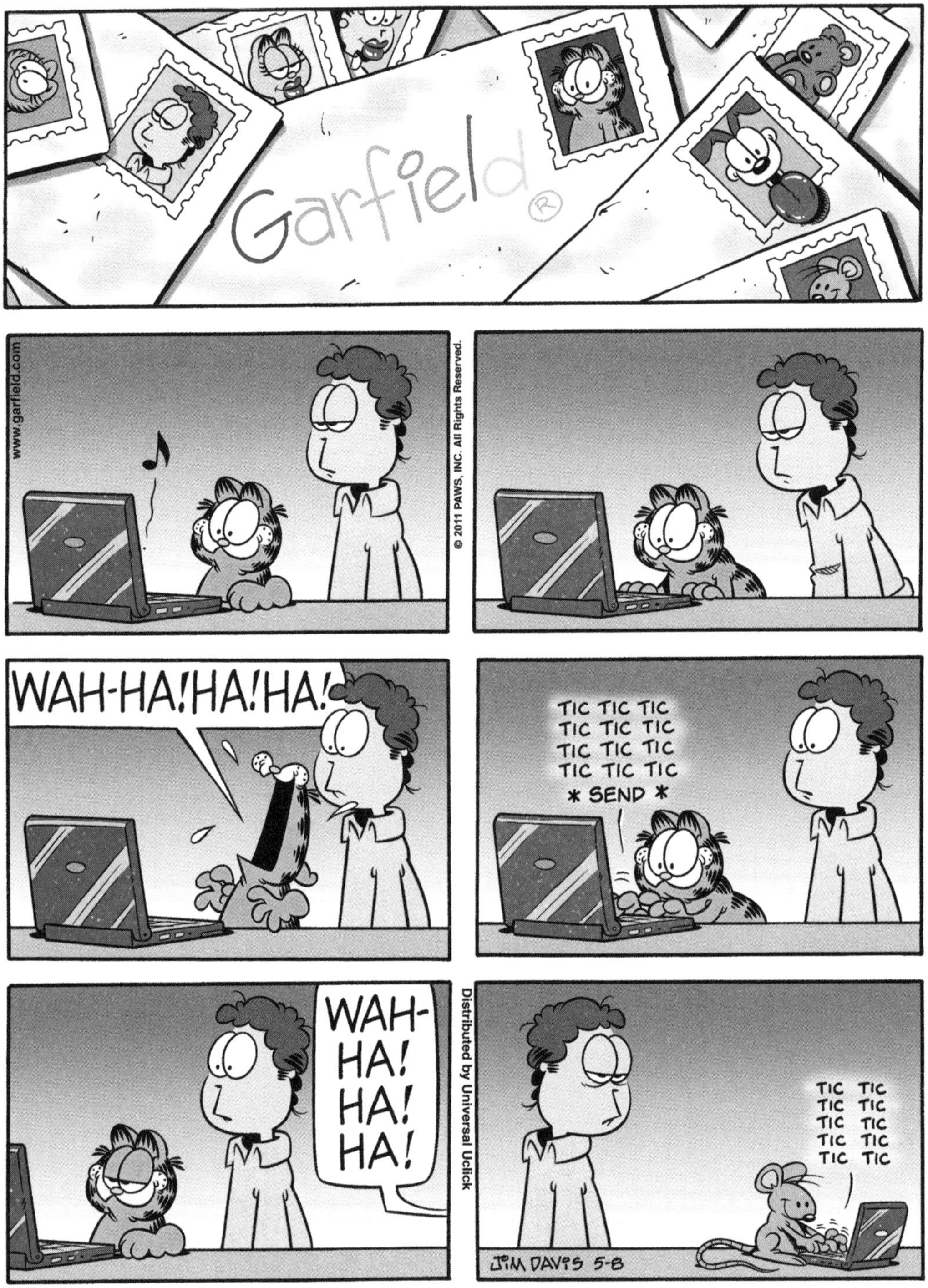
Garfield®
www.garfield.com
© 2011 PAWS, INC. All Rights Reserved.
WAH-HA!HA!HA!
TIC TIC TIC
TIC TIC TIC
TIC TIC TIC
TIC TIC TIC
* SEND *
WAH-
HA!
HA!
HA!
Distributed by Universal Uclick
TIC TIC
TIC TIC
TIC TIC
TIC TIC
TIC TIC
JIM DAVIS 5-8

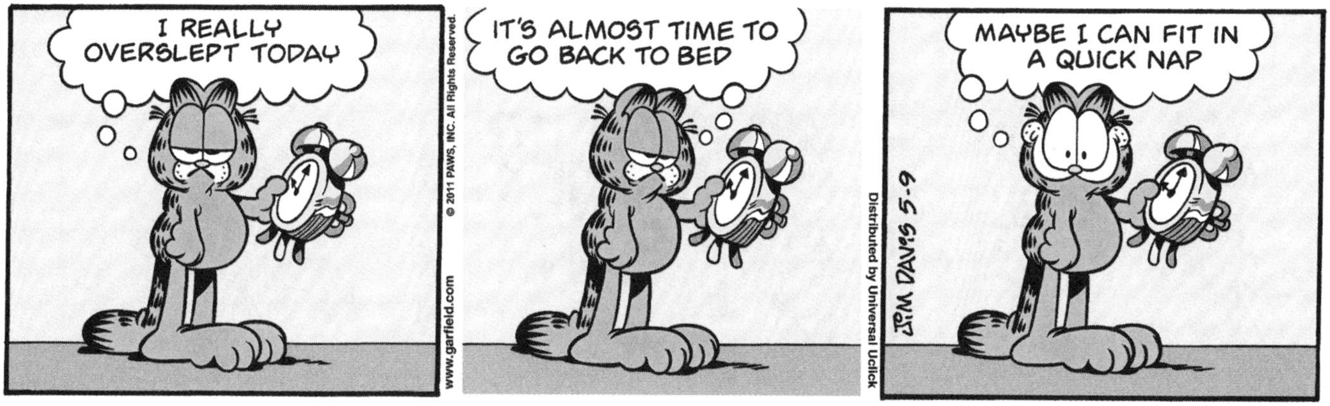
I REALLY OVERSLEPT TODAY
© 2011 PAWS, INC. All Rights Reserved.
www.garfield.com
IT'S ALMOST TIME TO GO BACK TO BED
MAYBE I CAN FIT IN A QUICK NAP
JIM DAVIS 5-9
Distributed by Universal Uclick

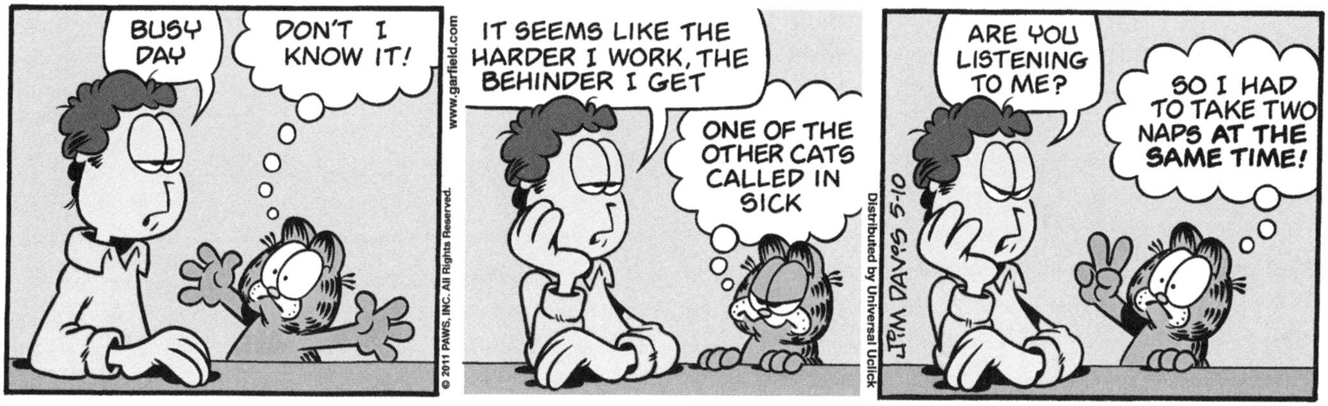
BUSY DAY
DON'T I KNOW IT!
© 2011 PAWS, INC. All Rights Reserved.
www.garfield.com
IT SEEMS LIKE THE HARDER I WORK, THE BEHINDER I GET
ONE OF THE OTHER CATS CALLED IN SICK
ARE YOU LISTENING TO ME?
SO I HAD TO TAKE TWO NAPS AT THE SAME TIME!
JIM DAVIS 5-10
Distributed by Universal Uclick

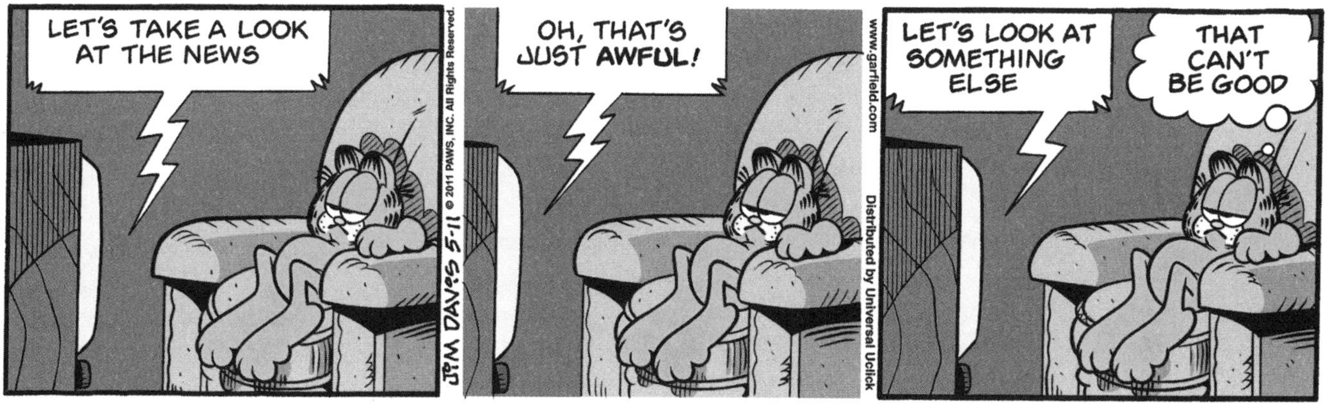
LET'S TAKE A LOOK AT THE NEWS
JIM DAVIS 5-11
© 2011 PAWS, INC. All Rights Reserved.
OH, THAT'S JUST AWFUL!
www.garfield.com
Distributed by Universal Uclick
LET'S LOOK AT SOMETHING ELSE
THAT CAN'T BE GOOD

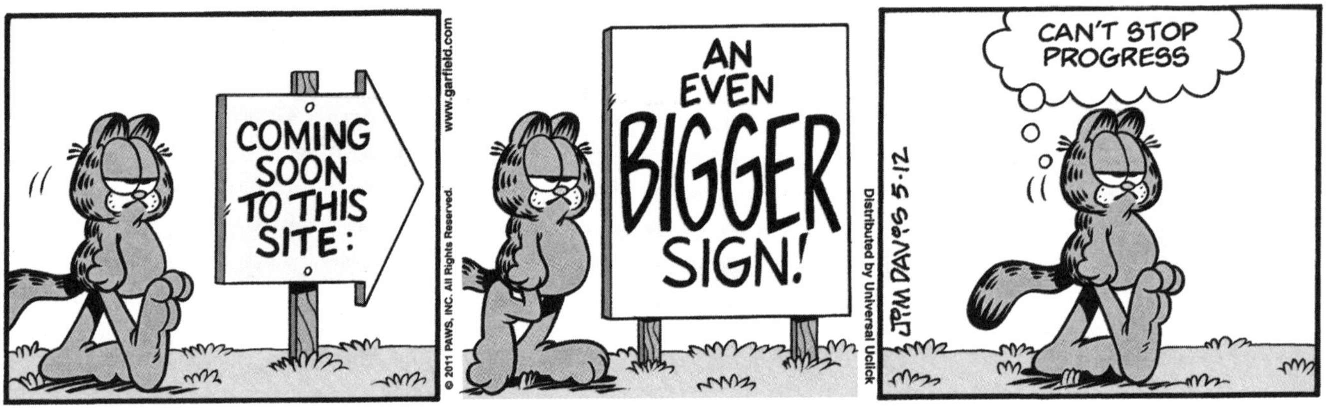
COMING SOON TO THIS SITE:
AN EVEN BIGGER SIGN!
CAN'T STOP PROGRESS
JPM DAV?S 5-12
© 2011 PAWS, INC. All Rights Reserved. www.garfield.com
Distributed by Universal Uclick

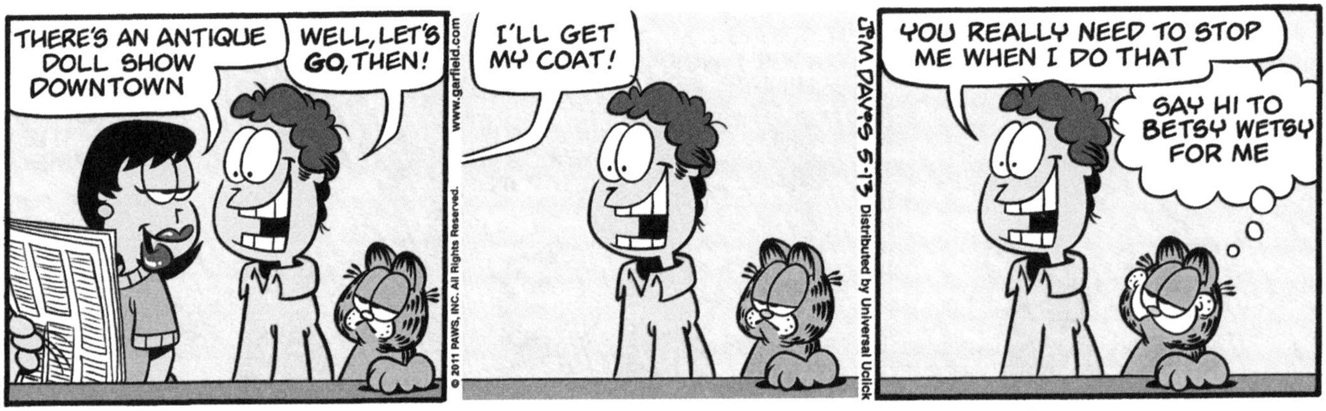
THERE'S AN ANTIQUE DOLL SHOW DOWNTOWN
WELL, LET'S GO, THEN!
I'LL GET MY COAT!
YOU REALLY NEED TO STOP ME WHEN I DO THAT
SAY HI TO BETSY WETSY FOR ME
JPM DAV?S 5-13
© 2011 PAWS, INC. All Rights Reserved. www.garfield.com
Distributed by Universal Uclick

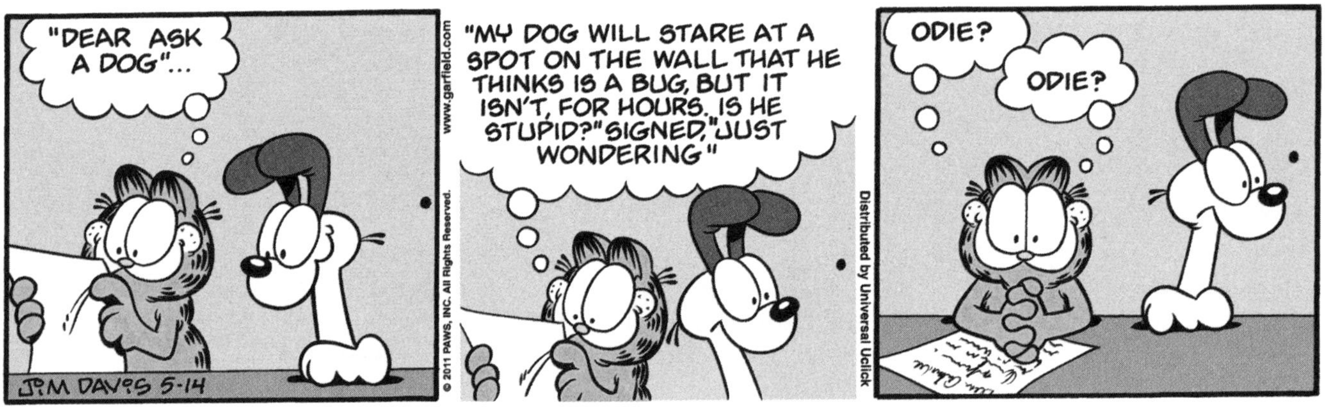
"DEAR ASK A DOG"...
"MY DOG WILL STARE AT A SPOT ON THE WALL THAT HE THINKS IS A BUG, BUT IT ISN'T, FOR HOURS. IS HE STUPID?" SIGNED, "JUST WONDERING"
ODIE?
ODIE?
JPM DAV?S 5-14
© 2011 PAWS, INC. All Rights Reserved. www.garfield.com
Distributed by Universal Uclick

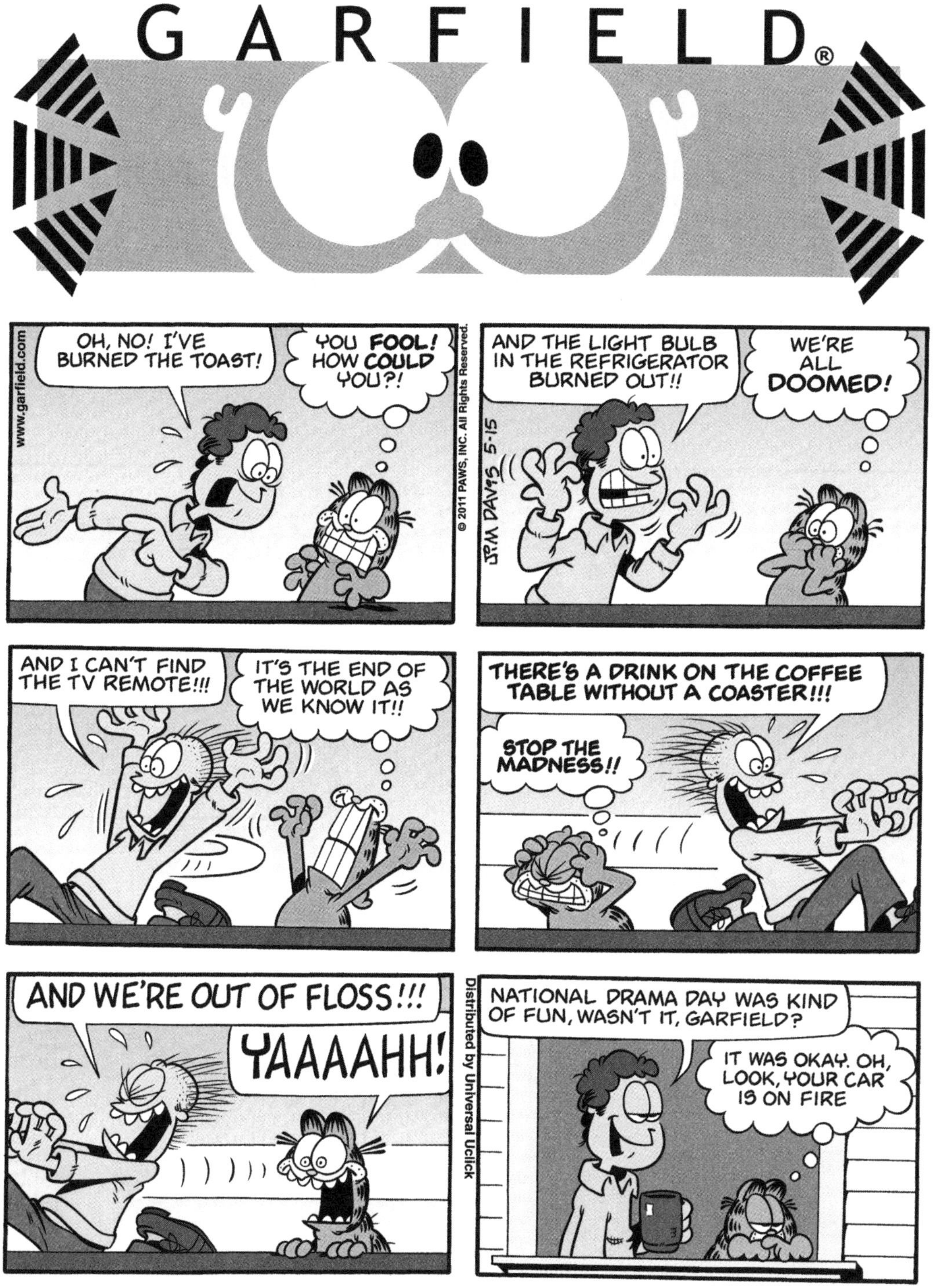
GARFIELD®
OH, NO! I'VE BURNED THE TOAST!
YOU FOOL! HOW COULD YOU?!
www.garfield.com
© 2011 PAWS, INC. All Rights Reserved.
JPM DAVIS 5-15
AND THE LIGHT BULB IN THE REFRIGERATOR BURNED OUT!!
WE'RE ALL DOOMED!
AND I CAN'T FIND THE TV REMOTE!!!
IT'S THE END OF THE WORLD AS WE KNOW IT!!
THERE'S A DRINK ON THE COFFEE TABLE WITHOUT A COASTER!!!
STOP THE MADNESS!!
AND WE'RE OUT OF FLOSS!!!
YAAAAHH!
Distributed by Universal Uclick
NATIONAL DRAMA DAY WAS KIND OF FUN, WASN'T IT, GARFIELD?
IT WAS OKAY. OH, LOOK, YOUR CAR IS ON FIRE

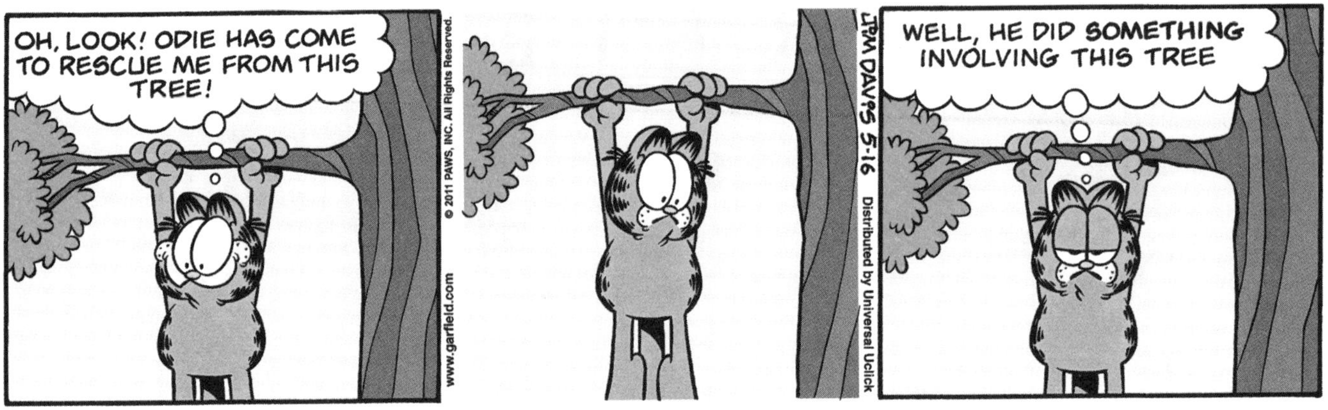
OH, LOOK! ODIE HAS COME TO RESCUE ME FROM THIS TREE!
© 2011 PAWS, INC. All Rights Reserved. www.garfield.com
JIM DAVIS 5-16
Distributed by Universal Uclick
WELL, HE DID SOMETHING INVOLVING THIS TREE

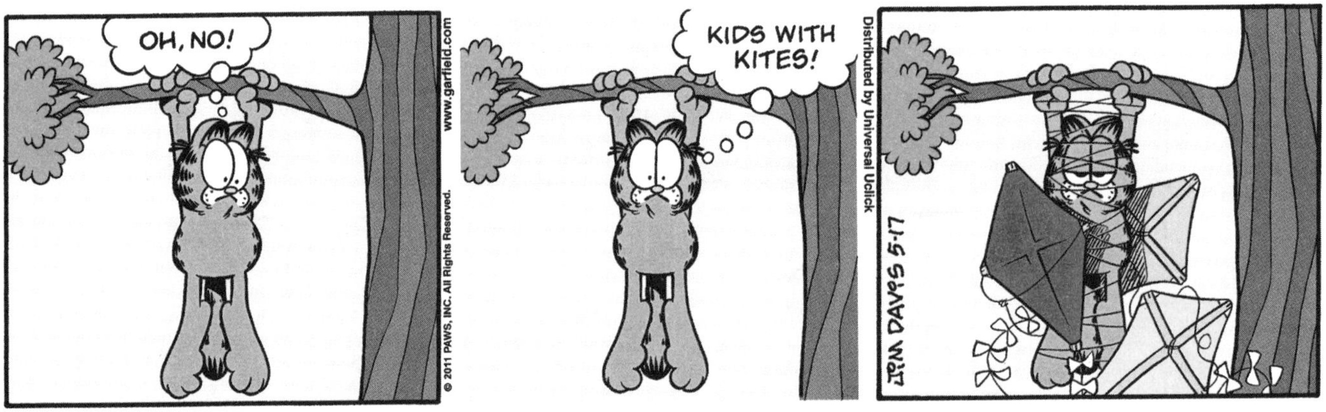
OH, NO!
© 2011 PAWS, INC. All Rights Reserved. www.garfield.com
KIDS WITH KITES!
Distributed by Universal Uclick
JIM DAVIS 5-17

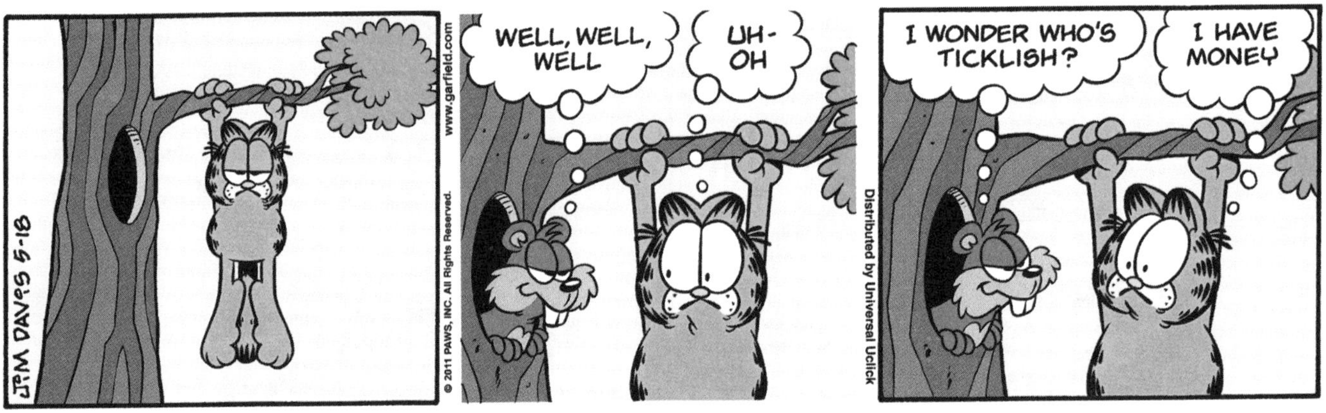
JIM DAVIS 5-18
© 2011 PAWS, INC. All Rights Reserved. www.garfield.com
WELL, WELL, WELL
UH-OH
Distributed by Universal Uclick
I WONDER WHO'S TICKLISH?
I HAVE MONEY

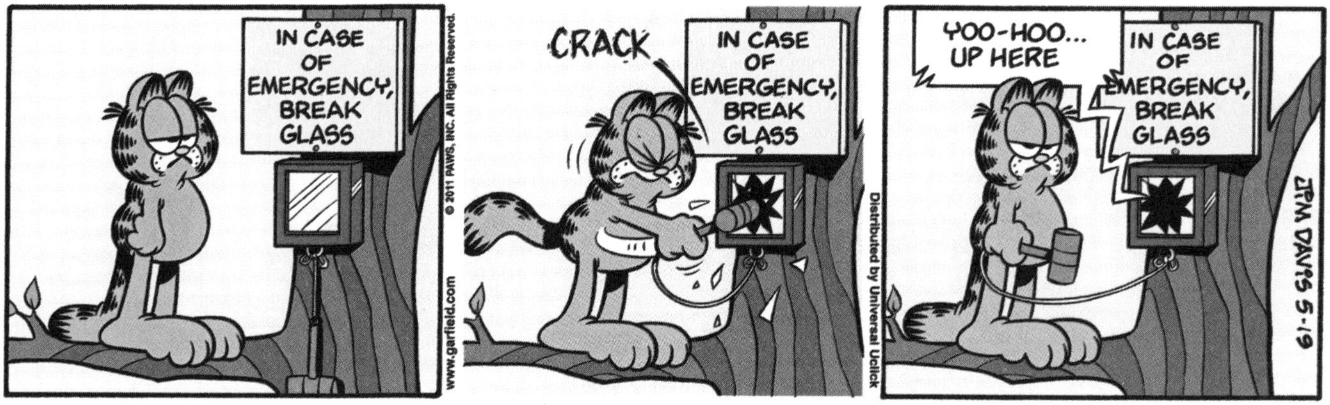
IN CASE OF EMERGENCY, BREAK GLASS
© 2011 PAWS, INC. All Rights Reserved.
www.garfield.com
CRACK
IN CASE OF EMERGENCY, BREAK GLASS
Distributed by Universal Uclick
YOO-HOO... UP HERE
IN CASE OF EMERGENCY, BREAK GLASS
JIM DAVIS 5-19

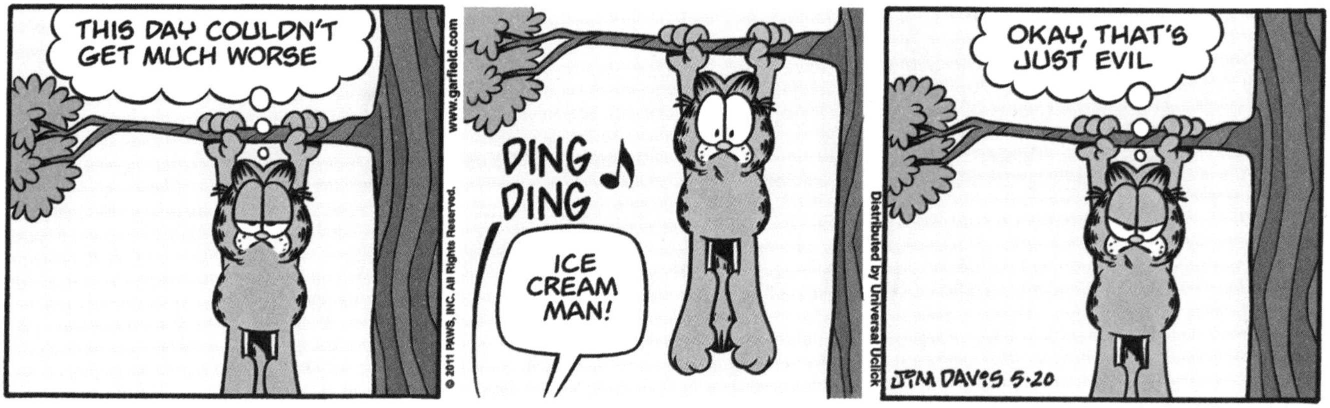
THIS DAY COULDN'T GET MUCH WORSE
www.garfield.com
© 2011 PAWS, INC. All Rights Reserved.
DING DING
ICE CREAM MAN!
Distributed by Universal Uclick
OKAY, THAT'S JUST EVIL
JIM DAVIS 5-20

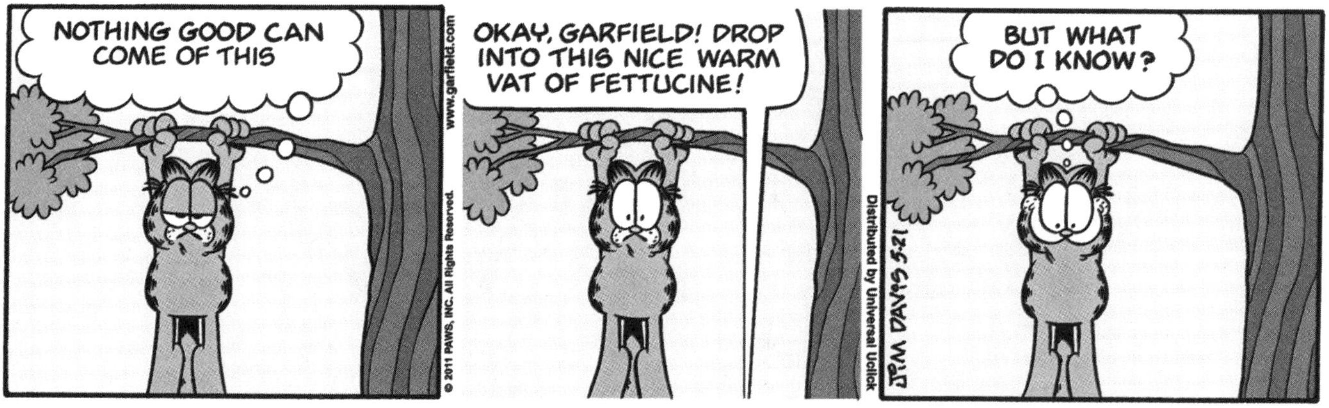
NOTHING GOOD CAN COME OF THIS
www.garfield.com
© 2011 PAWS, INC. All Rights Reserved.
OKAY, GARFIELD! DROP INTO THIS NICE WARM VAT OF FETTUCINE!
Distributed by Universal Uclick
BUT WHAT DO I KNOW?
JIM DAVIS 5-21

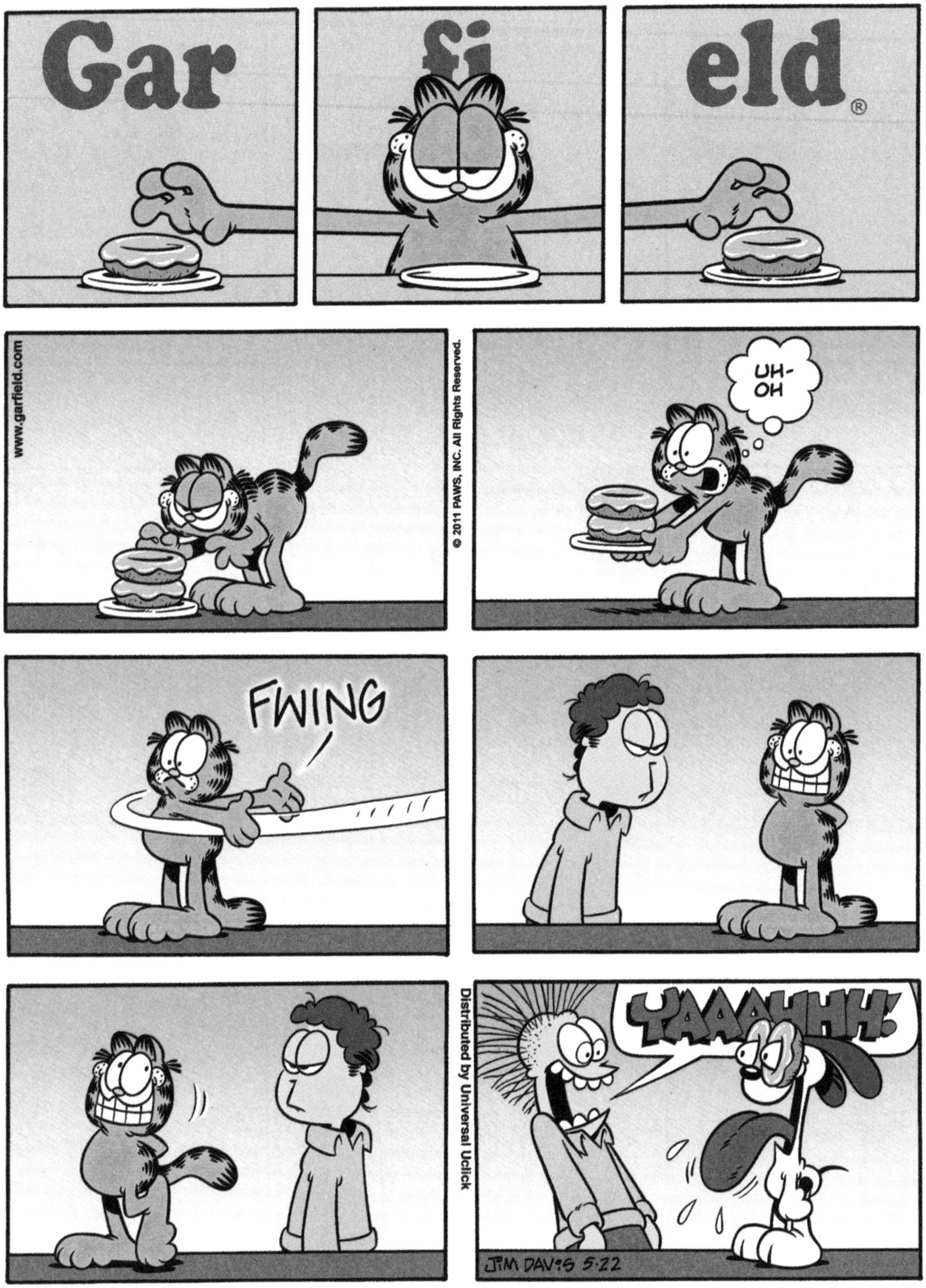
Garfield®
www.garfield.com
© 2011 PAWS, INC. All Rights Reserved.
UH-OH
FWING
Distributed by Universal Uclick
YAAAHHH!
JIM DAVIS 5-22

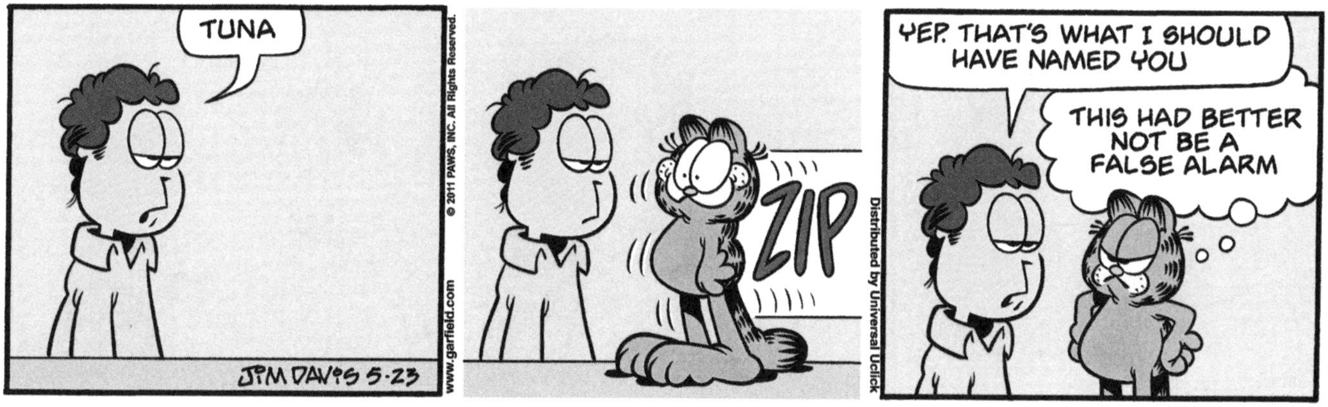
TUNA
JIM DAVIS 5-23
© 2011 PAWS, INC. All Rights Reserved.
www.garfield.com
ZIP
Distributed by Universal Uclick
YEP. THAT'S WHAT I SHOULD HAVE NAMED YOU
THIS HAD BETTER NOT BE A FALSE ALARM

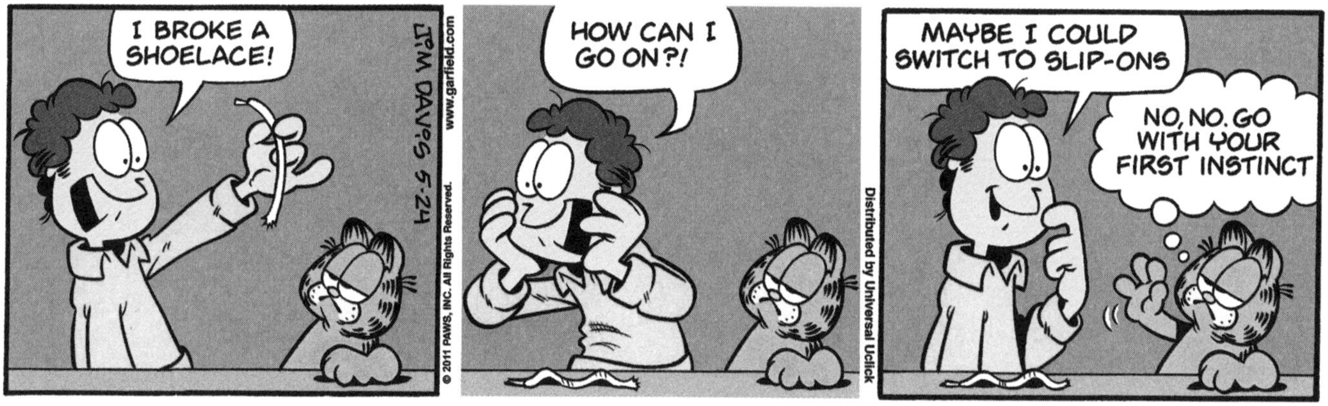
I BROKE A SHOELACE!
JIM DAVIS 5-24
www.garfield.com
© 2011 PAWS, INC. All Rights Reserved.
HOW CAN I GO ON?!
Distributed by Universal Uclick
MAYBE I COULD SWITCH TO SLIP-ONS
NO, NO. GO WITH YOUR FIRST INSTINCT

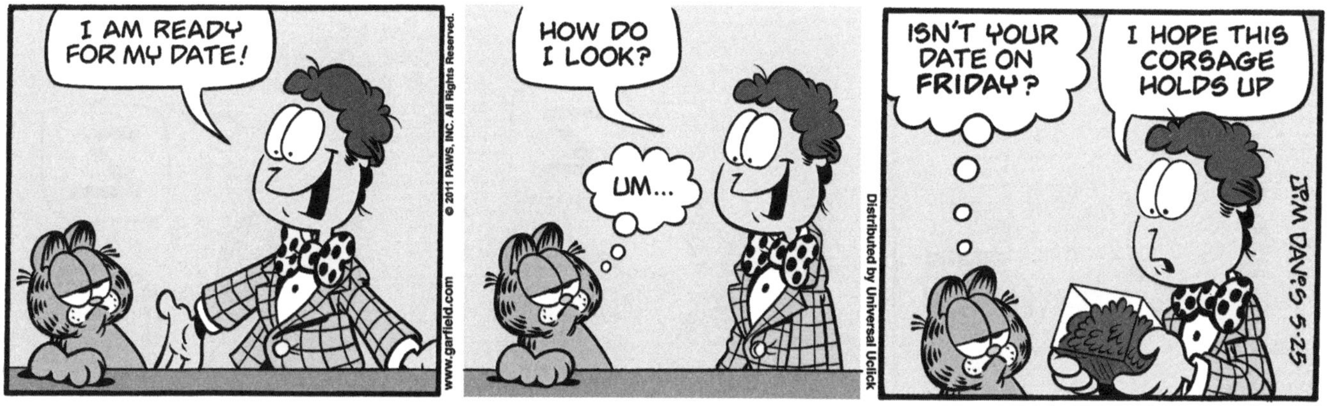
I AM READY FOR MY DATE!
© 2011 PAWS, INC. All Rights Reserved.
www.garfield.com
HOW DO I LOOK?
UM...
Distributed by Universal Uclick
ISN'T YOUR DATE ON FRIDAY?
I HOPE THIS CORSAGE HOLDS UP
JIM DAVIS 5-25

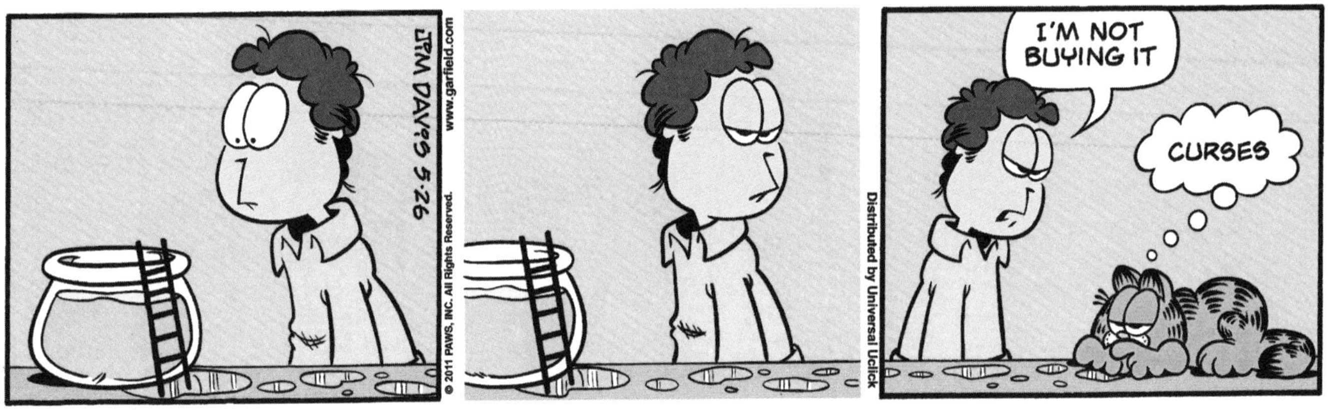
JIM DAVIS 5-26
I'M NOT BUYING IT
CURSES

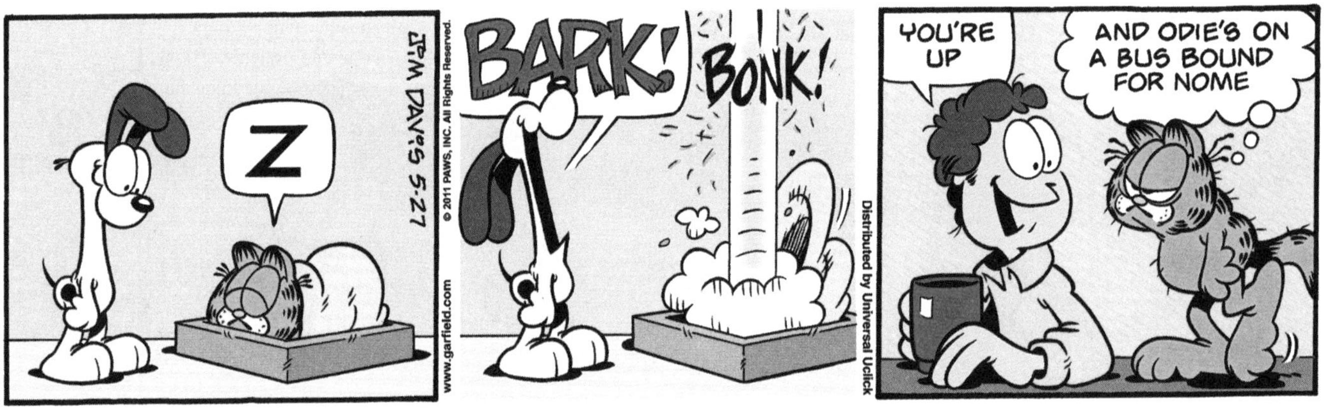
JIM DAVIS 5-27
Z
BARK!
BONK!
YOU'RE UP
AND ODIE'S ON A BUS BOUND FOR NOME

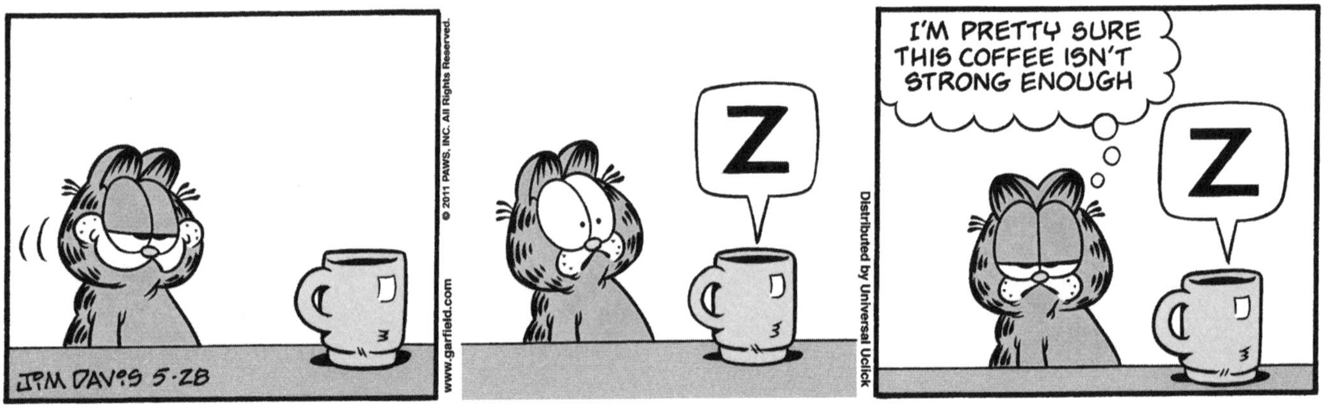
JIM DAVIS 5-28
Z
I'M PRETTY SURE THIS COFFEE ISN'T STRONG ENOUGH
Z

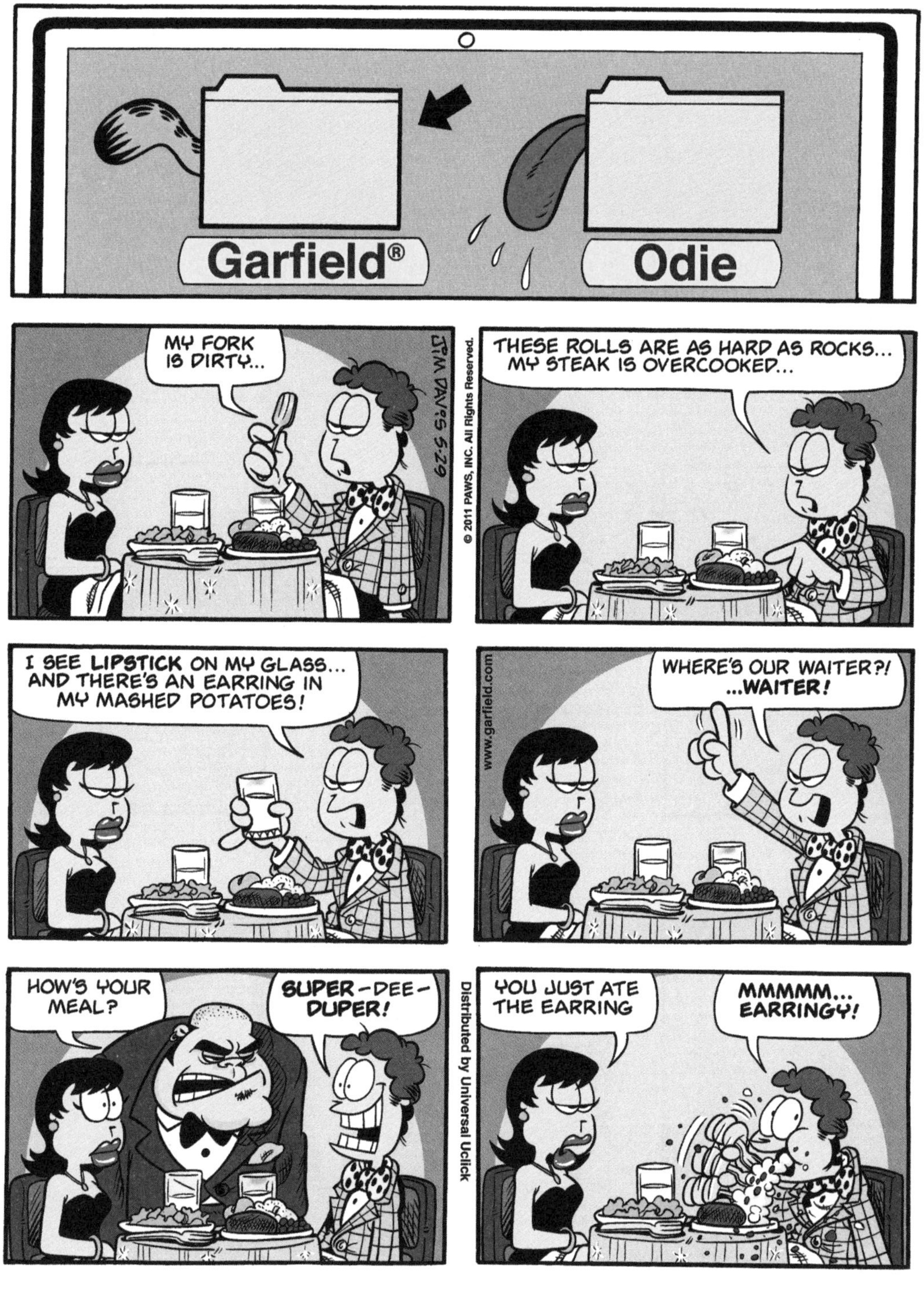
Garfield®
Odie
MY FORK IS DIRTY...
JIM DAVIS 5-29
© 2011 PAWS, INC. All Rights Reserved.
THESE ROLLS ARE AS HARD AS ROCKS... MY STEAK IS OVERCOOKED...
I SEE LIPSTICK ON MY GLASS... AND THERE'S AN EARRING IN MY MASHED POTATOES!
www.garfield.com
WHERE'S OUR WAITER?! ...WAITER!
HOW'S YOUR MEAL?
SUPER-DEE-DUPER!
Distributed by Universal Uclick
YOU JUST ATE THE EARRING
MMMMM... EARRINGY!

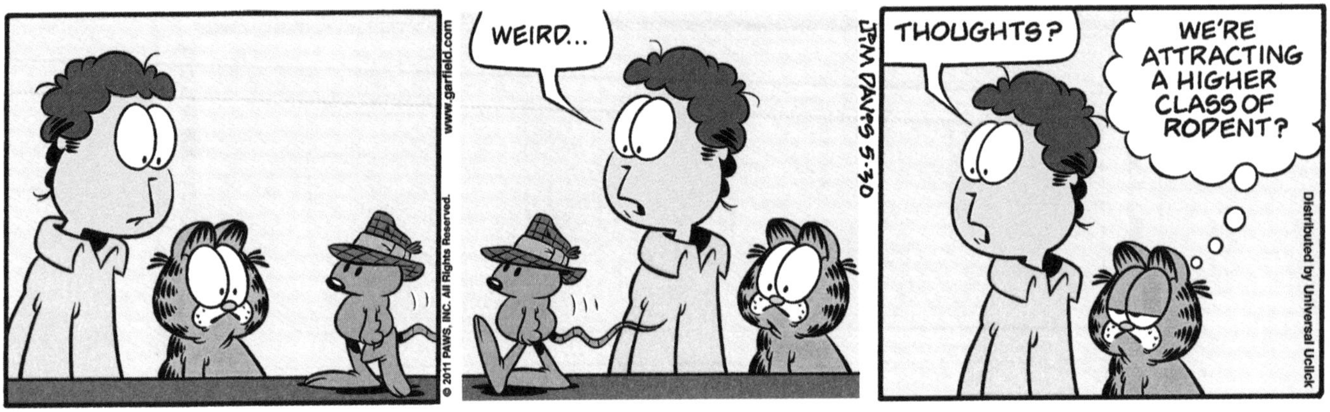

WEIRD...
THOUGHTS?
WE'RE ATTRACTING A HIGHER CLASS OF RODENT?
© 2011 PAWS, INC. All Rights Reserved.
www.garfield.com
Distributed by Universal Uclick

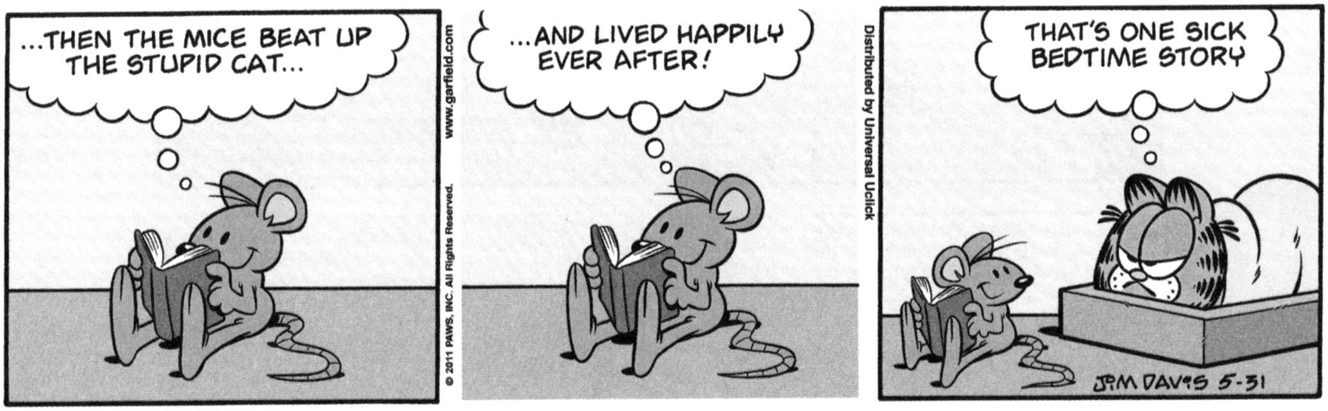

...THEN THE MICE BEAT UP THE STUPID CAT...
...AND LIVED HAPPILY EVER AFTER!
THAT'S ONE SICK BEDTIME STORY
© 2011 PAWS, INC. All Rights Reserved.
www.garfield.com
Distributed by Universal Uclick

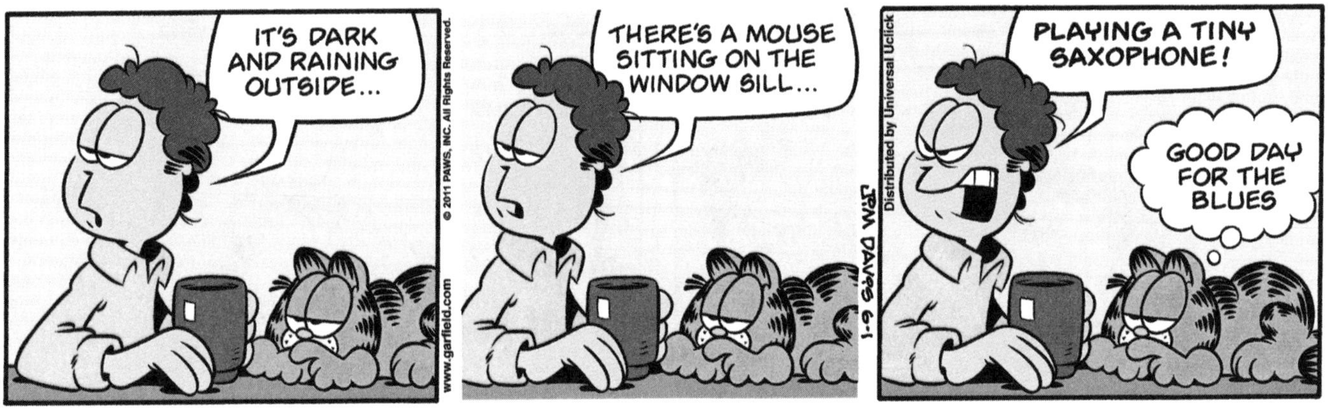

IT'S DARK AND RAINING OUTSIDE...
THERE'S A MOUSE SITTING ON THE WINDOW SILL...
PLAYING A TINY SAXOPHONE!
GOOD DAY FOR THE BLUES
© 2011 PAWS, INC. All Rights Reserved.
www.garfield.com
Distributed by Universal Uclick

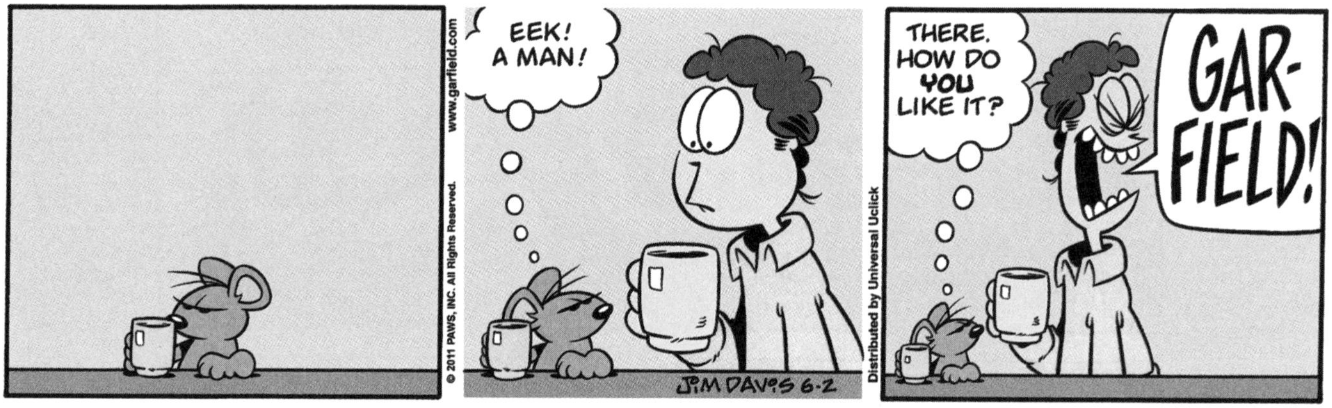
EEK! A MAN!
www.garfield.com
© 2011 PAWS, INC. All Rights Reserved.
JIM DAVIS 6-2
Distributed by Universal Uclick
THERE. HOW DO YOU LIKE IT?
GAR-FIELD!

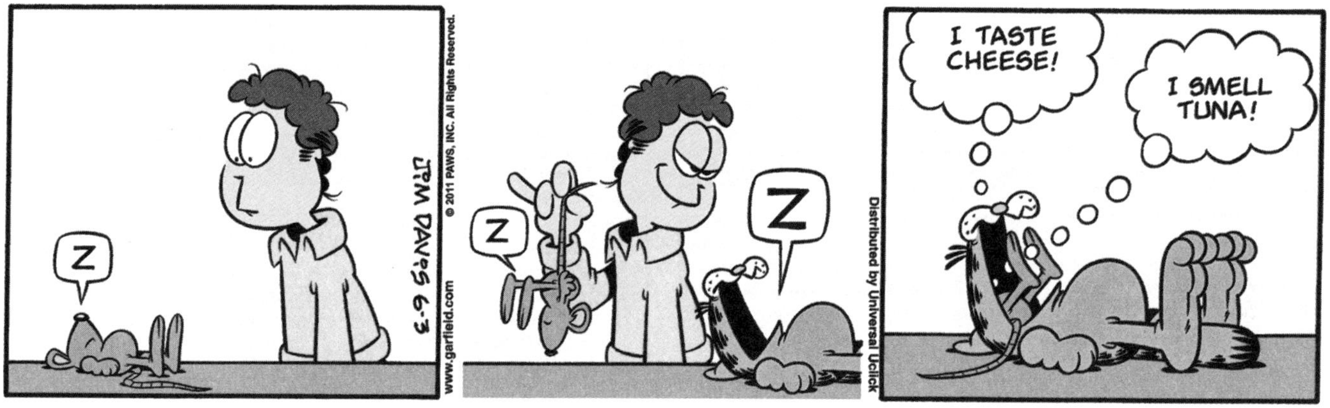
Z
JIM DAVIS 6-3
© 2011 PAWS, INC. All Rights Reserved.
www.garfield.com
Z
Z
Distributed by Universal Uclick
I TASTE CHEESE!
I SMELL TUNA!

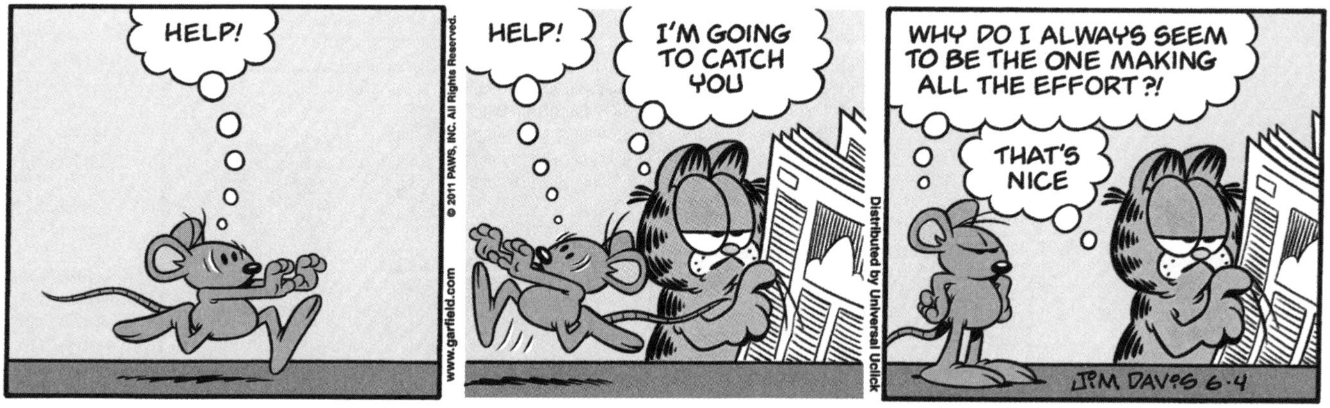
HELP!
www.garfield.com
© 2011 PAWS, INC. All Rights Reserved.
HELP!
I'M GOING TO CATCH YOU
Distributed by Universal Uclick
WHY DO I ALWAYS SEEM TO BE THE ONE MAKING ALL THE EFFORT?!
THAT'S NICE
JIM DAVIS 6-4

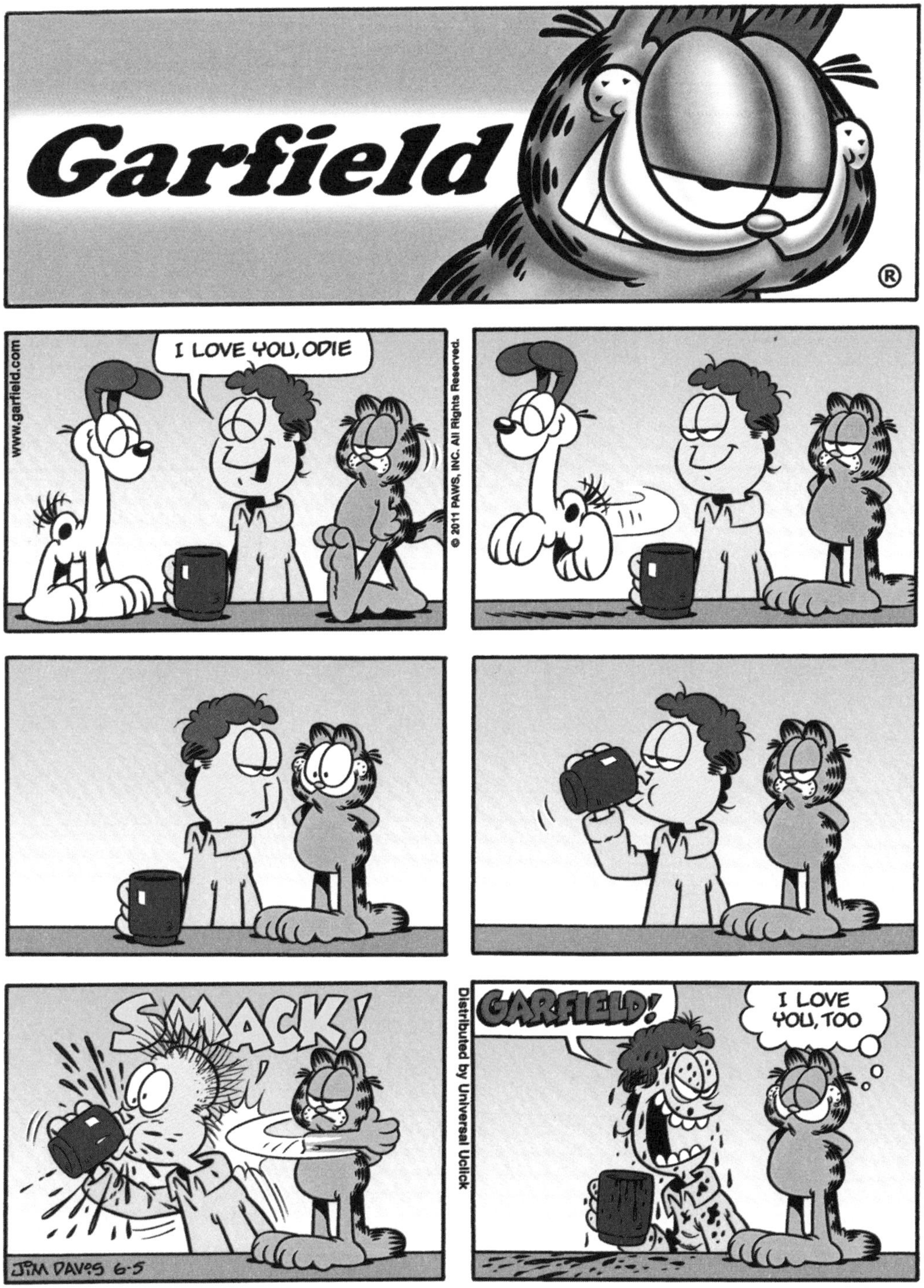
Garfield
®
www.garfield.com
I LOVE YOU, ODIE
© 2011 PAWS, INC. All Rights Reserved.
SMACK!
JIM DAVIS 6-5
Distributed by Universal Uclick
GARFIELD!
I LOVE YOU, TOO

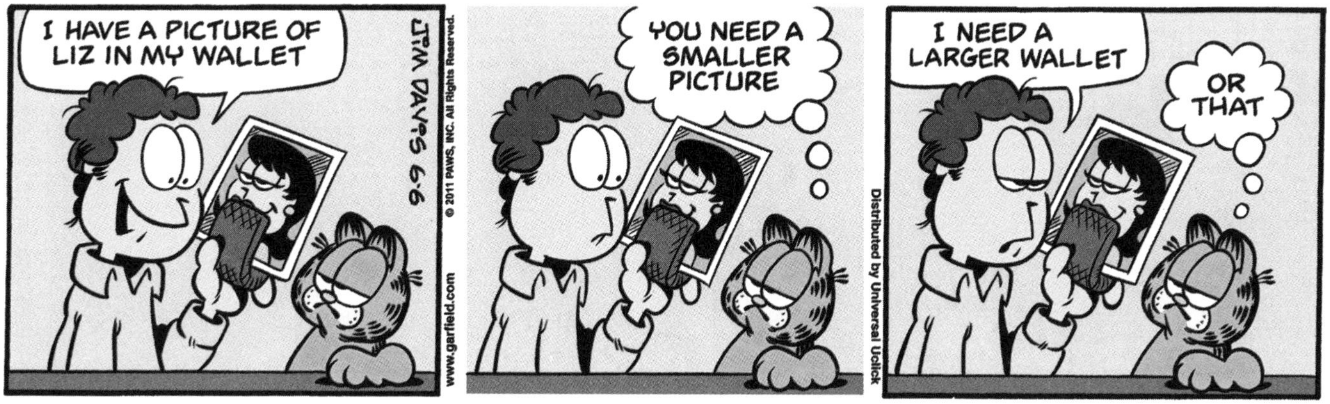
I HAVE A PICTURE OF LIZ IN MY WALLET
JIM DAVIS 6-6
© 2011 PAWS, INC. All Rights Reserved.
www.garfield.com
YOU NEED A SMALLER PICTURE
Distributed by Universal Uclick
I NEED A LARGER WALLET
OR THAT

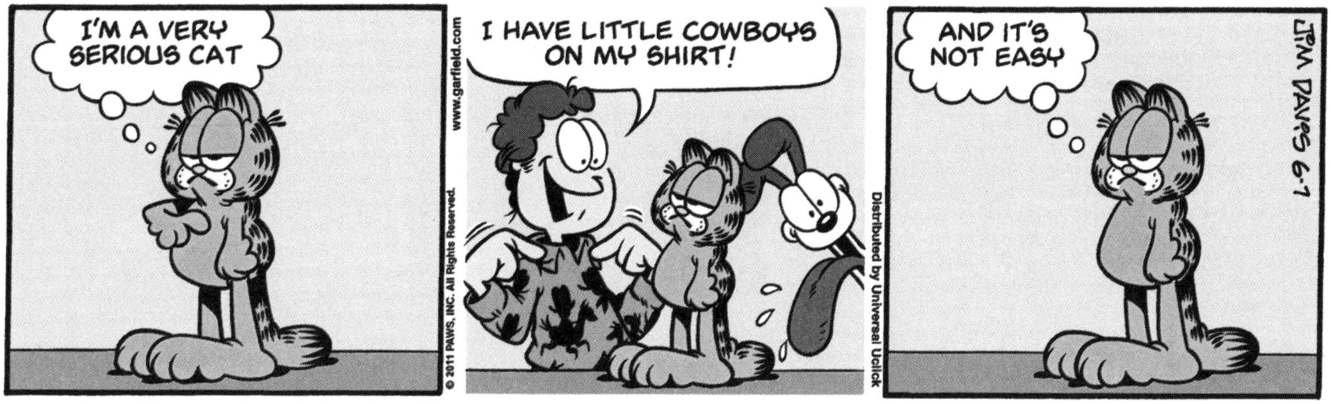
I'M A VERY SERIOUS CAT
www.garfield.com
© 2011 PAWS, INC. All Rights Reserved.
I HAVE LITTLE COWBOYS ON MY SHIRT!
Distributed by Universal Uclick
AND IT'S NOT EASY
JIM DAVIS 6-7

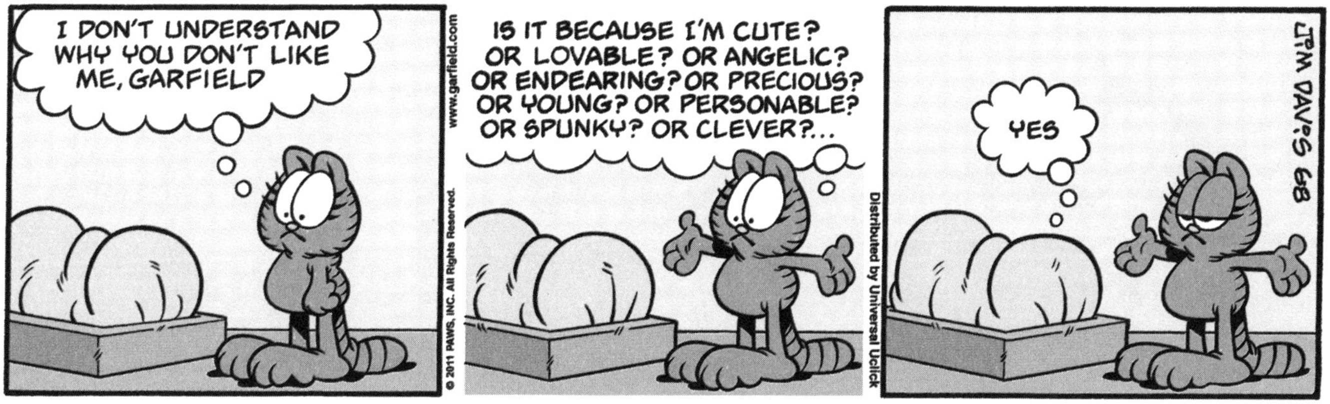
I DON'T UNDERSTAND WHY YOU DON'T LIKE ME, GARFIELD
www.garfield.com
© 2011 PAWS, INC. All Rights Reserved.
IS IT BECAUSE I'M CUTE? OR LOVABLE? OR ANGELIC? OR ENDEARING? OR PRECIOUS? OR YOUNG? OR PERSONABLE? OR SPUNKY? OR CLEVER?...
Distributed by Universal Uclick
YES
JIM DAVIS 6-8

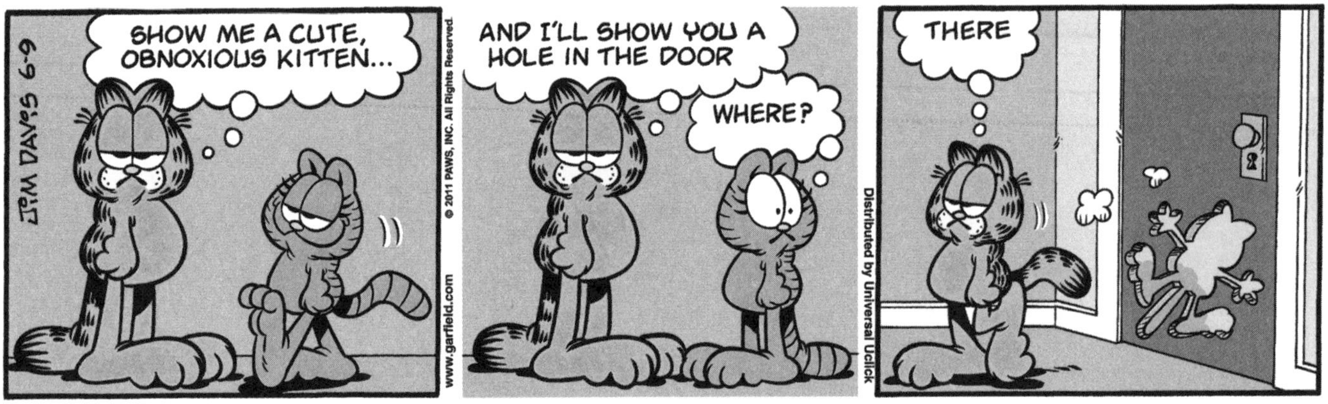
JIM DAVIS 6-9
SHOW ME A CUTE, OBNOXIOUS KITTEN...
© 2011 PAWS, INC. All Rights Reserved. www.garfield.com
AND I'LL SHOW YOU A HOLE IN THE DOOR
WHERE?
Distributed by Universal Uclick
THERE

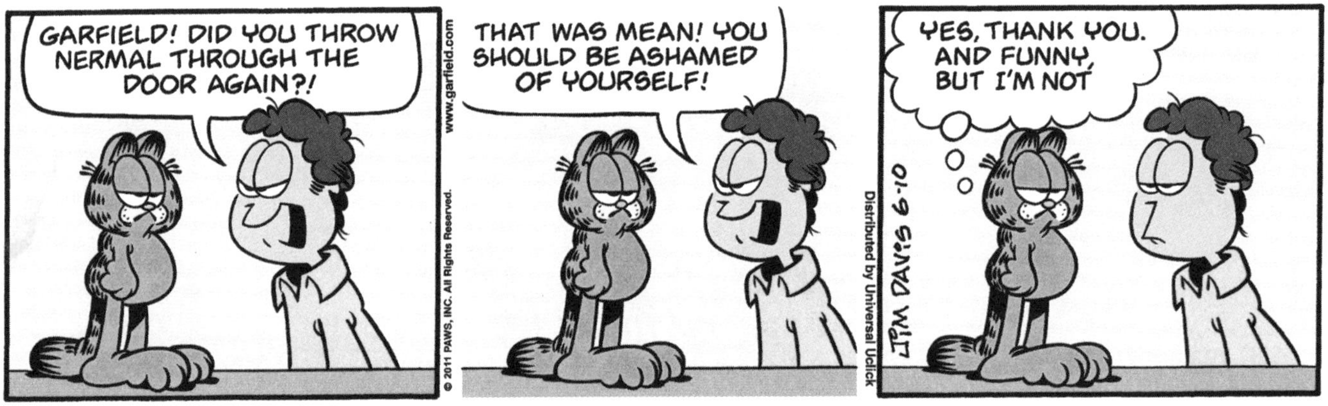
GARFIELD! DID YOU THROW NERMAL THROUGH THE DOOR AGAIN?!
© 2011 PAWS, INC. All Rights Reserved. www.garfield.com
THAT WAS MEAN! YOU SHOULD BE ASHAMED OF YOURSELF!
Distributed by Universal Uclick
JIM DAVIS 6-10
YES, THANK YOU. AND FUNNY, BUT I'M NOT

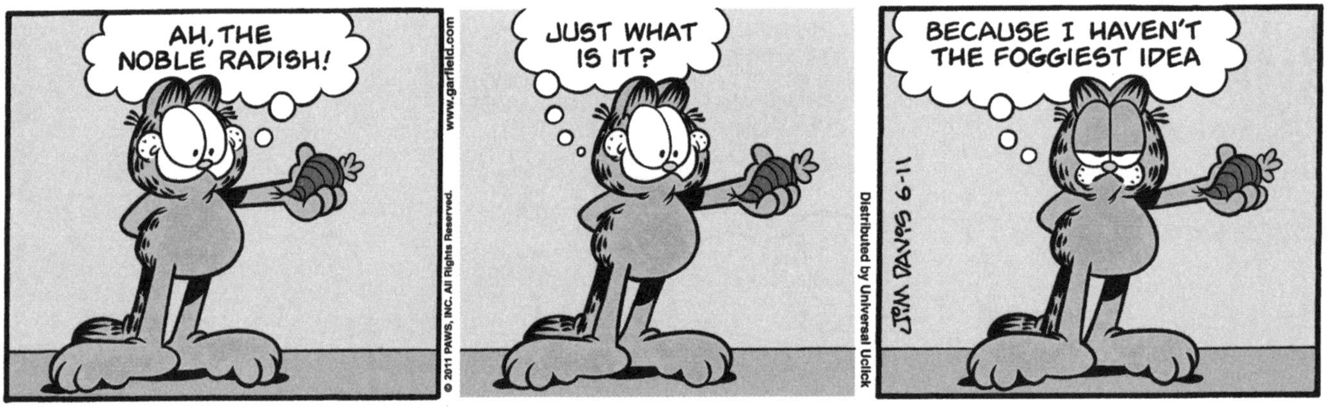
AH, THE NOBLE RADISH!
© 2011 PAWS, INC. All Rights Reserved. www.garfield.com
JUST WHAT IS IT?
Distributed by Universal Uclick
JIM DAVIS 6-11
BECAUSE I HAVEN'T THE FOGGIEST IDEA

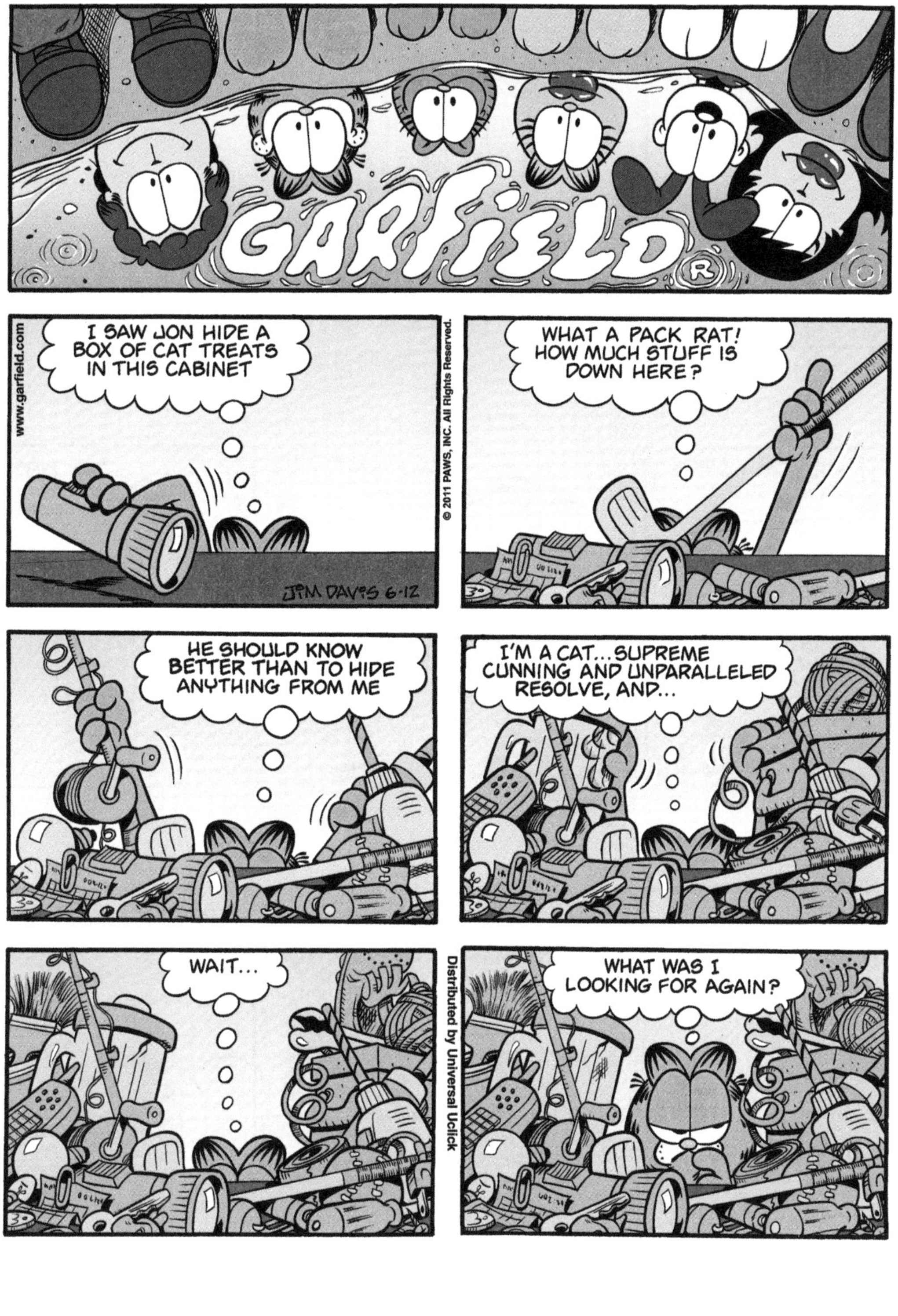
GARFIELD
I SAW JON HIDE A BOX OF CAT TREATS IN THIS CABINET
WHAT A PACK RAT! HOW MUCH STUFF IS DOWN HERE?
HE SHOULD KNOW BETTER THAN TO HIDE ANYTHING FROM ME
I'M A CAT...SUPREME CUNNING AND UNPARALLELED RESOLVE, AND...
WAIT...
WHAT WAS I LOOKING FOR AGAIN?
JIM DAVIS 6-12
www.garfield.com
© 2011 PAWS, INC. All Rights Reserved.
Distributed by Universal Uclick

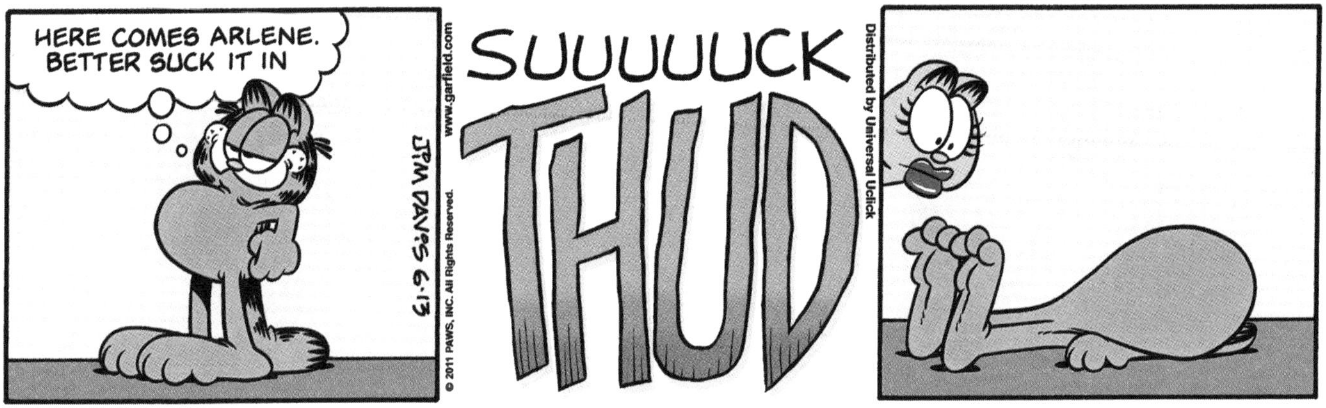
HERE COMES ARLENE. BETTER SUCK IT IN
SUUUUUCK
THUD
JIM DAVIS 6-13
© 2011 PAWS, INC. All Rights Reserved. www.garfield.com
Distributed by Universal Uclick

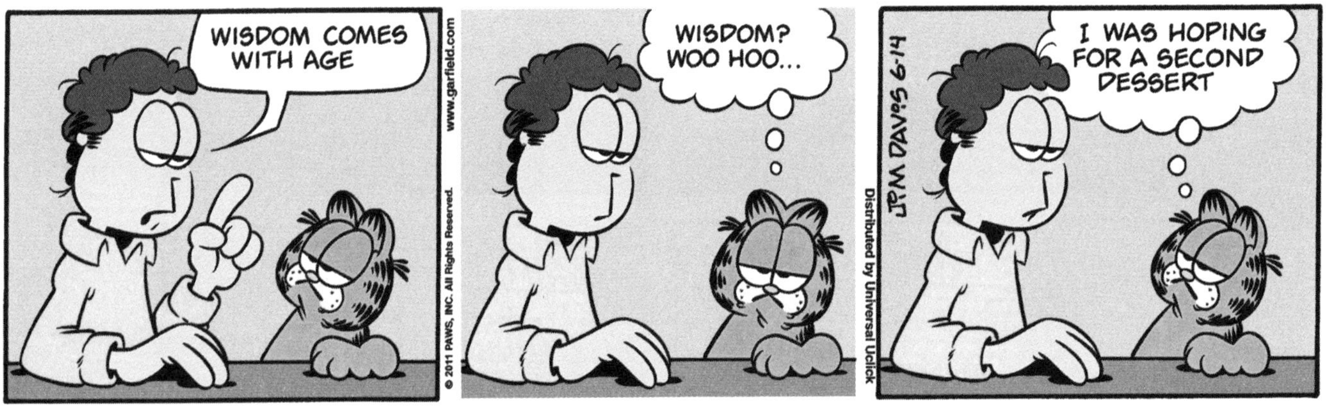
WISDOM COMES WITH AGE
WISDOM? WOO HOO...
I WAS HOPING FOR A SECOND DESSERT
JIM DAVIS 6-14
© 2011 PAWS, INC. All Rights Reserved. www.garfield.com
Distributed by Universal Uclick

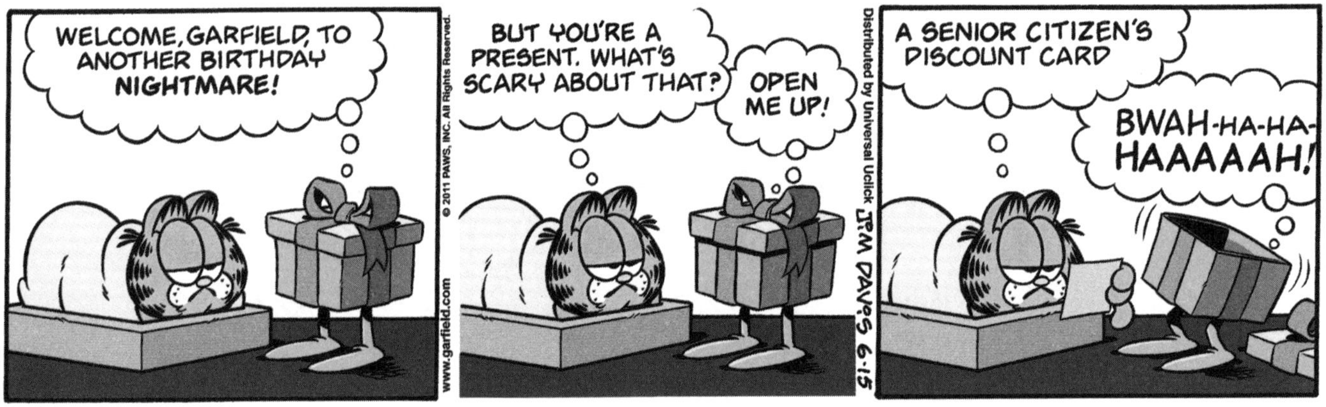
WELCOME, GARFIELD, TO ANOTHER BIRTHDAY NIGHTMARE!
BUT YOU'RE A PRESENT. WHAT'S SCARY ABOUT THAT?
OPEN ME UP!
A SENIOR CITIZEN'S DISCOUNT CARD
BWAH-HA-HA-HAAAAAH!
JIM DAVIS 6-15
© 2011 PAWS, INC. All Rights Reserved. www.garfield.com
Distributed by Universal Uclick

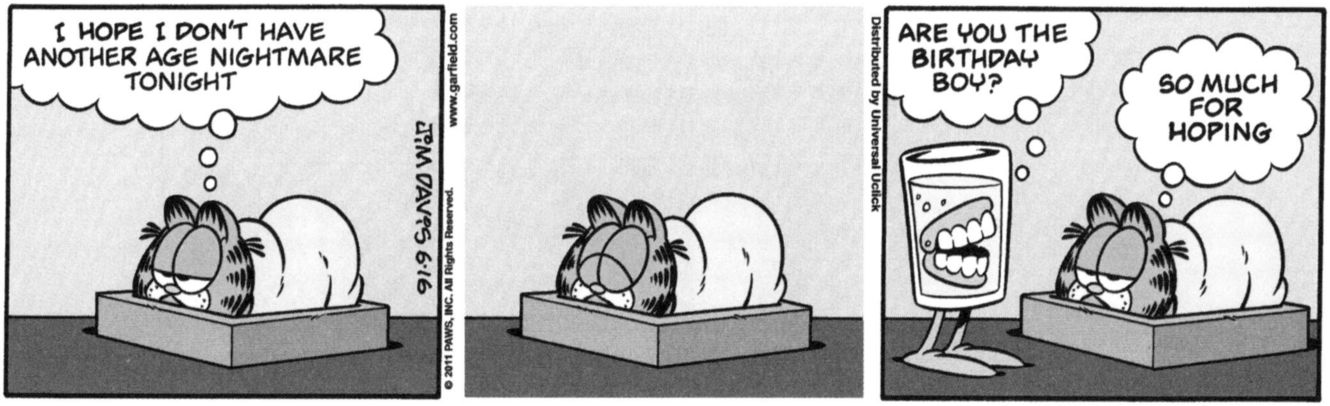
I HOPE I DON'T HAVE ANOTHER AGE NIGHTMARE TONIGHT
JIM DAVIS 6-16
www.garfield.com
© 2011 PAWS, INC. All Rights Reserved.
Distributed by Universal Uclick
ARE YOU THE BIRTHDAY BOY?
SO MUCH FOR HOPING

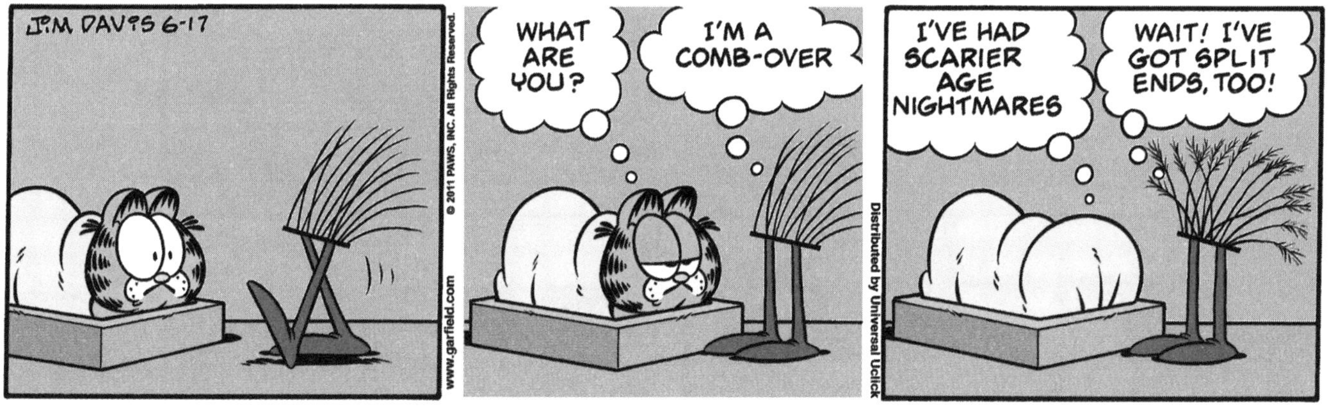
JIM DAVIS 6-17
© 2011 PAWS, INC. All Rights Reserved.
www.garfield.com
WHAT ARE YOU?
I'M A COMB-OVER
Distributed by Universal Uclick
I'VE HAD SCARIER AGE NIGHTMARES
WAIT! I'VE GOT SPLIT ENDS, TOO!

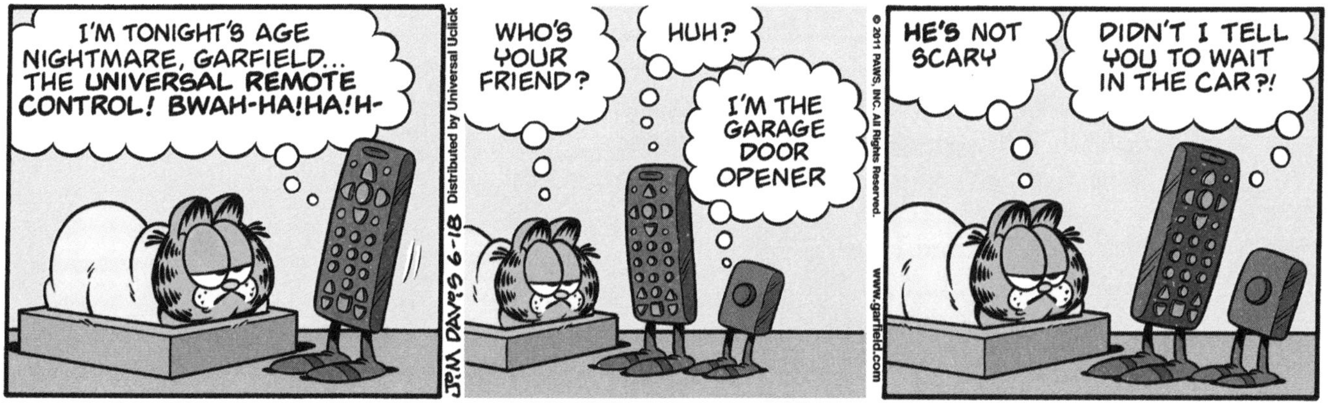
I'M TONIGHT'S AGE NIGHTMARE, GARFIELD... THE UNIVERSAL REMOTE CONTROL! BWAH-HA!HA!H-
JIM DAVIS 6-18
Distributed by Universal Uclick
WHO'S YOUR FRIEND?
HUH?
I'M THE GARAGE DOOR OPENER
© 2011 PAWS, INC. All Rights Reserved.
www.garfield.com
HE'S NOT SCARY
DIDN'T I TELL YOU TO WAIT IN THE CAR?!

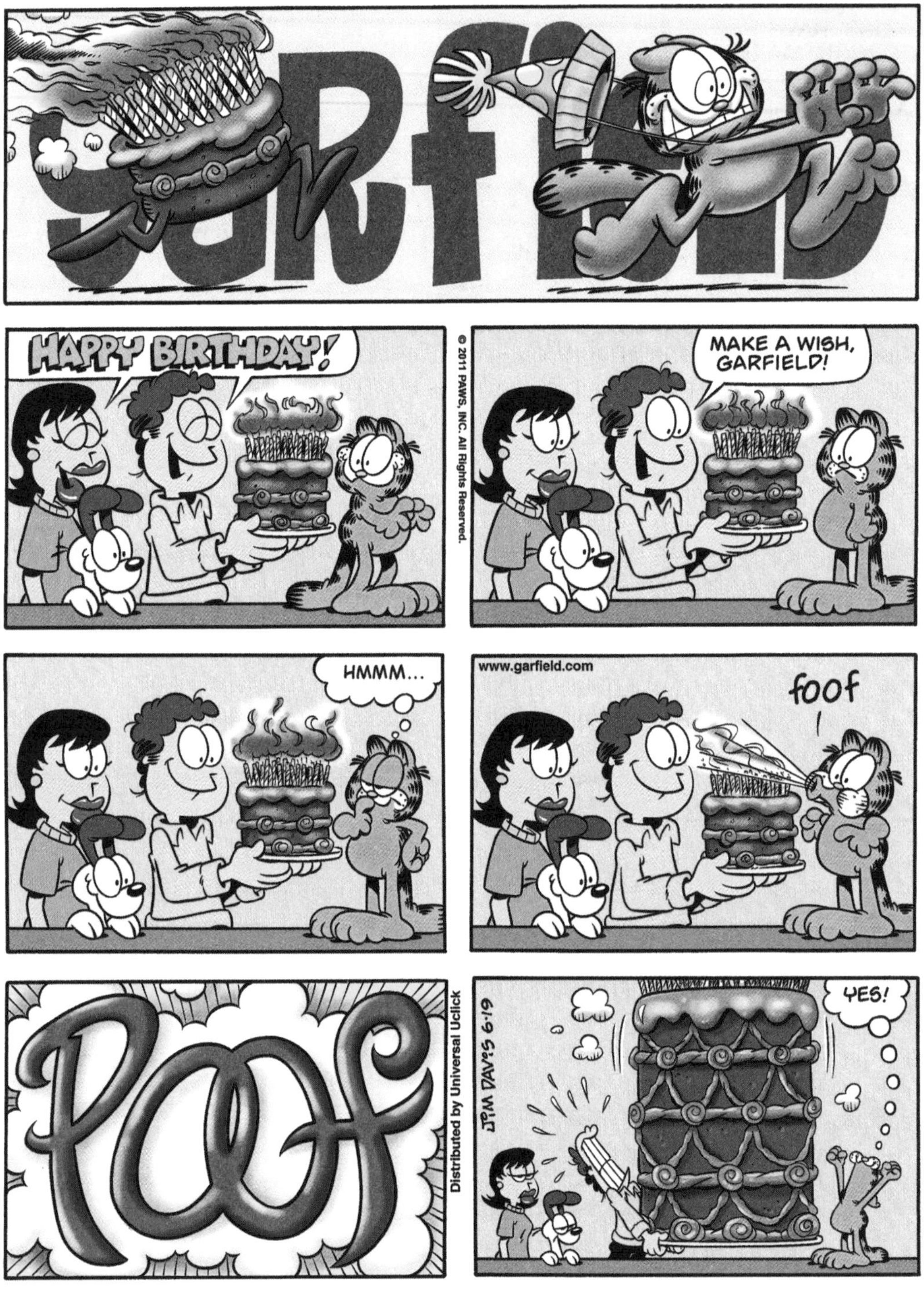

GARFIELD
HAPPY BIRTHDAY!
© 2011 PAWS, INC. All Rights Reserved.
MAKE A WISH, GARFIELD!
HMMM...
www.garfield.com
foof
POOF
Distributed by Universal Uclick
JPM DAVPS 6-19
YES!

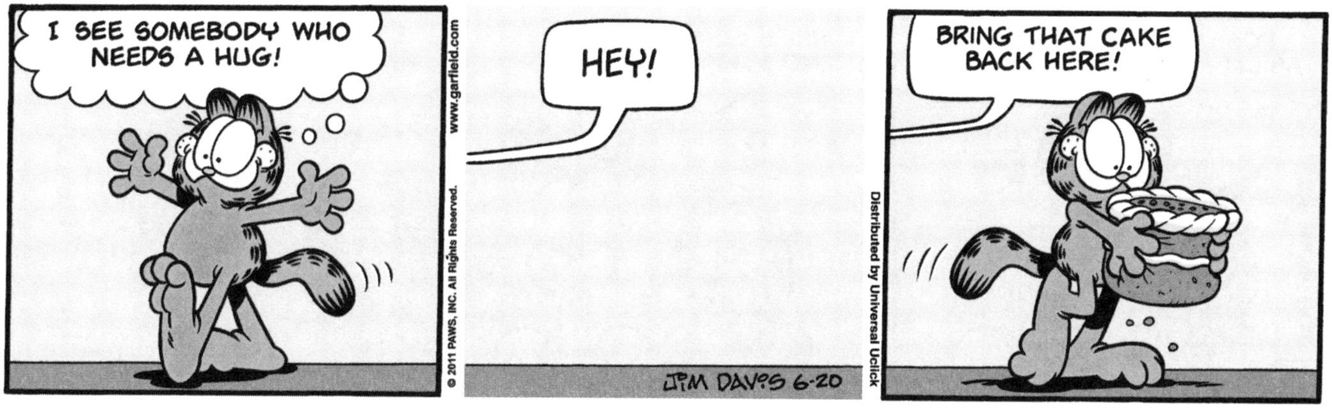
I SEE SOMEBODY WHO NEEDS A HUG!
HEY!
BRING THAT CAKE BACK HERE!
JIM DAVIS 6-20
© 2011 PAWS, INC. All Rights Reserved.
www.garfield.com
Distributed by Universal Uclick

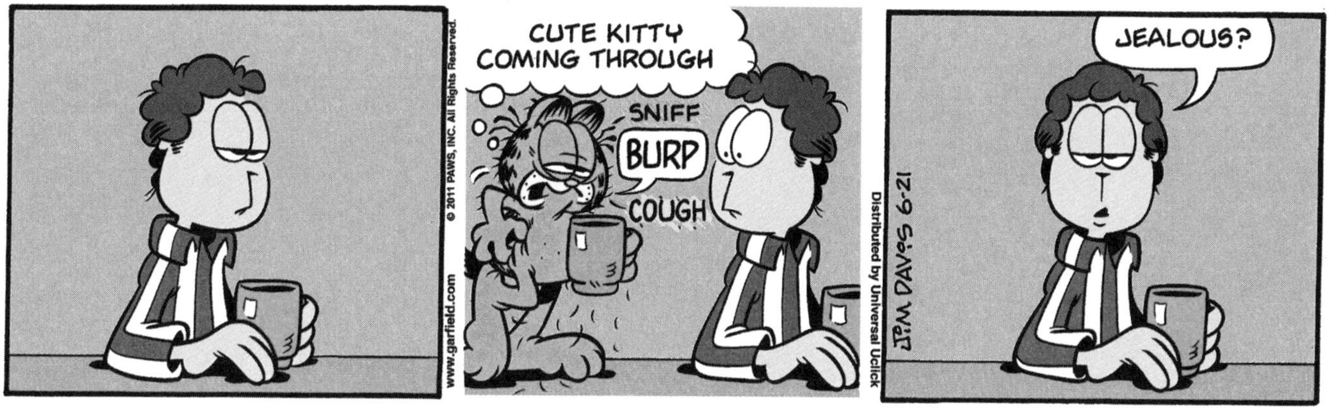
CUTE KITTY COMING THROUGH
SNIFF
BURP
COUGH
JEALOUS?
JIM DAVIS 6-21
© 2011 PAWS, INC. All Rights Reserved.
www.garfield.com
Distributed by Universal Uclick

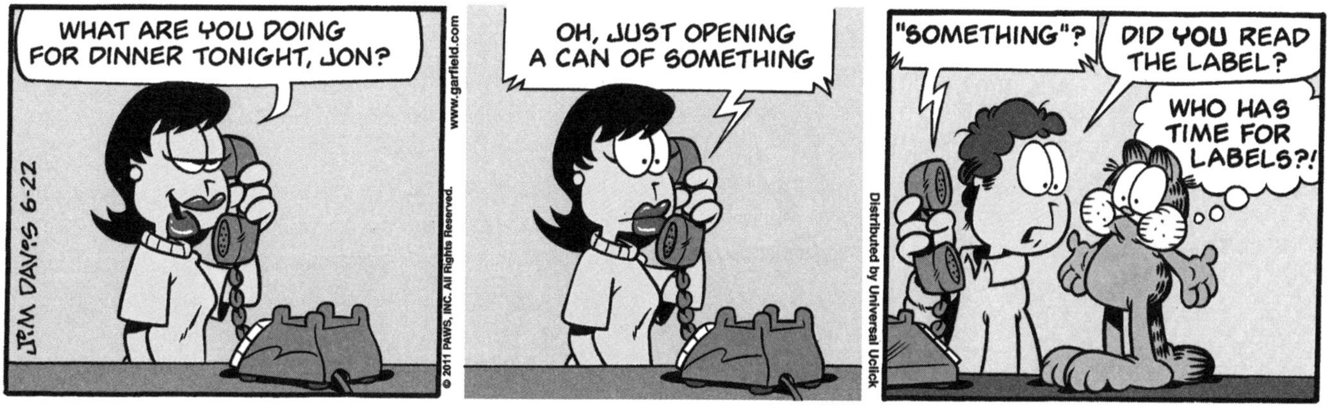
WHAT ARE YOU DOING FOR DINNER TONIGHT, JON?
OH, JUST OPENING A CAN OF SOMETHING
"SOMETHING"?
DID YOU READ THE LABEL?
WHO HAS TIME FOR LABELS?!
JIM DAVIS 6-22
© 2011 PAWS, INC. All Rights Reserved.
www.garfield.com
Distributed by Universal Uclick

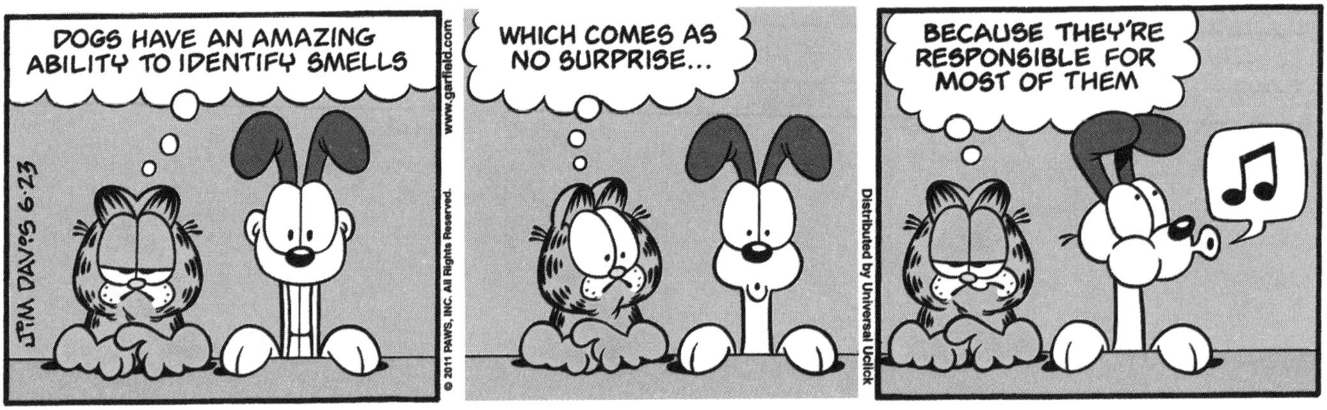
JIM DAVIS 6·23
DOGS HAVE AN AMAZING ABILITY TO IDENTIFY SMELLS
© 2011 PAWS, INC. All Rights Reserved. www.garfield.com
WHICH COMES AS NO SURPRISE...
Distributed by Universal Uclick
BECAUSE THEY'RE RESPONSIBLE FOR MOST OF THEM

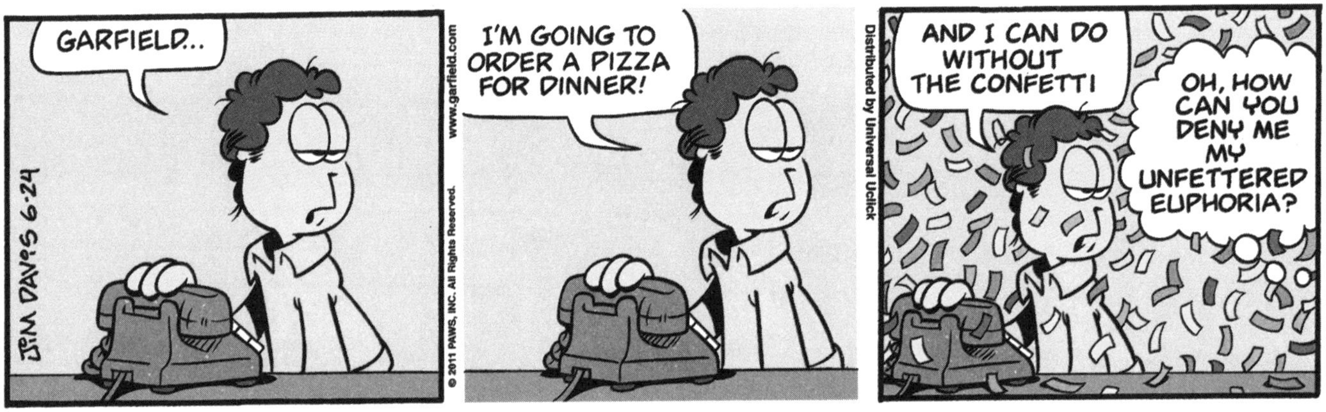
JIM DAVIS 6·24
GARFIELD...
© 2011 PAWS, INC. All Rights Reserved. www.garfield.com
I'M GOING TO ORDER A PIZZA FOR DINNER!
Distributed by Universal Uclick
AND I CAN DO WITHOUT THE CONFETTI
OH, HOW CAN YOU DENY ME MY UNFETTERED EUPHORIA?

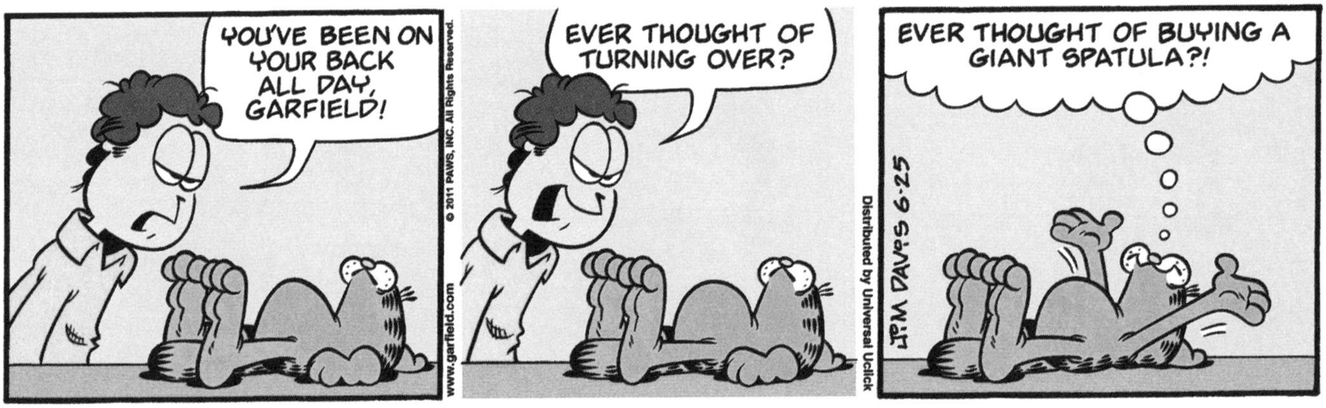
YOU'VE BEEN ON YOUR BACK ALL DAY, GARFIELD!
© 2011 PAWS, INC. All Rights Reserved. www.garfield.com
EVER THOUGHT OF TURNING OVER?
Distributed by Universal Uclick
JIM DAVIS 6·25
EVER THOUGHT OF BUYING A GIANT SPATULA?!

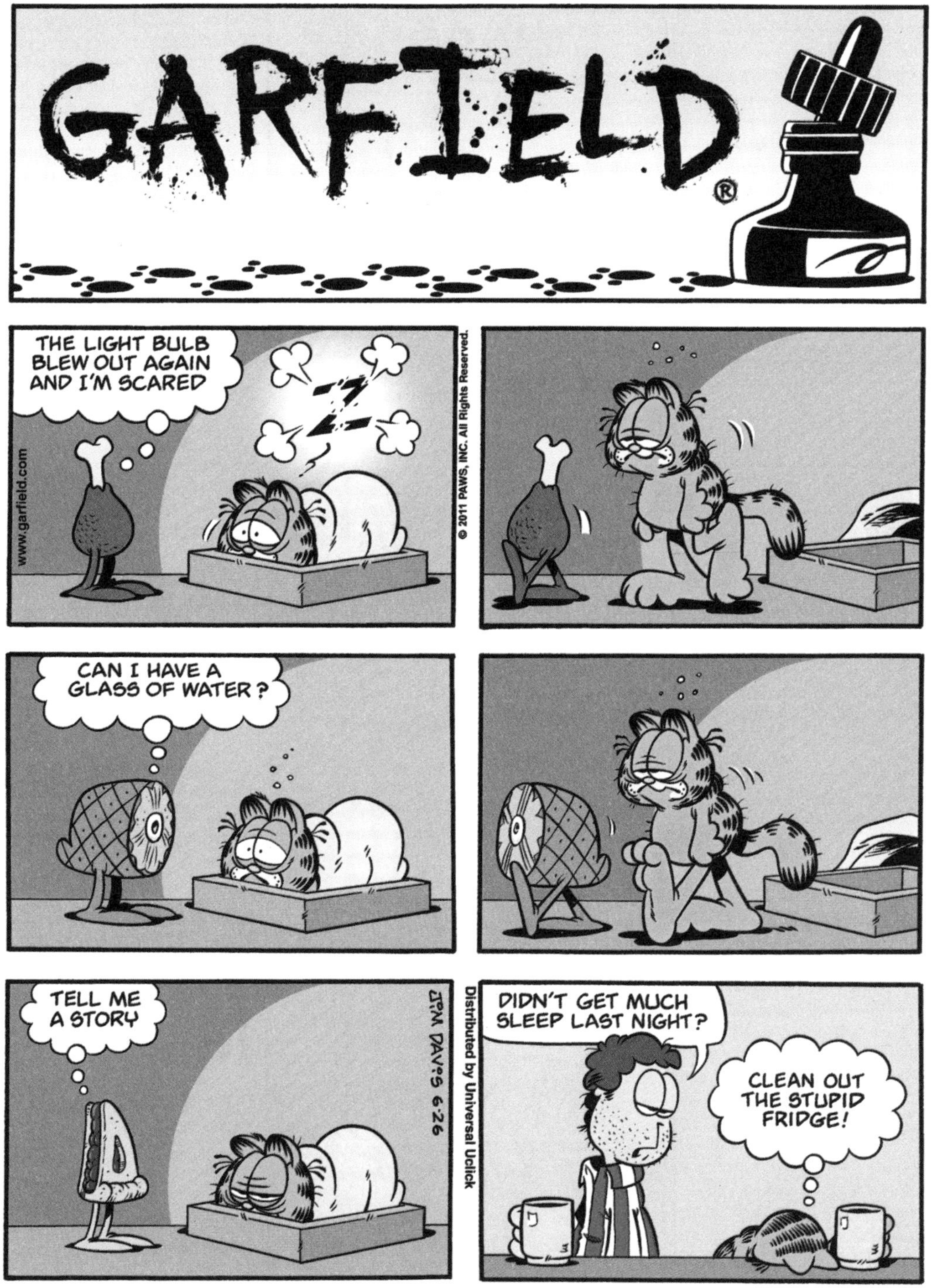
GARFIELD®
THE LIGHT BULB BLEW OUT AGAIN AND I'M SCARED
Z
www.garfield.com
© 2011 PAWS, INC. All Rights Reserved.
CAN I HAVE A GLASS OF WATER?
TELL ME A STORY
JIM DAVIS 6-26
Distributed by Universal Uclick
DIDN'T GET MUCH SLEEP LAST NIGHT?
CLEAN OUT THE STUPID FRIDGE!

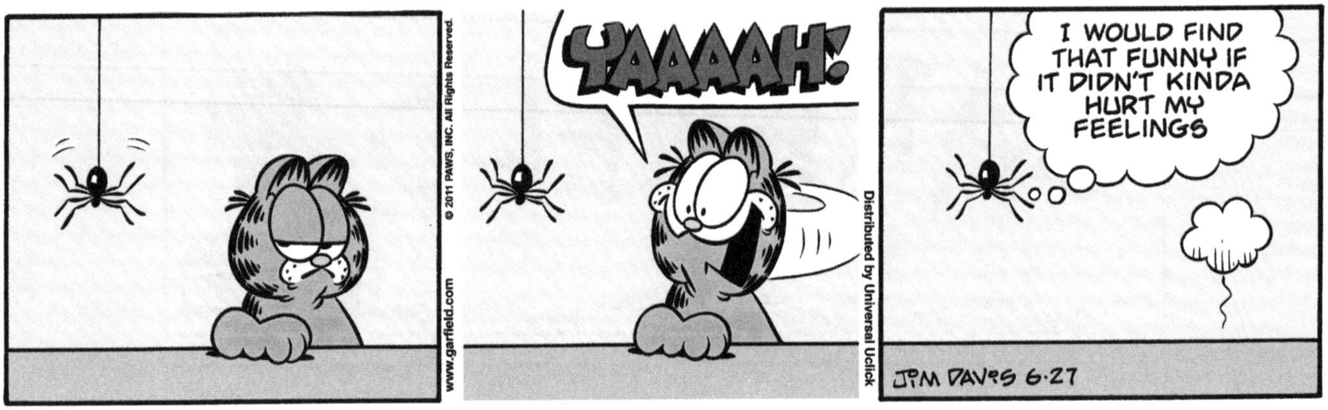
YAAAAH!
I WOULD FIND THAT FUNNY IF IT DIDN'T KINDA HURT MY FEELINGS
JIM DAVIS 6-27
© 2011 PAWS, INC. All Rights Reserved.
www.garfield.com
Distributed by Universal Uclick

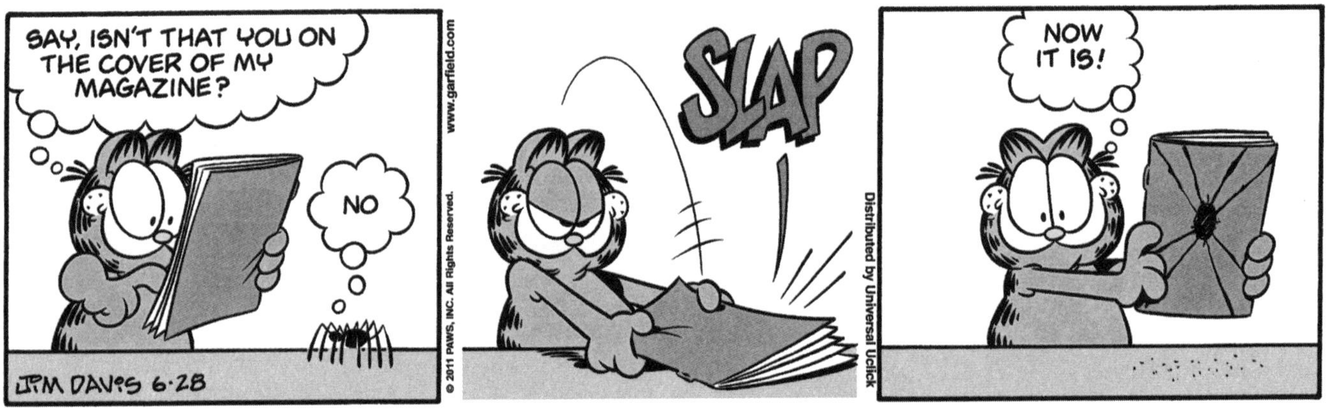
SAY, ISN'T THAT YOU ON THE COVER OF MY MAGAZINE?
NO
SLAP
NOW IT IS!
JIM DAVIS 6-28
© 2011 PAWS, INC. All Rights Reserved.
www.garfield.com
Distributed by Universal Uclick

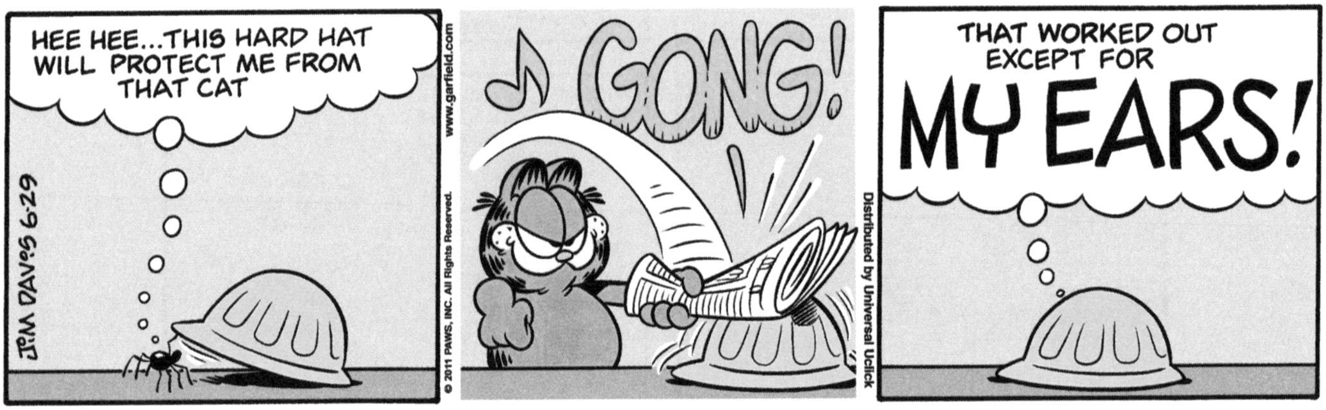
HEE HEE...THIS HARD HAT WILL PROTECT ME FROM THAT CAT
GONG!
THAT WORKED OUT EXCEPT FOR MY EARS!
JIM DAVIS 6-29
© 2011 PAWS, INC. All Rights Reserved.
www.garfield.com
Distributed by Universal Uclick

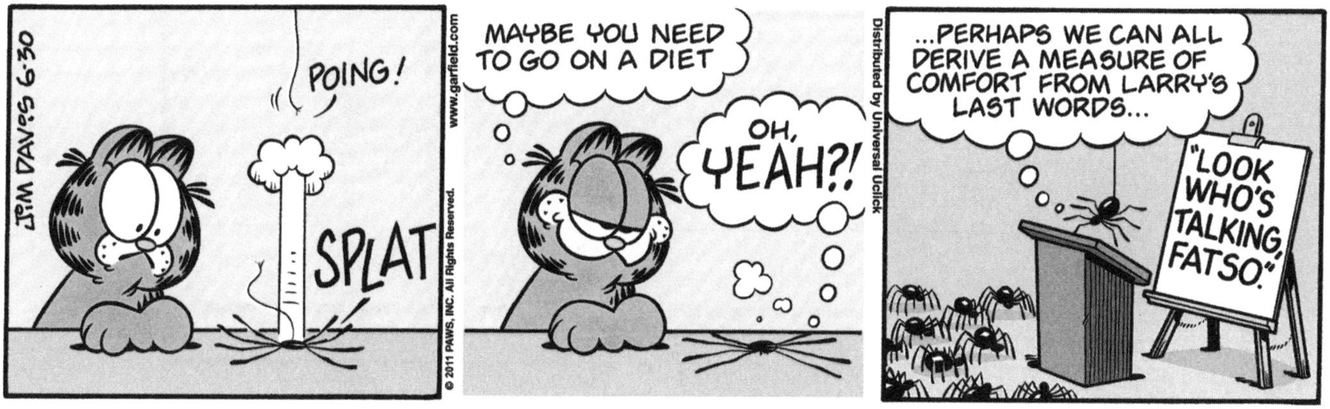
JIM DAVIS 6·30
POING!
SPLAT
© 2011 PAWS, INC. All Rights Reserved.
www.garfield.com
MAYBE YOU NEED TO GO ON A DIET
OH, YEAH?!
Distributed by Universal Uclick
...PERHAPS WE CAN ALL DERIVE A MEASURE OF COMFORT FROM LARRY'S LAST WORDS...
"LOOK WHO'S TALKING, FATSO."

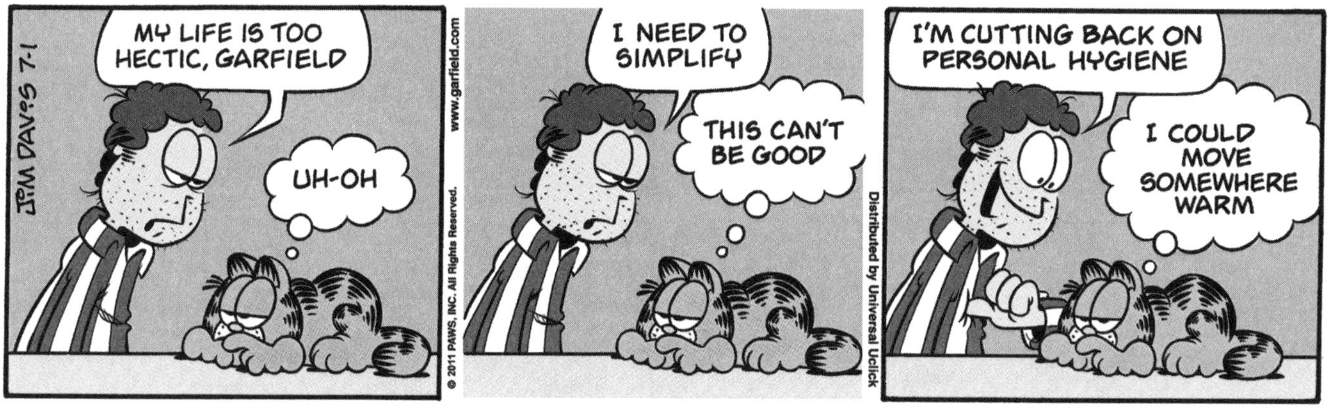
JIM DAVIS 7·1
MY LIFE IS TOO HECTIC, GARFIELD
UH-OH
© 2011 PAWS, INC. All Rights Reserved.
www.garfield.com
I NEED TO SIMPLIFY
THIS CAN'T BE GOOD
Distributed by Universal Uclick
I'M CUTTING BACK ON PERSONAL HYGIENE
I COULD MOVE SOMEWHERE WARM

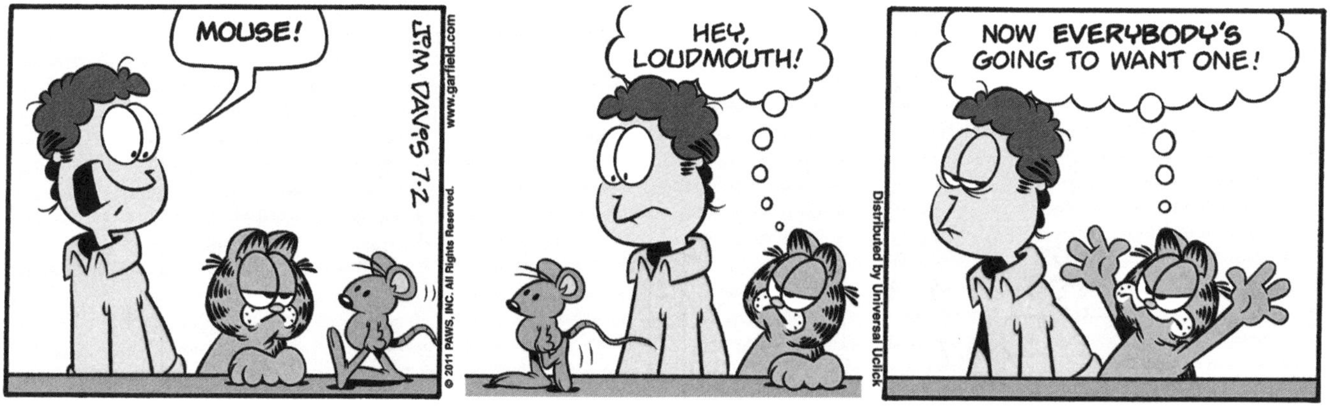
MOUSE!
JIM DAVIS 7·2
www.garfield.com
© 2011 PAWS, INC. All Rights Reserved.
HEY, LOUDMOUTH!
Distributed by Universal Uclick
NOW EVERYBODY'S GOING TO WANT ONE!

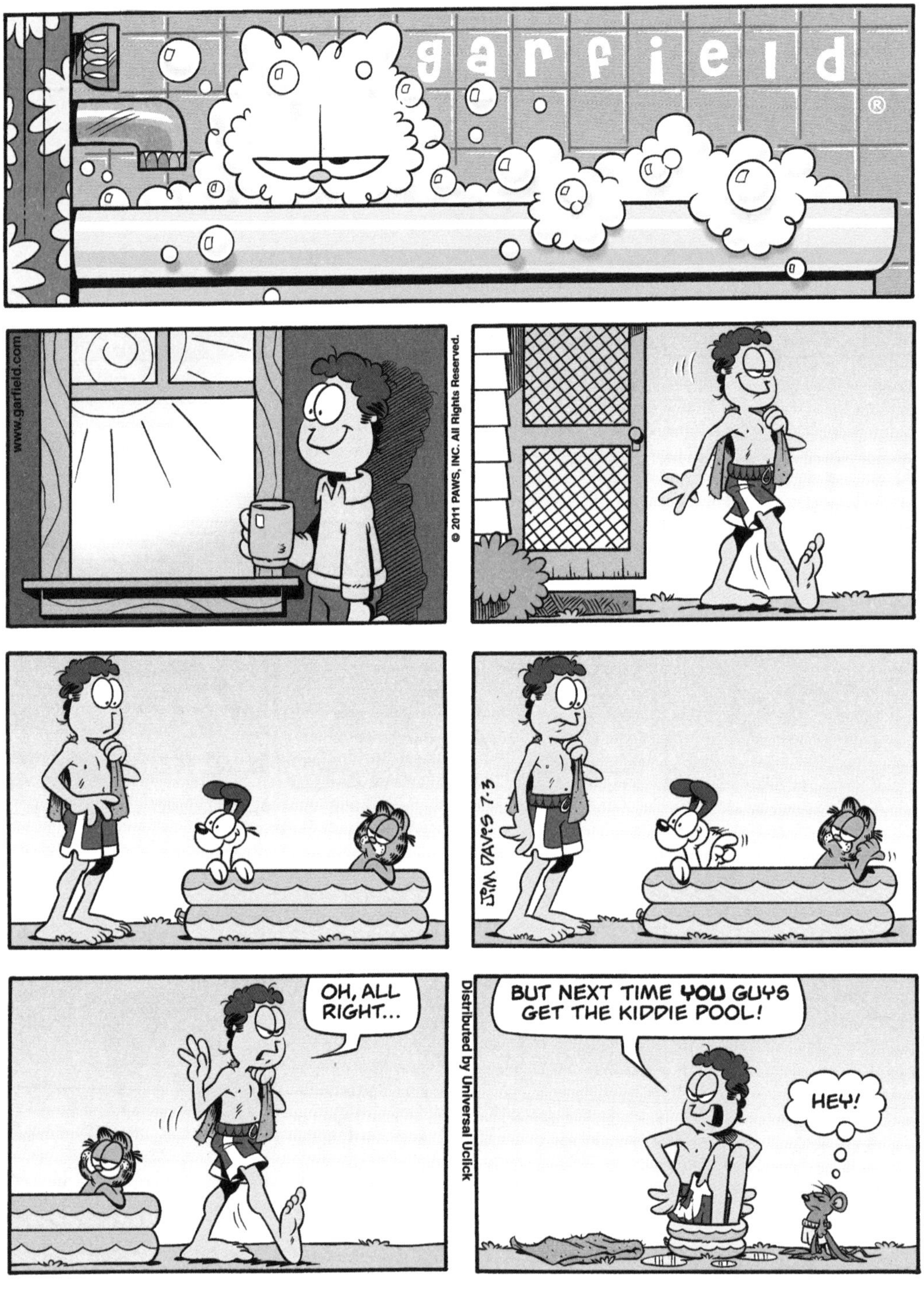
garfield®
www.garfield.com
© 2011 PAWS, INC. All Rights Reserved.
JIM DAVIS 7-3
OH, ALL RIGHT...
Distributed by Universal Uclick
BUT NEXT TIME YOU GUYS GET THE KIDDIE POOL!
HEY!

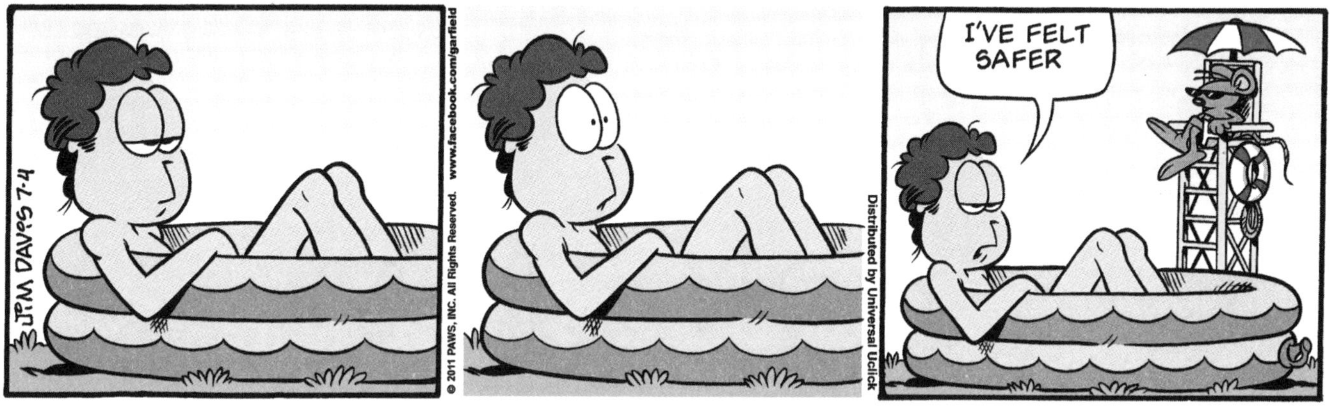
JPM DAVPS 7-4
© 2011 PAWS, INC. All Rights Reserved. www.facebook.com/garfield
Distributed by Universal Uclick
I'VE FELT SAFER

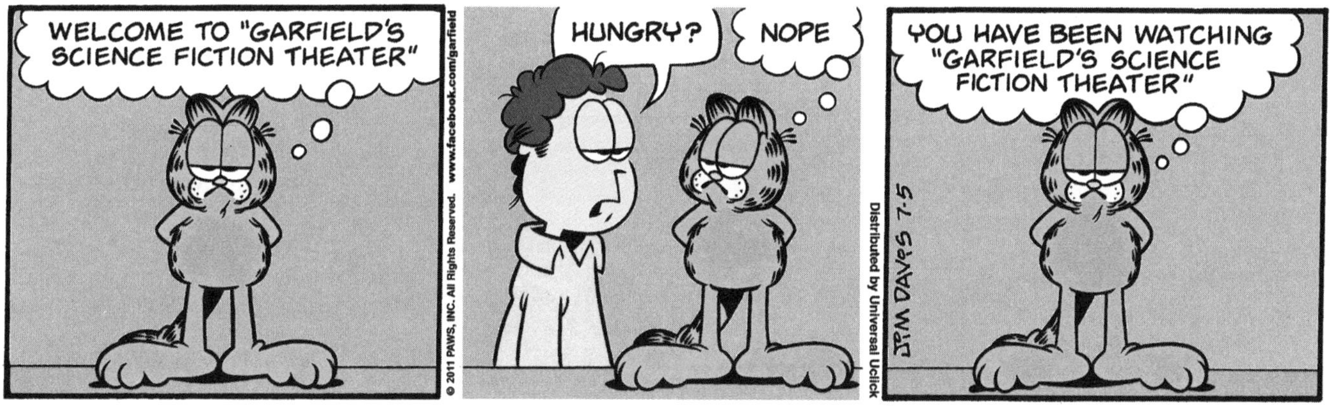
WELCOME TO "GARFIELD'S SCIENCE FICTION THEATER"
© 2011 PAWS, INC. All Rights Reserved. www.facebook.com/garfield
HUNGRY?
NOPE
Distributed by Universal Uclick
JPM DAVPS 7-5
YOU HAVE BEEN WATCHING "GARFIELD'S SCIENCE FICTION THEATER"

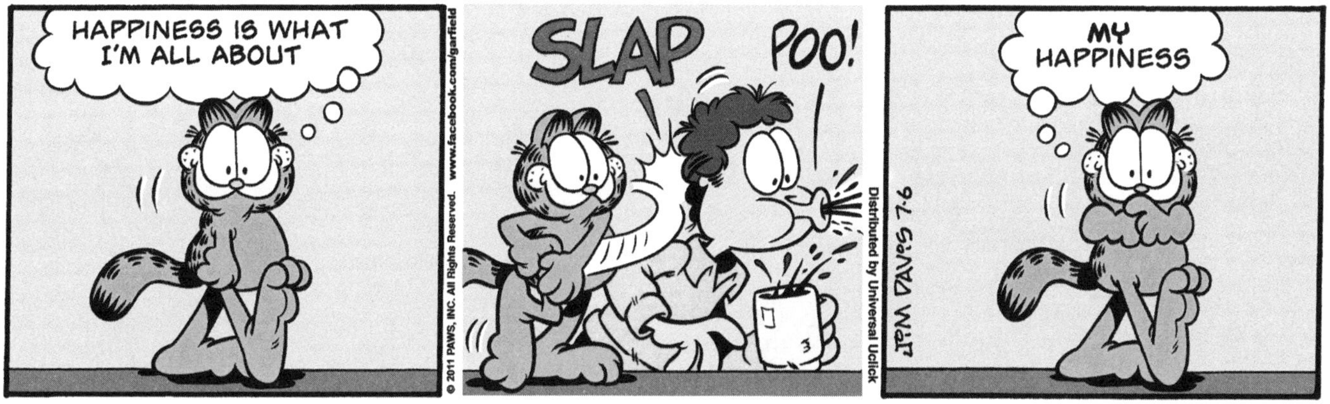
HAPPINESS IS WHAT I'M ALL ABOUT
© 2011 PAWS, INC. All Rights Reserved. www.facebook.com/garfield
SLAP
POO!
Distributed by Universal Uclick
JPM DAVPS 7-6
MY HAPPINESS

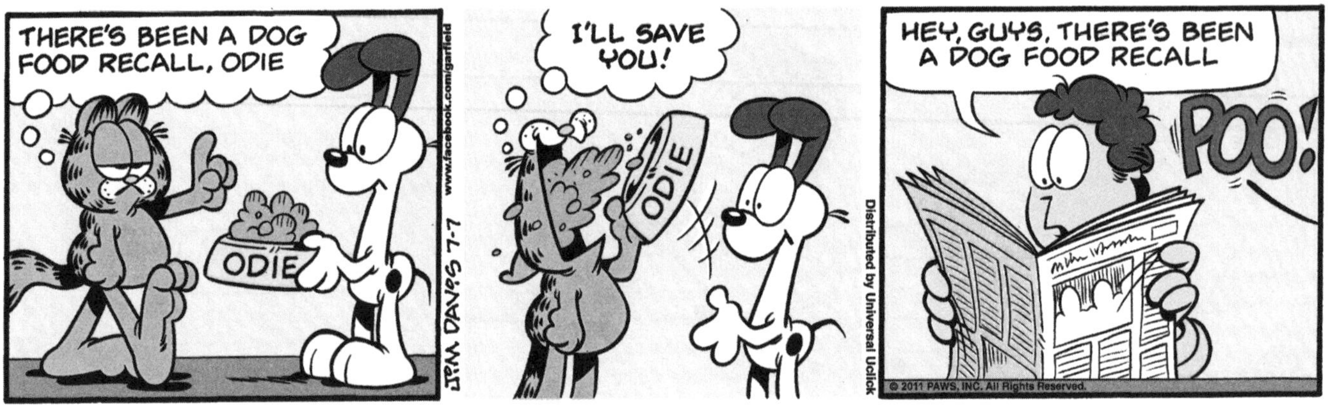
THERE'S BEEN A DOG FOOD RECALL, ODIE
ODIE
JPM DAVPS 7-7
www.facebook.com/garfield
I'LL SAVE YOU!
ODIE
Distributed by Universal Uclick
HEY, GUYS, THERE'S BEEN A DOG FOOD RECALL
POO!
© 2011 PAWS, INC. All Rights Reserved.

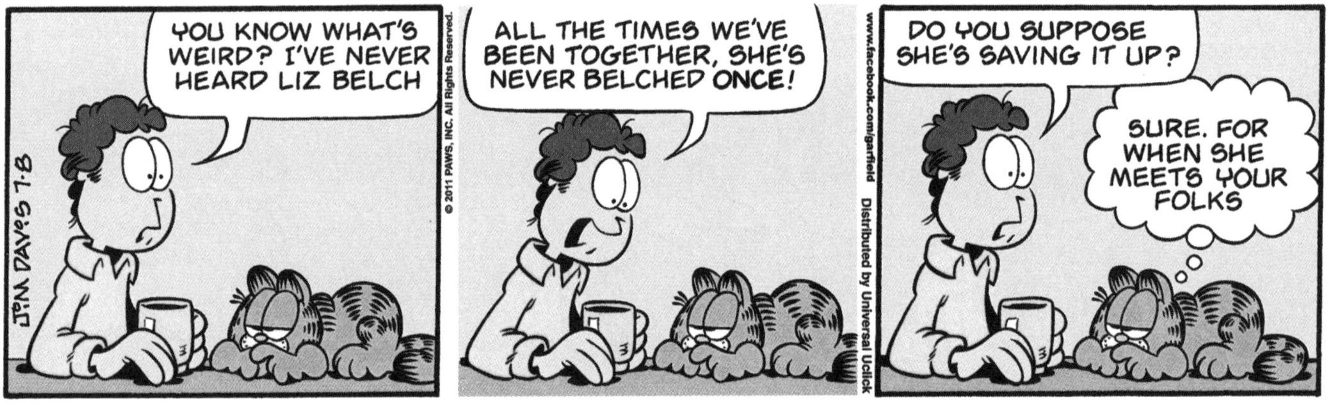
JPM DAVPS 7-8
YOU KNOW WHAT'S WEIRD? I'VE NEVER HEARD LIZ BELCH
© 2011 PAWS, INC. All Rights Reserved.
ALL THE TIMES WE'VE BEEN TOGETHER, SHE'S NEVER BELCHED ONCE!
www.facebook.com/garfield
Distributed by Universal Uclick
DO YOU SUPPOSE SHE'S SAVING IT UP?
SURE. FOR WHEN SHE MEETS YOUR FOLKS

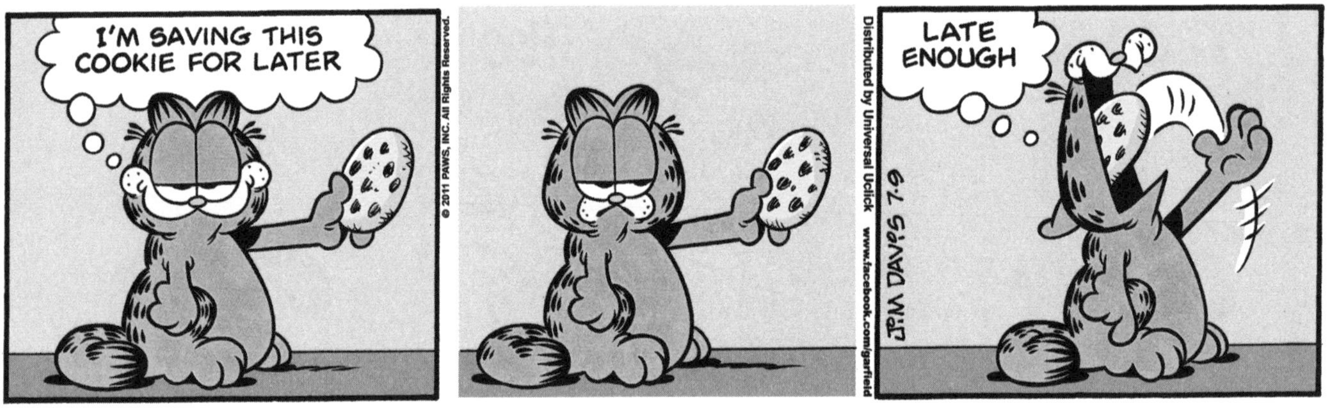
I'M SAVING THIS COOKIE FOR LATER
© 2011 PAWS, INC. All Rights Reserved.
Distributed by Universal Uclick
LATE ENOUGH
JPM DAVPS 7-9
www.facebook.com/garfield

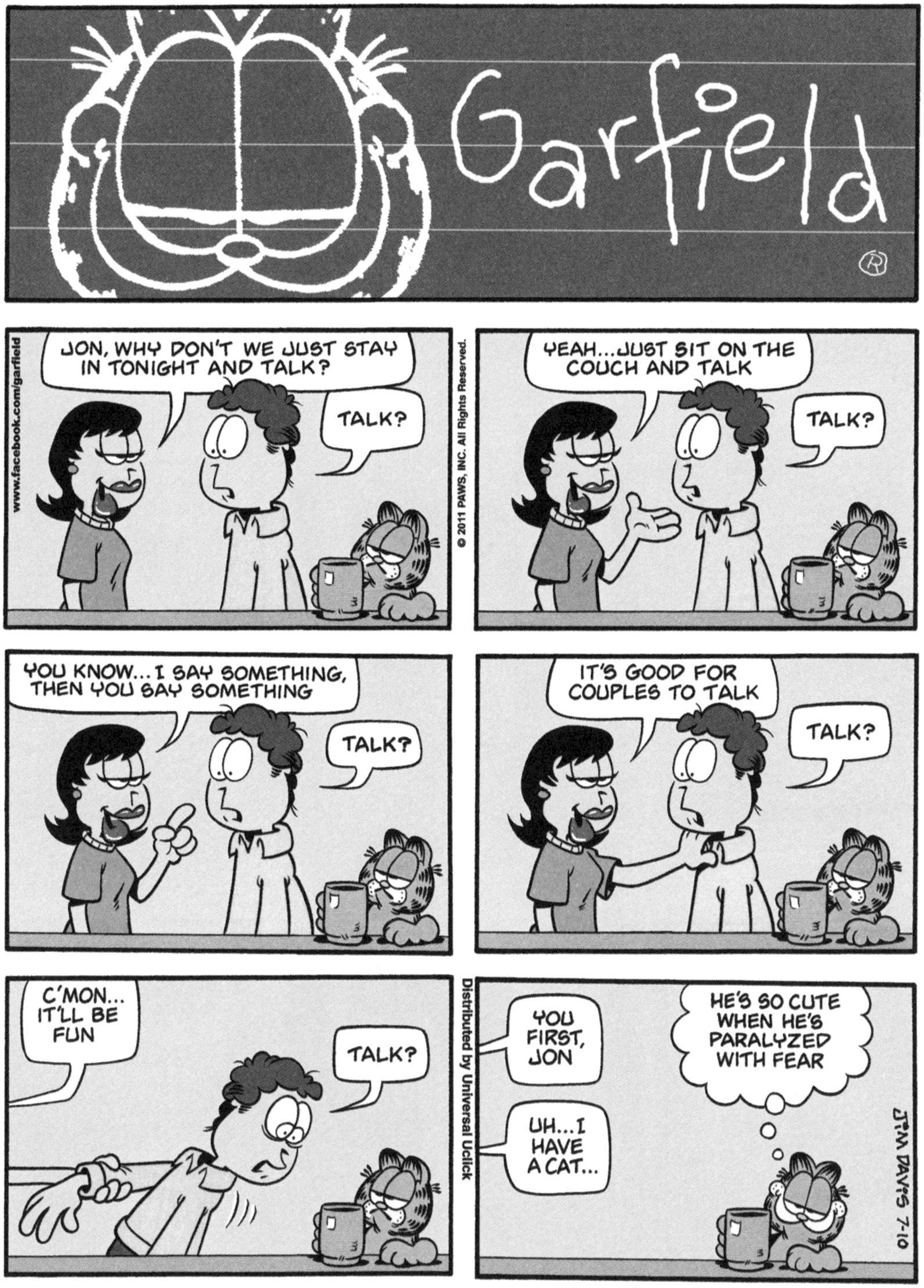
Garfield
www.facebook.com/garfield
JON, WHY DON'T WE JUST STAY IN TONIGHT AND TALK?
TALK?
© 2011 PAWS, INC. All Rights Reserved.
YEAH...JUST SIT ON THE COUCH AND TALK
TALK?
YOU KNOW... I SAY SOMETHING, THEN YOU SAY SOMETHING
TALK?
IT'S GOOD FOR COUPLES TO TALK
TALK?
C'MON... IT'LL BE FUN
TALK?
Distributed by Universal Uclick
YOU FIRST, JON
UH...I HAVE A CAT...
HE'S SO CUTE WHEN HE'S PARALYZED WITH FEAR
JIM DAVIS 7-10

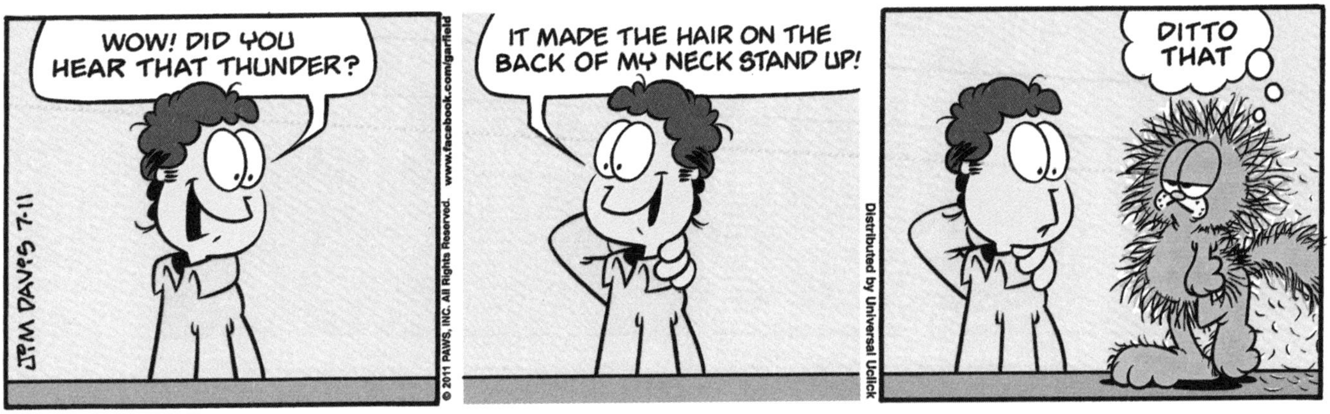
WOW! DID YOU HEAR THAT THUNDER?
JIM DAVIS 7-11
© 2011 PAWS, INC. All Rights Reserved. www.facebook.com/garfield
IT MADE THE HAIR ON THE BACK OF MY NECK STAND UP!
Distributed by Universal Uclick
DITTO THAT

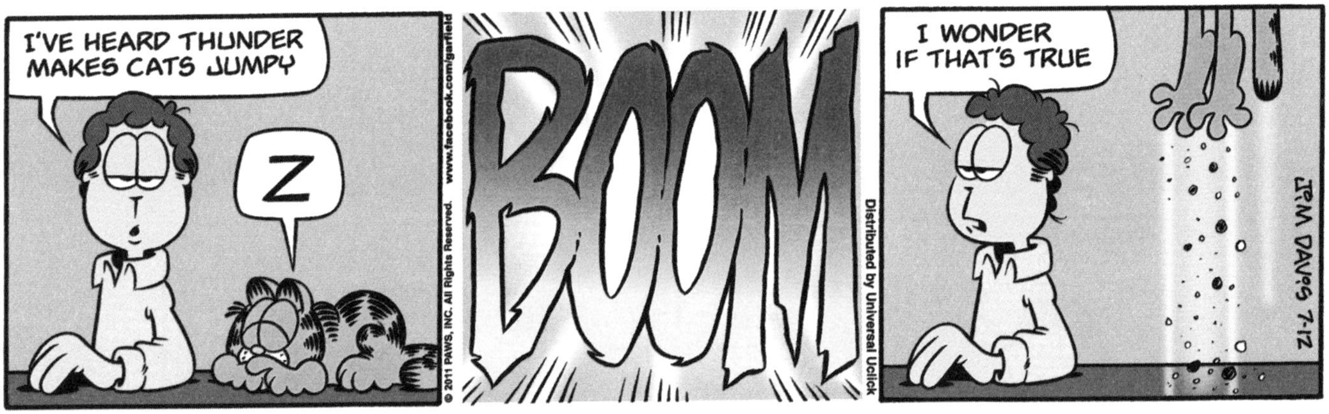
I'VE HEARD THUNDER MAKES CATS JUMPY
Z
© 2011 PAWS, INC. All Rights Reserved. www.facebook.com/garfield
BOOM
Distributed by Universal Uclick
I WONDER IF THAT'S TRUE
JIM DAVIS 7-12

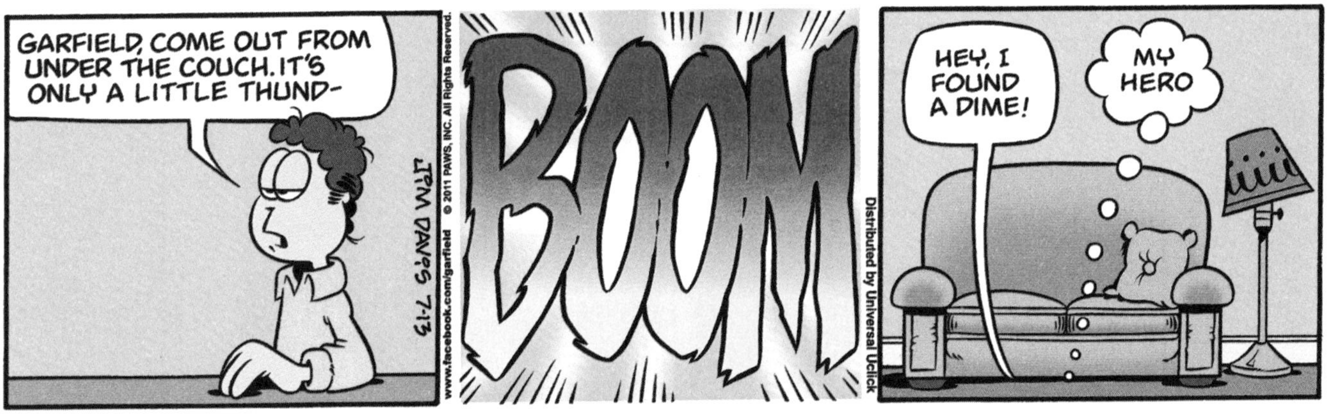
GARFIELD, COME OUT FROM UNDER THE COUCH. IT'S ONLY A LITTLE THUND-
JIM DAVIS 7-13
© 2011 PAWS, INC. All Rights Reserved. www.facebook.com/garfield
BOOM
Distributed by Universal Uclick
HEY, I FOUND A DIME!
MY HERO

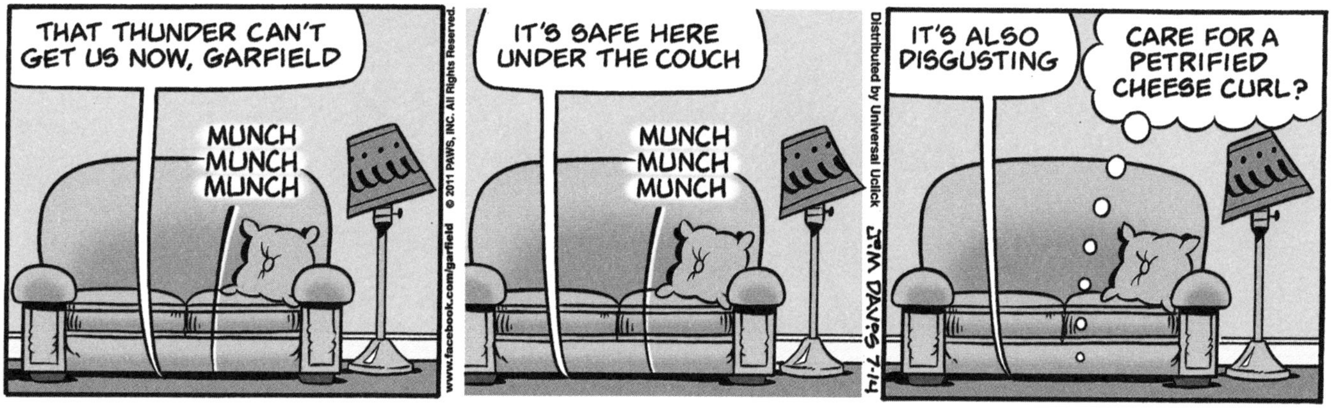
THAT THUNDER CAN'T GET US NOW, GARFIELD
MUNCH MUNCH MUNCH
IT'S SAFE HERE UNDER THE COUCH
MUNCH MUNCH MUNCH
IT'S ALSO DISGUSTING
CARE FOR A PETRIFIED CHEESE CURL?
www.facebook.com/garfield © 2011 PAWS, INC. All Rights Reserved.
Distributed by Universal Uclick
JIM DAVIS 7-14

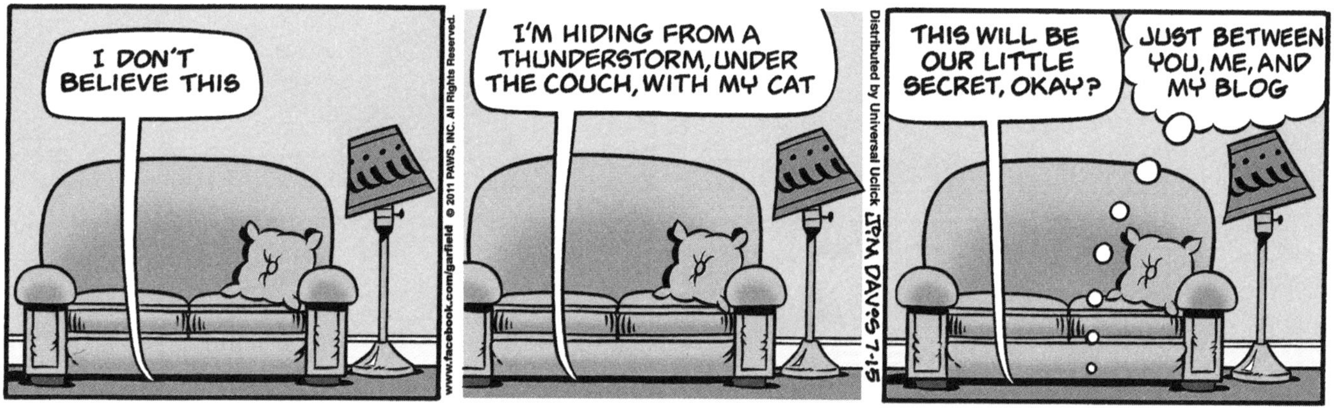
I DON'T BELIEVE THIS
I'M HIDING FROM A THUNDERSTORM, UNDER THE COUCH, WITH MY CAT
THIS WILL BE OUR LITTLE SECRET, OKAY?
JUST BETWEEN YOU, ME, AND MY BLOG
www.facebook.com/garfield © 2011 PAWS, INC. All Rights Reserved.
Distributed by Universal Uclick
JIM DAVIS 7-15

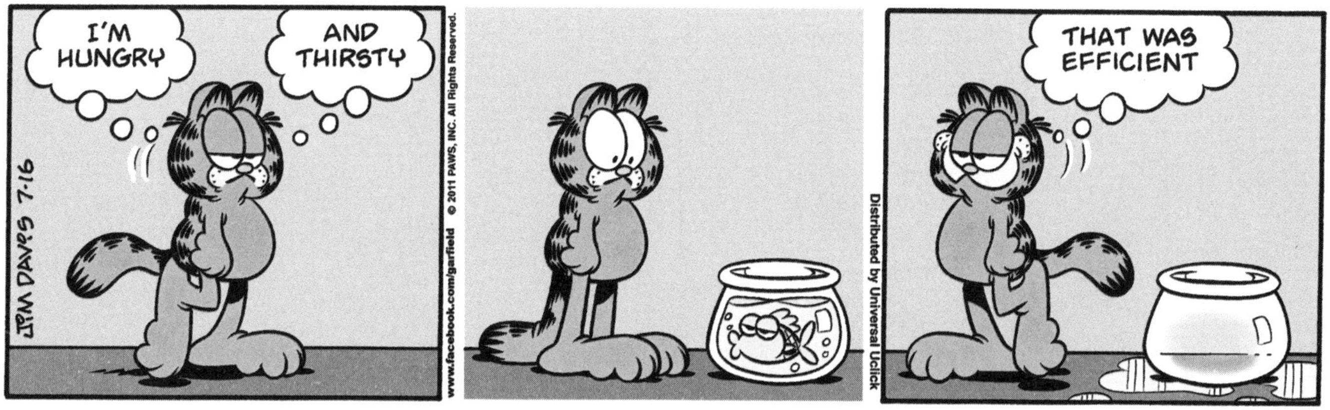
I'M HUNGRY
AND THIRSTY
THAT WAS EFFICIENT
JIM DAVIS 7-16
www.facebook.com/garfield © 2011 PAWS, INC. All Rights Reserved.
Distributed by Universal Uclick

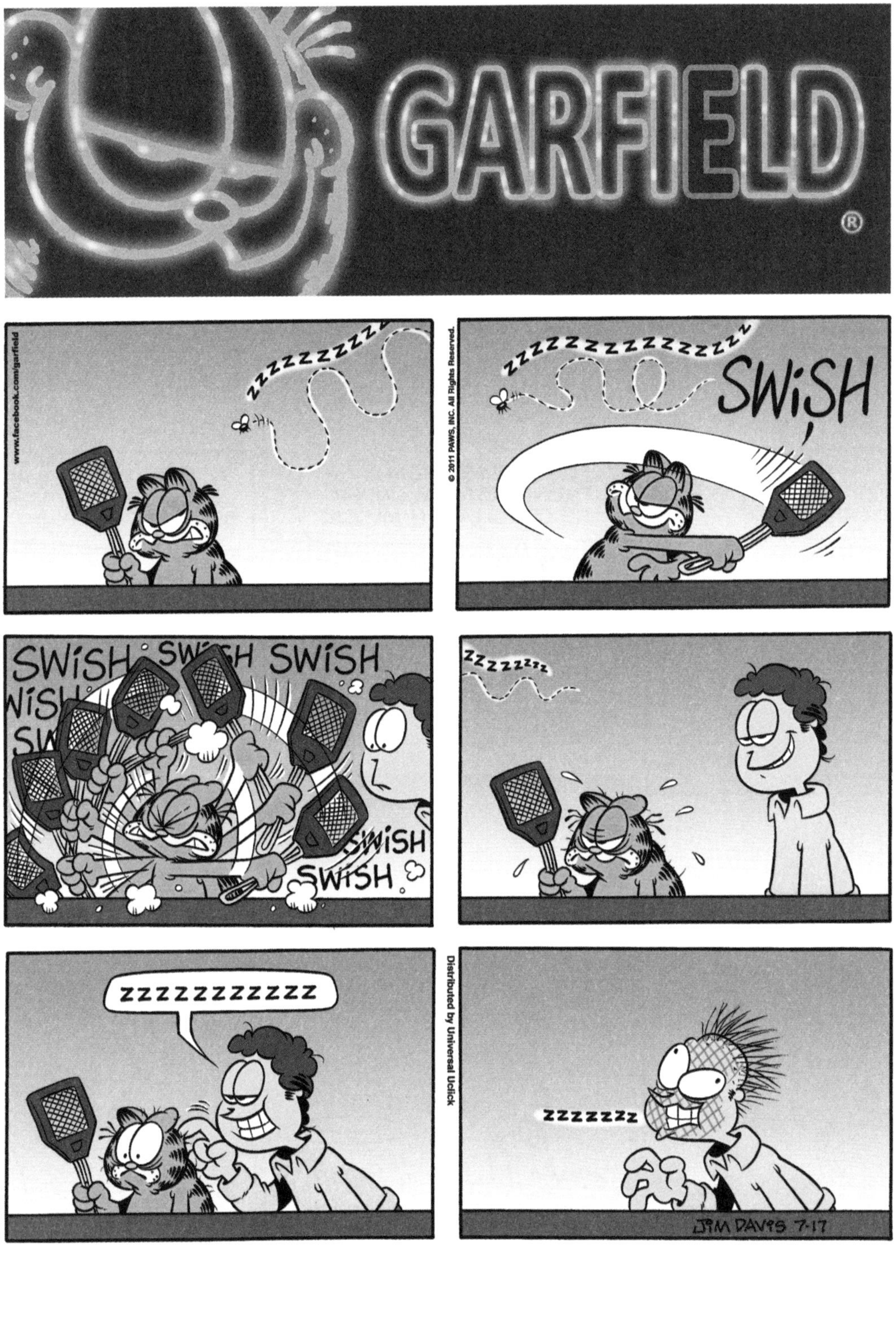

GARFIELD®
www.facebook.com/garfield
© 2011 PAWS, INC. All Rights Reserved.
SWISH
SWISH SWISH SWISH
SWISH
SWISH
ZZZZZZZZZZZ
Distributed by Universal Uclick
ZZZZZZZ
JIM DAVIS 7-17

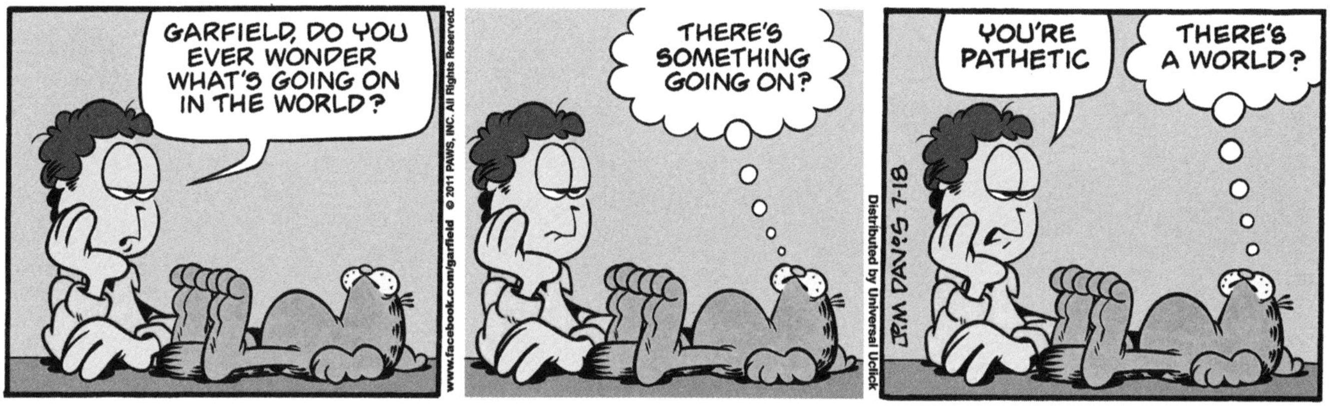
GARFIELD, DO YOU EVER WONDER WHAT'S GOING ON IN THE WORLD?
THERE'S SOMETHING GOING ON?
YOU'RE PATHETIC
THERE'S A WORLD?
© 2011 PAWS, INC. All Rights Reserved. www.facebook.com/garfield
Distributed by Universal Uclick
JPM DAVPS 7-18

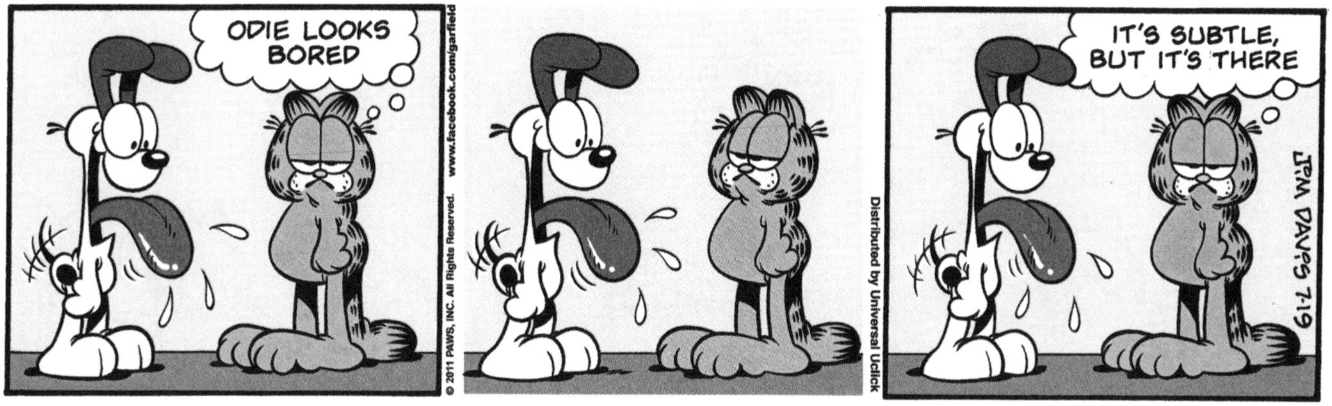
ODIE LOOKS BORED
IT'S SUBTLE, BUT IT'S THERE
© 2011 PAWS, INC. All Rights Reserved. www.facebook.com/garfield
Distributed by Universal Uclick
JPM DAVPS 7-19

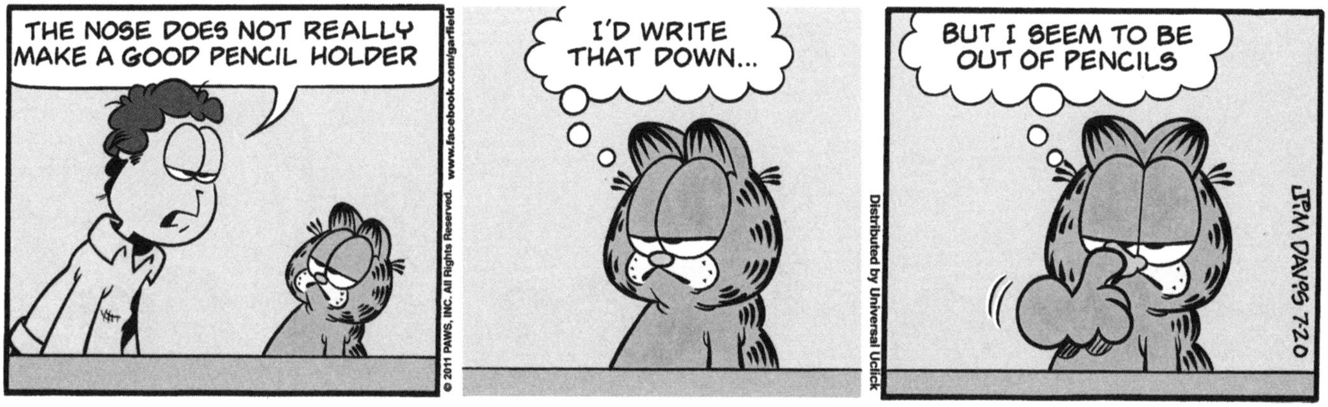
THE NOSE DOES NOT REALLY MAKE A GOOD PENCIL HOLDER
I'D WRITE THAT DOWN...
BUT I SEEM TO BE OUT OF PENCILS
© 2011 PAWS, INC. All Rights Reserved. www.facebook.com/garfield
Distributed by Universal Uclick
JPM DAVPS 7-20

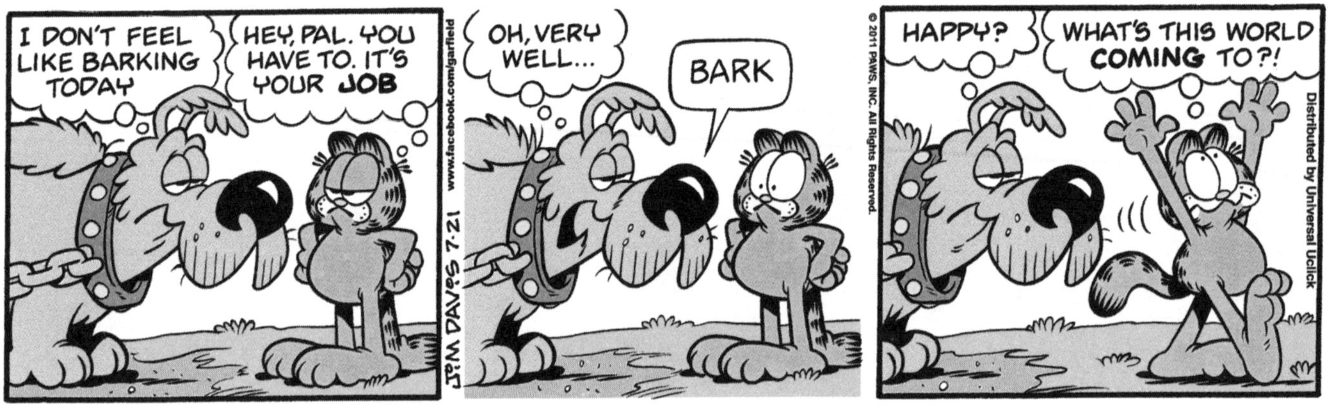
I DON'T FEEL LIKE BARKING TODAY
HEY, PAL. YOU HAVE TO. IT'S YOUR **JOB**
OH, VERY WELL...
BARK
HAPPY?
WHAT'S THIS WORLD **COMING** TO?!
JPM DAVPS 7·21
www.facebook.com/garfield
© 2011 PAWS, INC. All Rights Reserved.
Distributed by Universal Uclick

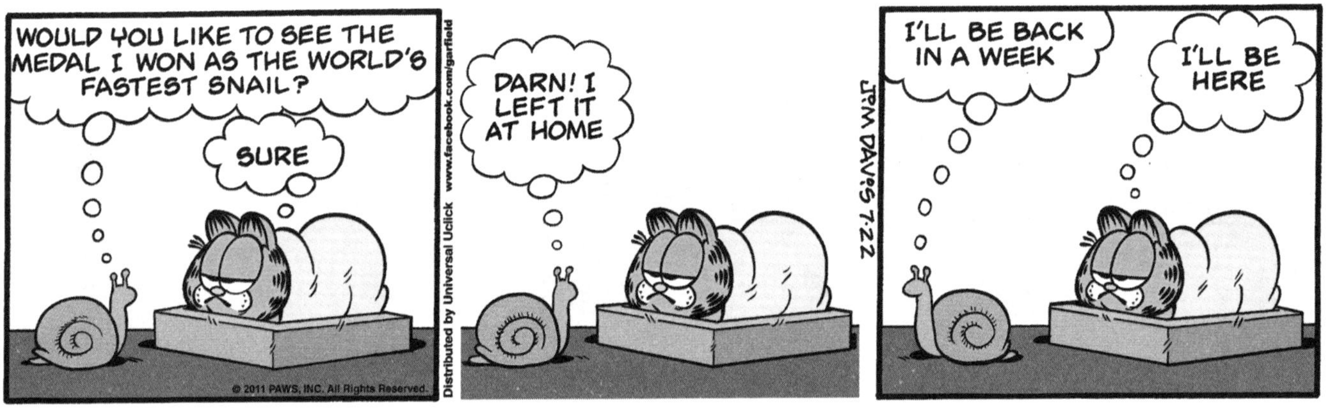
WOULD YOU LIKE TO SEE THE MEDAL I WON AS THE WORLD'S FASTEST SNAIL?
SURE
DARN! I LEFT IT AT HOME
I'LL BE BACK IN A WEEK
I'LL BE HERE
JPM DAVPS 7·22
www.facebook.com/garfield
Distributed by Universal Uclick
© 2011 PAWS, INC. All Rights Reserved.

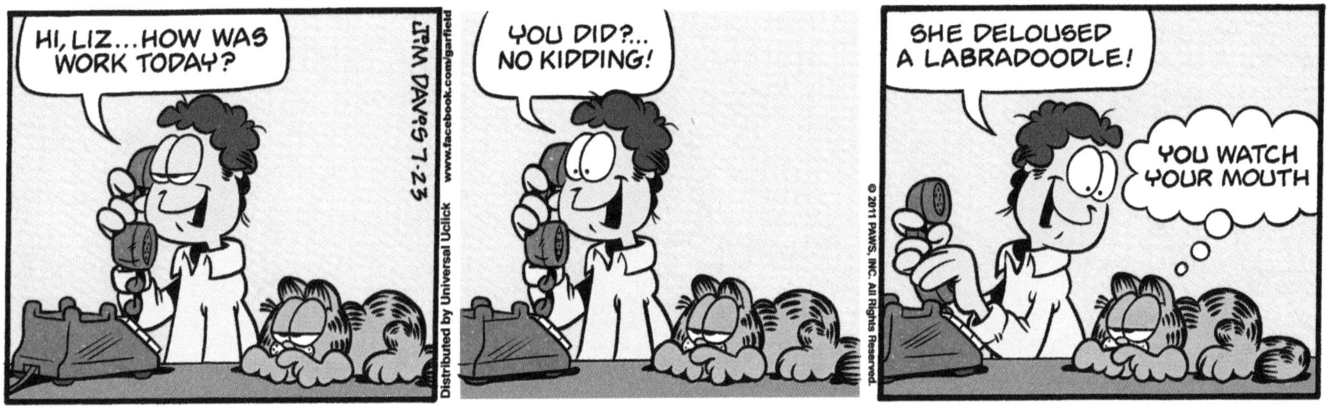
HI, LIZ...HOW WAS WORK TODAY?
YOU DID?... NO KIDDING!
SHE DELOUSED A LABRADOODLE!
YOU WATCH YOUR MOUTH
JPM DAVPS 7·23
www.facebook.com/garfield
Distributed by Universal Uclick
© 2011 PAWS, INC. All Rights Reserved.

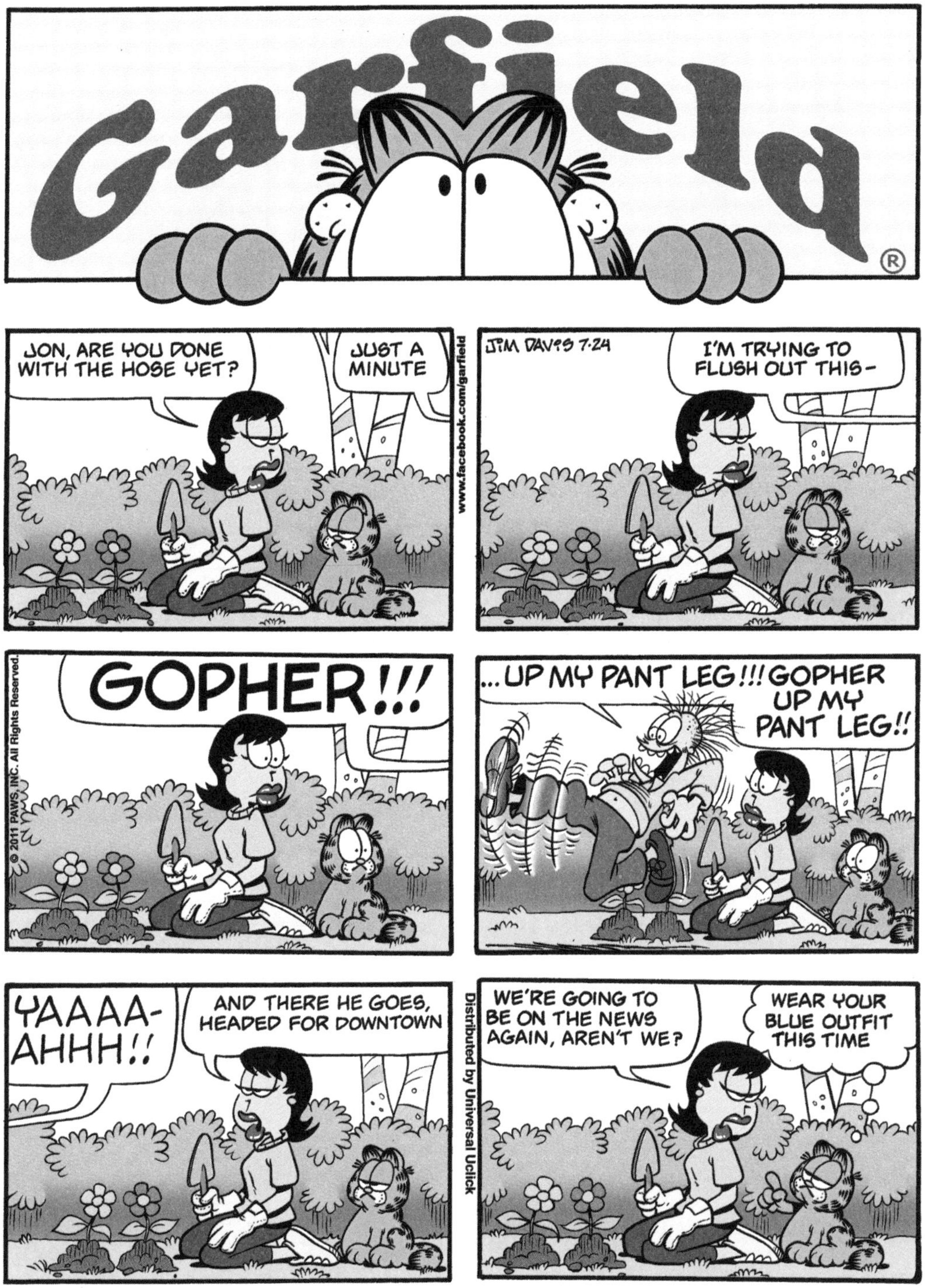
Garfield®
JIM DAVIS 7·24
JON, ARE YOU DONE WITH THE HOSE YET?
JUST A MINUTE
I'M TRYING TO FLUSH OUT THIS–
GOPHER!!!
...UP MY PANT LEG!!!
GOPHER UP MY PANT LEG!!
YAAAA-AHHH!!
AND THERE HE GOES, HEADED FOR DOWNTOWN
WE'RE GOING TO BE ON THE NEWS AGAIN, AREN'T WE?
WEAR YOUR BLUE OUTFIT THIS TIME
www.facebook.com/garfield
Distributed by Universal Uclick

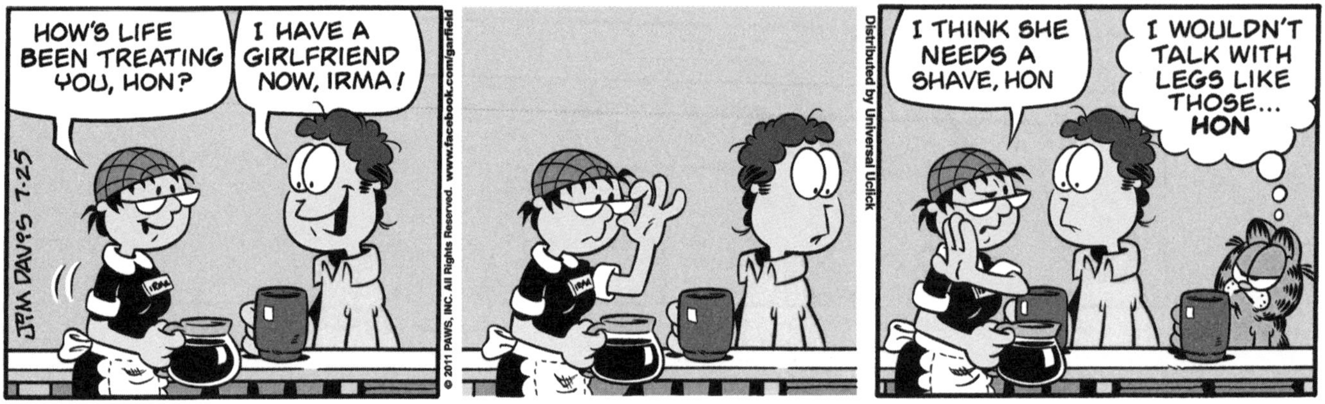
HOW'S LIFE BEEN TREATING YOU, HON?
I HAVE A GIRLFRIEND NOW, IRMA!
JIM DAVIS 7-25
© 2011 PAWS, INC. All Rights Reserved. www.facebook.com/garfield
Distributed by Universal Uclick
I THINK SHE NEEDS A SHAVE, HON
I WOULDN'T TALK WITH LEGS LIKE THOSE... **HON**

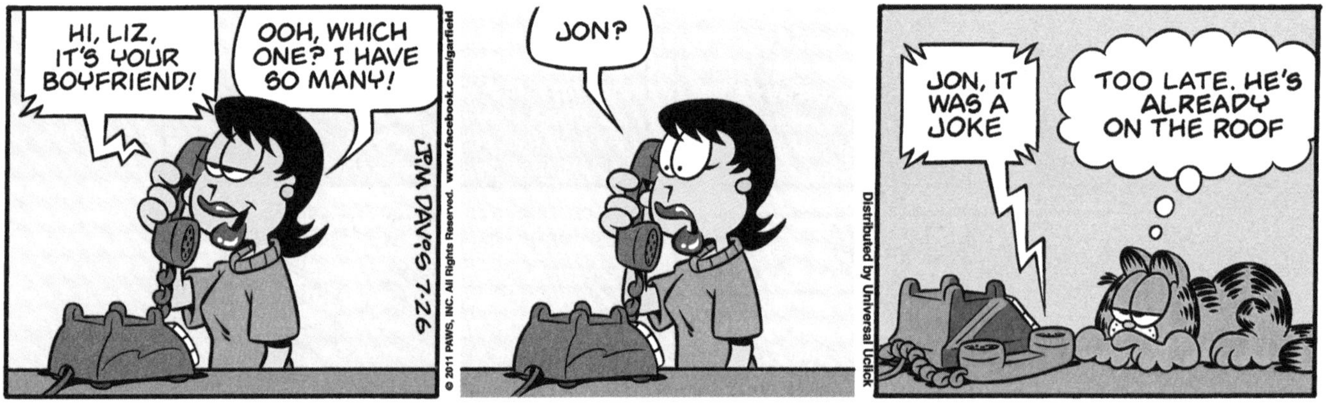
HI, LIZ, IT'S YOUR BOYFRIEND!
OOH, WHICH ONE? I HAVE SO MANY!
JIM DAVIS 7-26
© 2011 PAWS, INC. All Rights Reserved. www.facebook.com/garfield
JON?
Distributed by Universal Uclick
JON, IT WAS A JOKE
TOO LATE. HE'S ALREADY ON THE ROOF

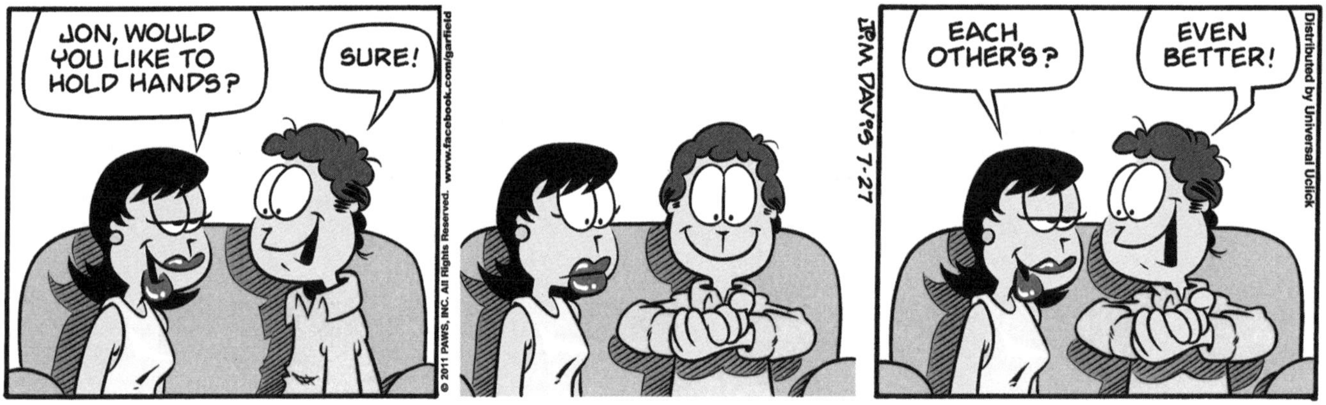
JON, WOULD YOU LIKE TO HOLD HANDS?
SURE!
© 2011 PAWS, INC. All Rights Reserved. www.facebook.com/garfield
JIM DAVIS 7-27
EACH OTHER'S?
EVEN BETTER!
Distributed by Universal Uclick

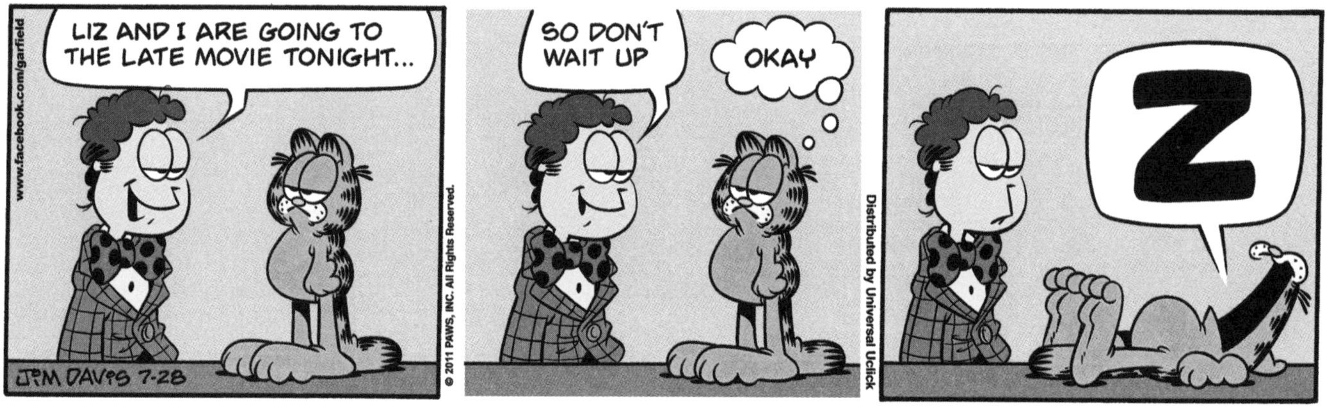
www.facebook.com/garfield
LIZ AND I ARE GOING TO THE LATE MOVIE TONIGHT...
JIM DAVIS 7-28
© 2011 PAWS, INC. All Rights Reserved.
SO DON'T WAIT UP
OKAY
Distributed by Universal Uclick
Z

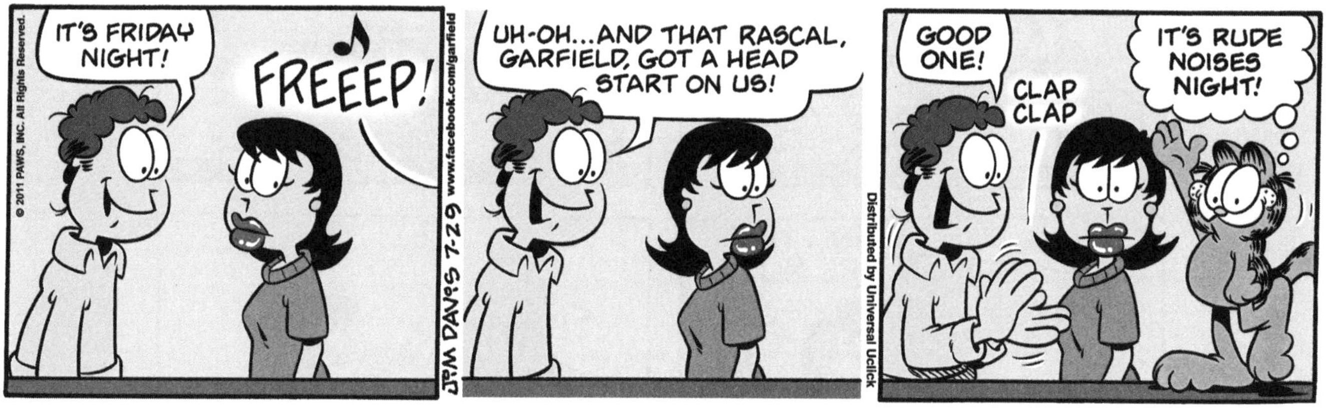
© 2011 PAWS, INC. All Rights Reserved.
IT'S FRIDAY NIGHT!
FREEEP!
JIM DAVIS 7-29
www.facebook.com/garfield
UH-OH...AND THAT RASCAL, GARFIELD, GOT A HEAD START ON US!
Distributed by Universal Uclick
GOOD ONE!
CLAP CLAP
IT'S RUDE NOISES NIGHT!

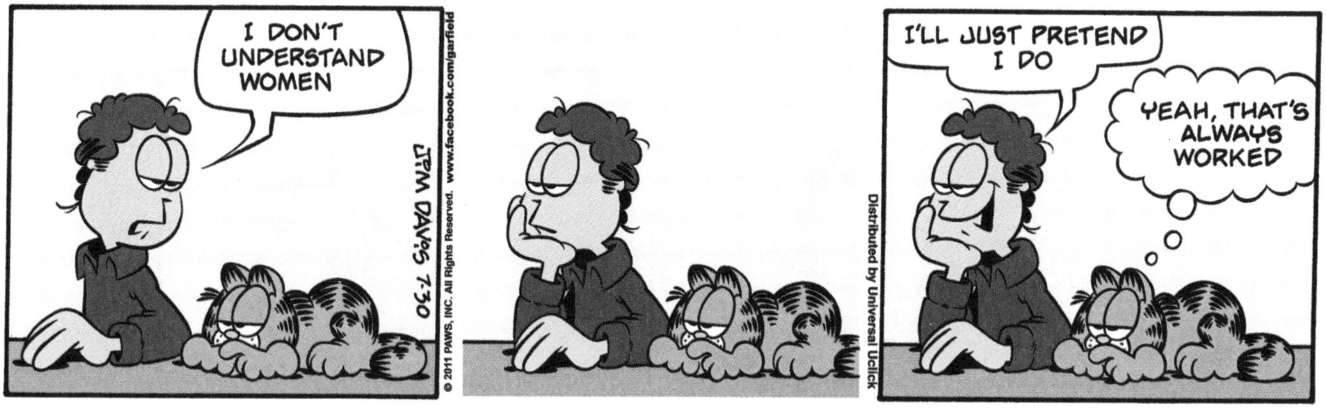
I DON'T UNDERSTAND WOMEN
JIM DAVIS 7-30
© 2011 PAWS, INC. All Rights Reserved. www.facebook.com/garfield
Distributed by Universal Uclick
I'LL JUST PRETEND I DO
YEAH, THAT'S ALWAYS WORKED

Garfield

www.facebook.com/garfield
GARFIELD! THE DONUT BARN IS HAVING A CLEARANCE SALE!
© 2011 PAWS, INC. All Rights Reserved.
EEEEEEEEEE!
OH, FOR PETE'S SAKE!
EEEEEEEEEEEE
YOU TWO ARE NUTS!
SLAM
BEEP
BEEP
BOOP
BEEP
BEEP
Distributed by Universal Uclick
HELLO?
I WANT SPRINKLES
JPM DAVIS 7-31

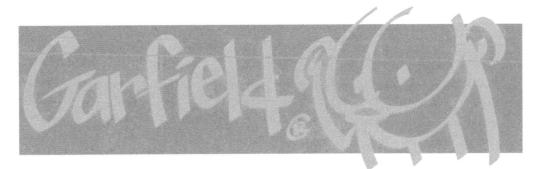

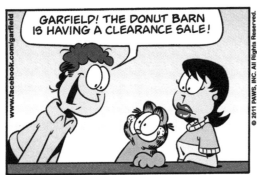

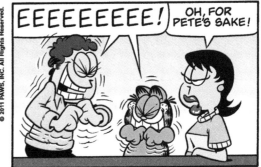

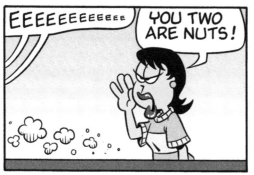

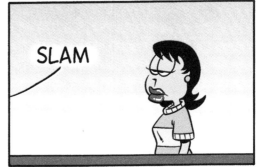

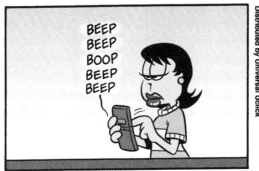

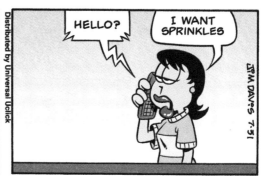

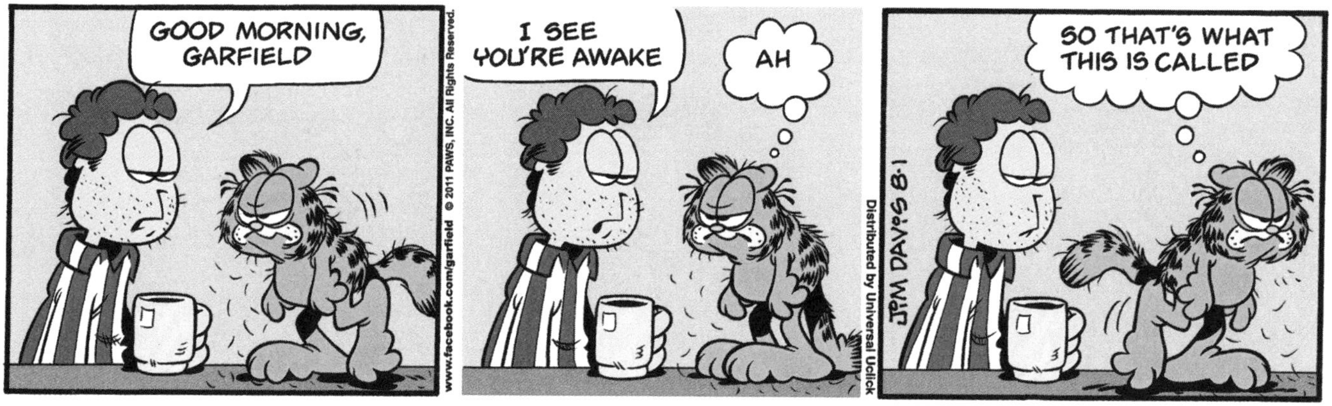
GOOD MORNING, GARFIELD
www.facebook.com/garfield © 2011 PAWS, INC. All Rights Reserved.
I SEE YOU'RE AWAKE
AH
Distributed by Universal Uclick
JPM DAVIS 8-1
SO THAT'S WHAT THIS IS CALLED

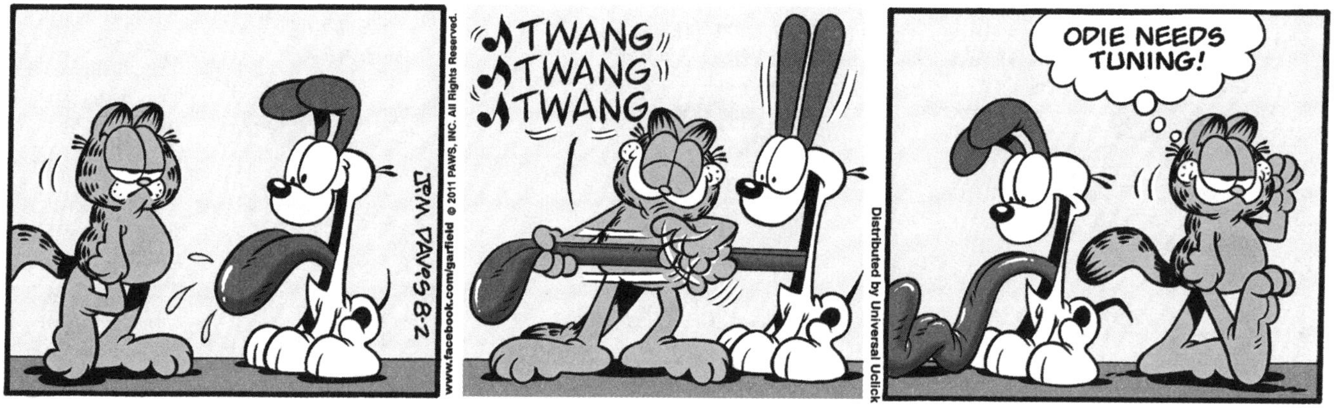
JPM DAVIS 8-2
www.facebook.com/garfield © 2011 PAWS, INC. All Rights Reserved.
TWANG
TWANG
TWANG
Distributed by Universal Uclick
ODIE NEEDS TUNING!

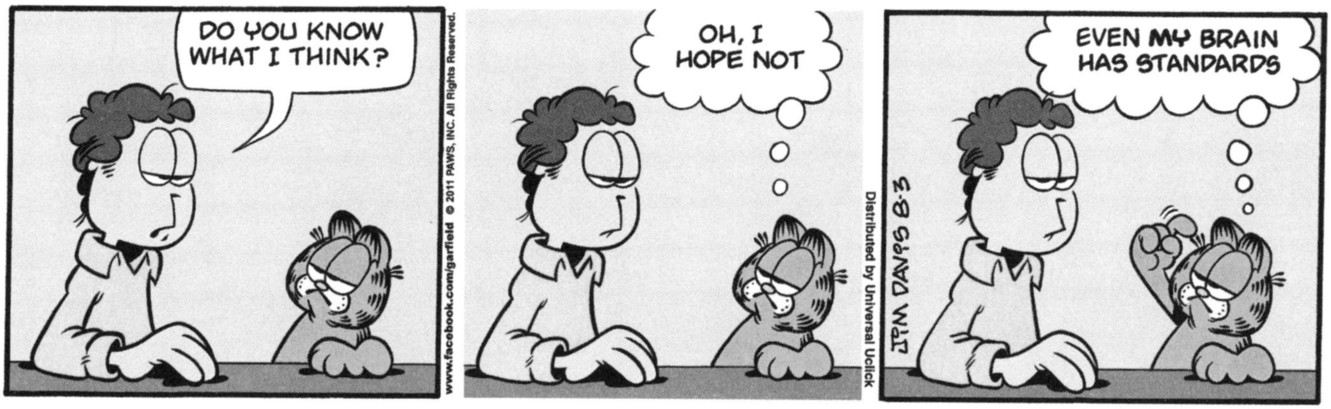
DO YOU KNOW WHAT I THINK?
www.facebook.com/garfield © 2011 PAWS, INC. All Rights Reserved.
OH, I HOPE NOT
Distributed by Universal Uclick
JPM DAVIS 8-3
EVEN MY BRAIN HAS STANDARDS

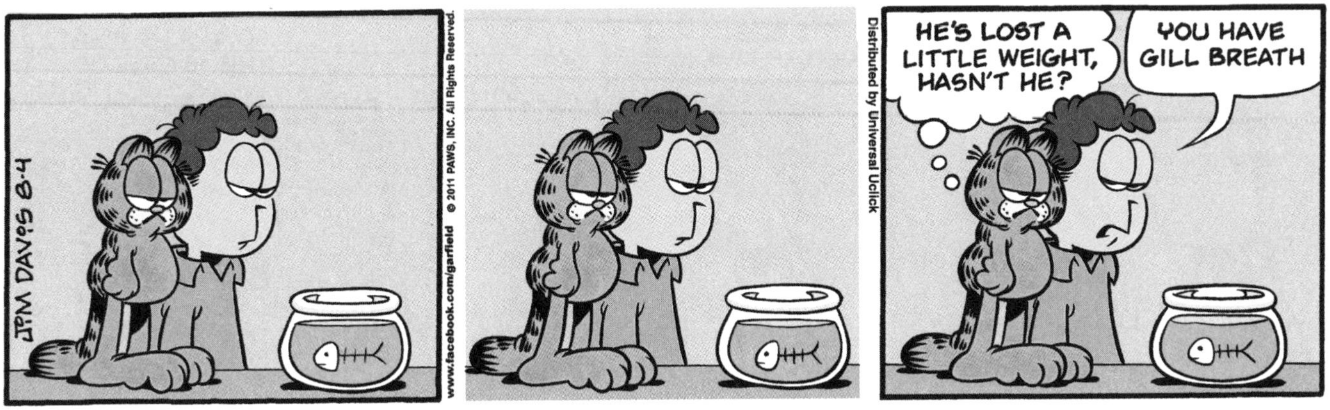
HE'S LOST A LITTLE WEIGHT, HASN'T HE?
YOU HAVE GILL BREATH

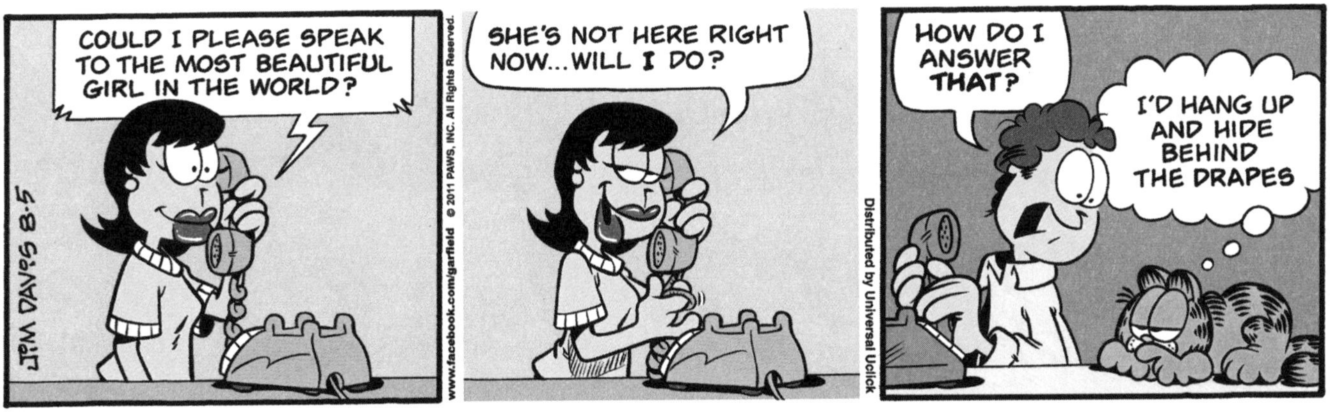
COULD I PLEASE SPEAK TO THE MOST BEAUTIFUL GIRL IN THE WORLD?
SHE'S NOT HERE RIGHT NOW... WILL I DO?
HOW DO I ANSWER THAT?
I'D HANG UP AND HIDE BEHIND THE DRAPES

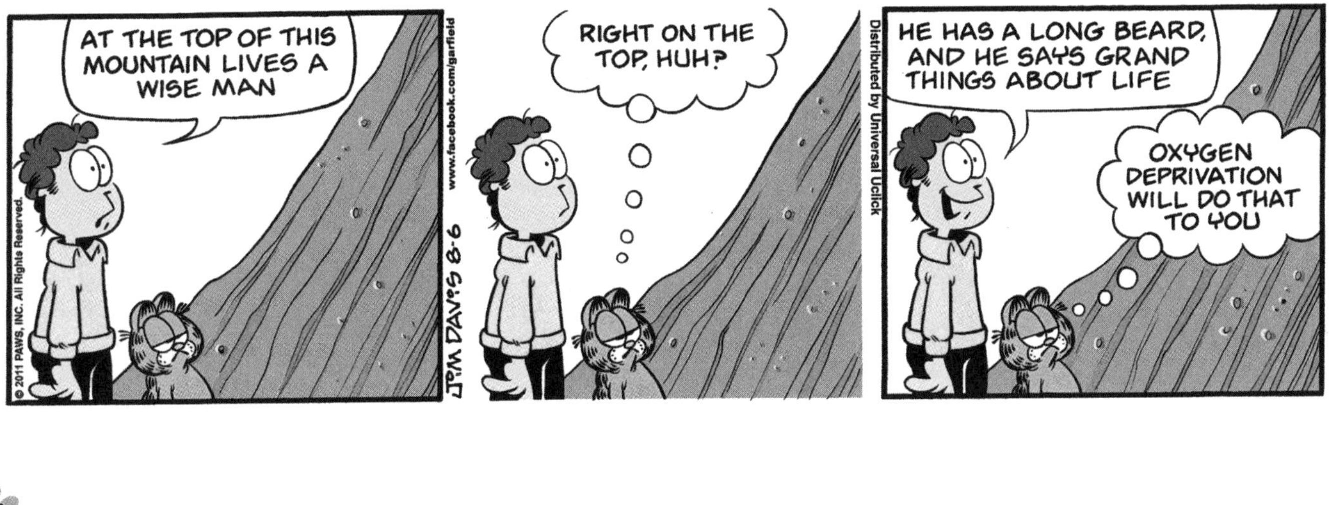
AT THE TOP OF THIS MOUNTAIN LIVES A WISE MAN
RIGHT ON THE TOP, HUH?
HE HAS A LONG BEARD, AND HE SAYS GRAND THINGS ABOUT LIFE
OXYGEN DEPRIVATION WILL DO THAT TO YOU

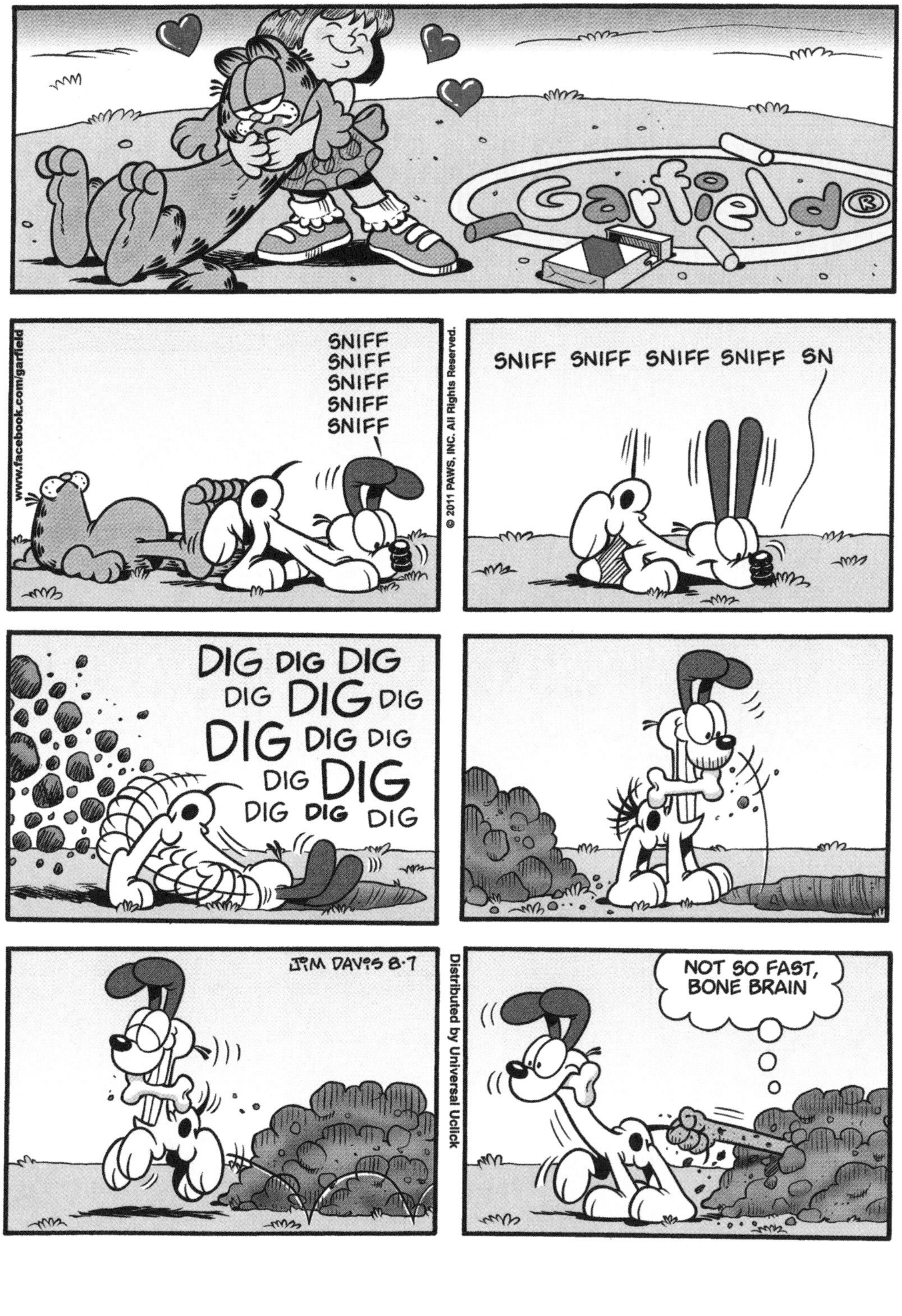
Garfield®
www.facebook.com/garfield
SNIFF SNIFF SNIFF SNIFF SNIFF
© 2011 PAWS, INC. All Rights Reserved.
SNIFF SNIFF SNIFF SNIFF SN
DIG DIG DIG DIG DIG DIG DIG DIG DIG DIG DIG DIG DIG DIG DIG
JIM DAVIS 8-7
Distributed by Universal Uclick
NOT SO FAST, BONE BRAIN

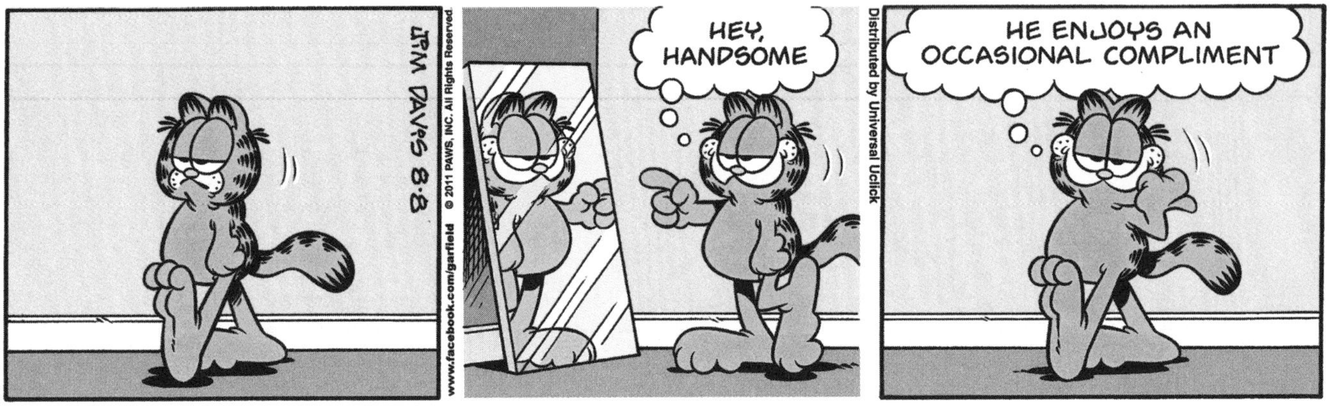
JIM DAVIS 8-8
HEY, HANDSOME
HE ENJOYS AN OCCASIONAL COMPLIMENT
© 2011 PAWS, INC. All Rights Reserved. www.facebook.com/garfield
Distributed by Universal Uclick

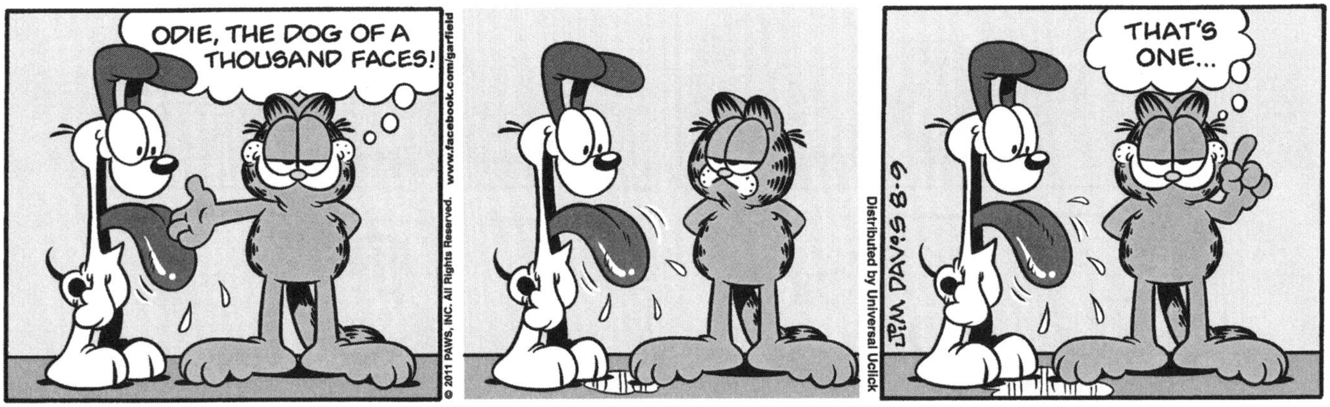
ODIE, THE DOG OF A THOUSAND FACES!
THAT'S ONE...
JIM DAVIS 8-9
© 2011 PAWS, INC. All Rights Reserved. www.facebook.com/garfield
Distributed by Universal Uclick

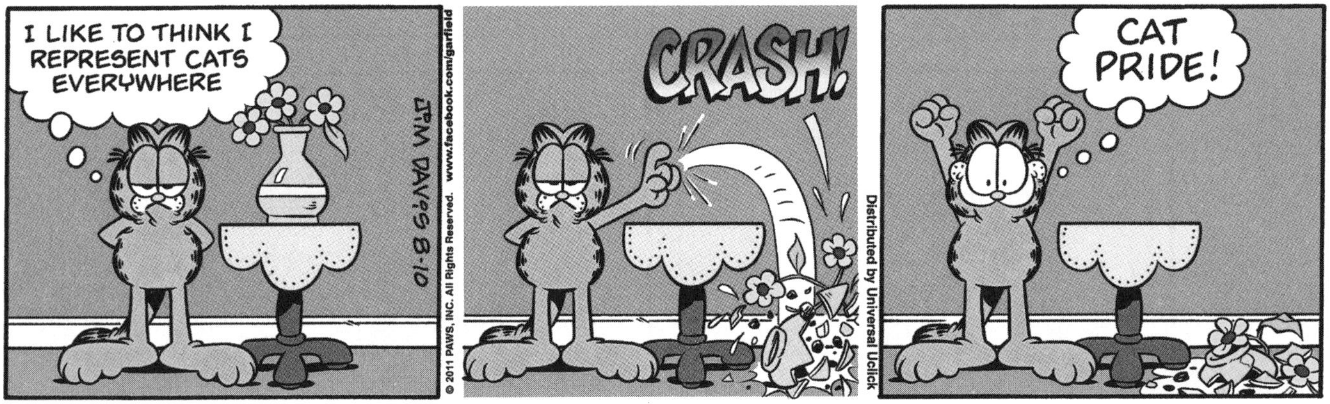
I LIKE TO THINK I REPRESENT CATS EVERYWHERE
JIM DAVIS 8-10
CRASH!
CAT PRIDE!
© 2011 PAWS, INC. All Rights Reserved. www.facebook.com/garfield
Distributed by Universal Uclick

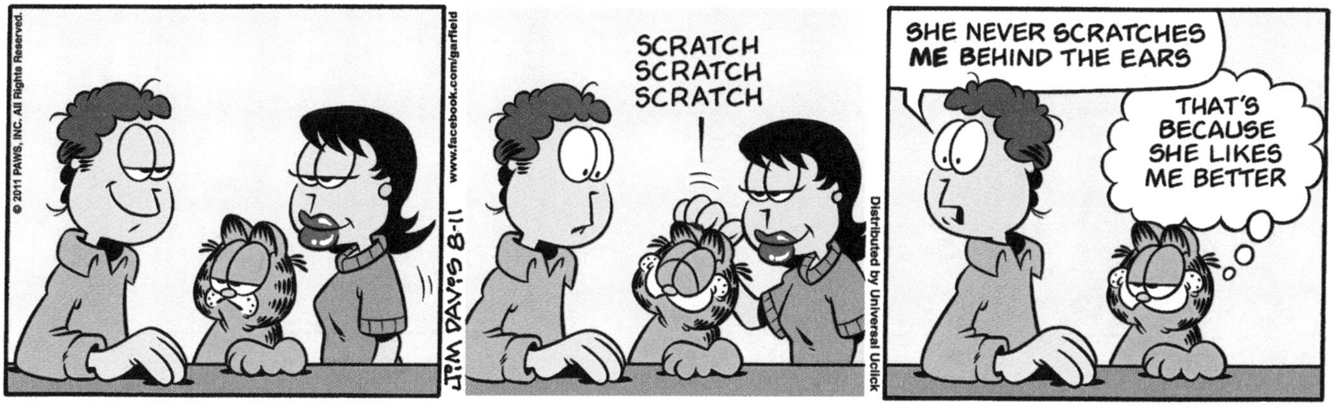
© 2011 PAWS, INC. All Rights Reserved.
www.facebook.com/garfield
SCRATCH SCRATCH SCRATCH
Distributed by Universal Uclick
SHE NEVER SCRATCHES ME BEHIND THE EARS
THAT'S BECAUSE SHE LIKES ME BETTER

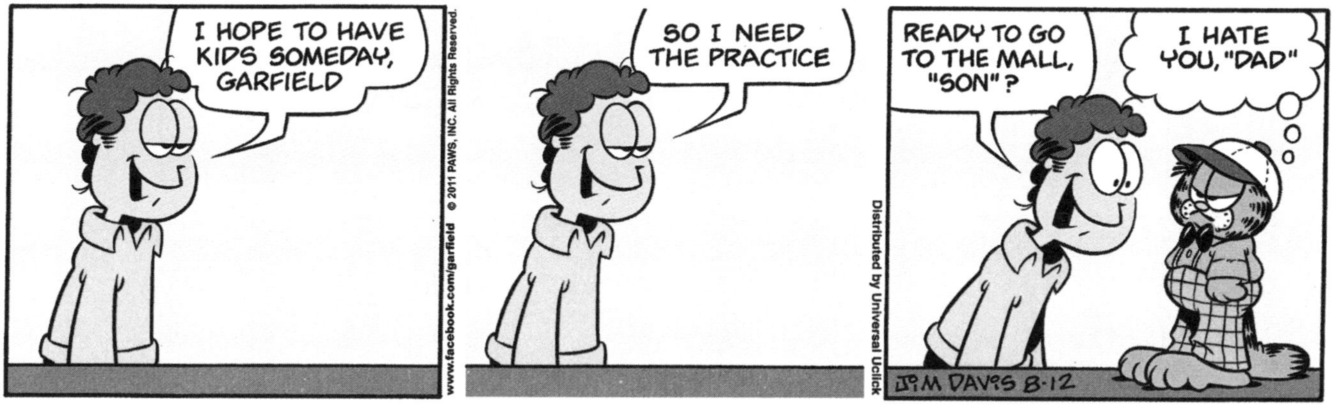
I HOPE TO HAVE KIDS SOMEDAY, GARFIELD
www.facebook.com/garfield © 2011 PAWS, INC. All Rights Reserved.
SO I NEED THE PRACTICE
Distributed by Universal Uclick
READY TO GO TO THE MALL, "SON"?
I HATE YOU, "DAD"

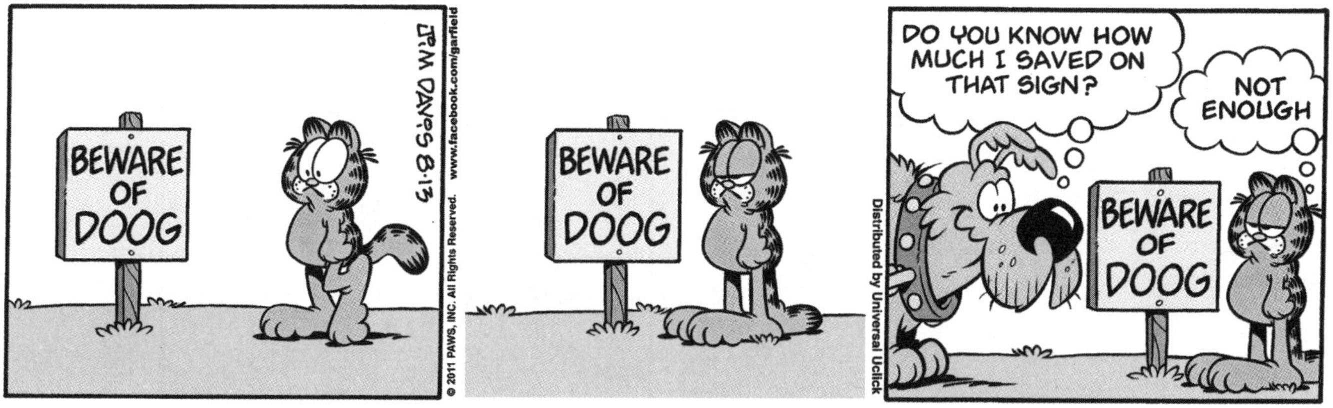
BEWARE OF DOOG
www.facebook.com/garfield
© 2011 PAWS, INC. All Rights Reserved.
BEWARE OF DOOG
Distributed by Universal Uclick
DO YOU KNOW HOW MUCH I SAVED ON THAT SIGN?
NOT ENOUGH
BEWARE OF DOOG

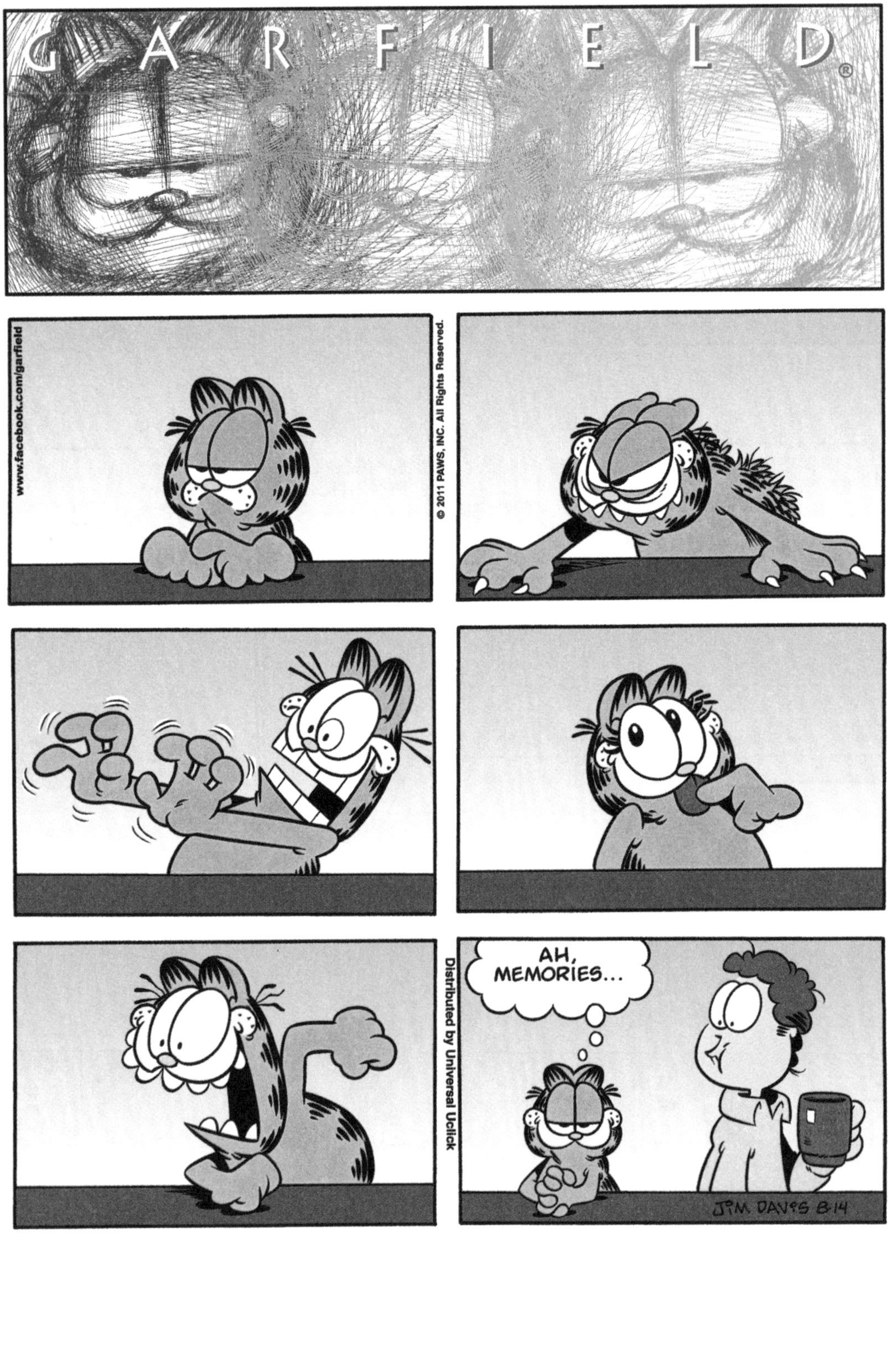
GARFIELD®
www.facebook.com/garfield
© 2011 PAWS, INC. All Rights Reserved.
Distributed by Universal Uclick
AH, MEMORIES...
JIM DAVIS 8-14

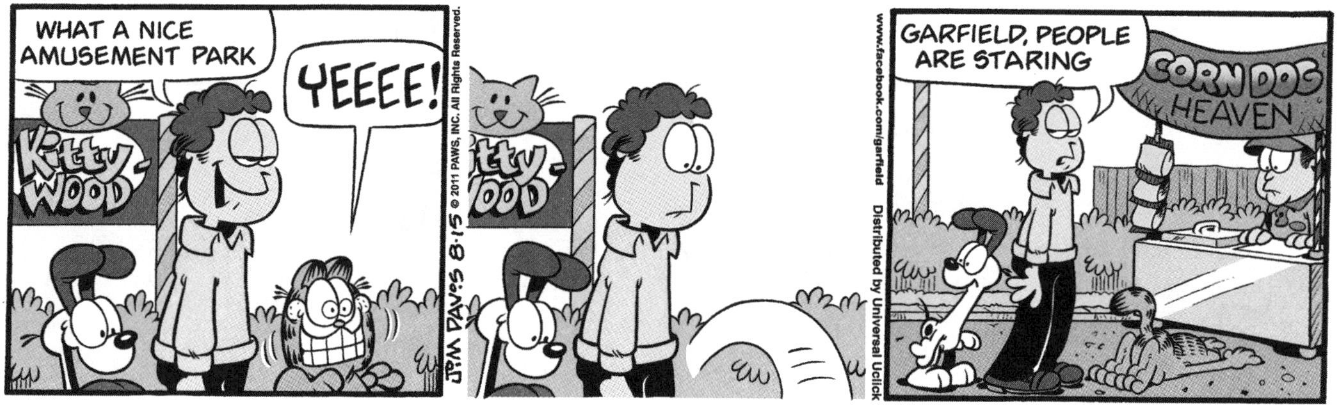
WHAT A NICE AMUSEMENT PARK
YEEEE!
Kitty-WOOD
JIM DAVIS 8·15
© 2011 PAWS, INC. All Rights Reserved.
www.facebook.com/garfield
Distributed by Universal Uclick
GARFIELD, PEOPLE ARE STARING
CORN DOG HEAVEN

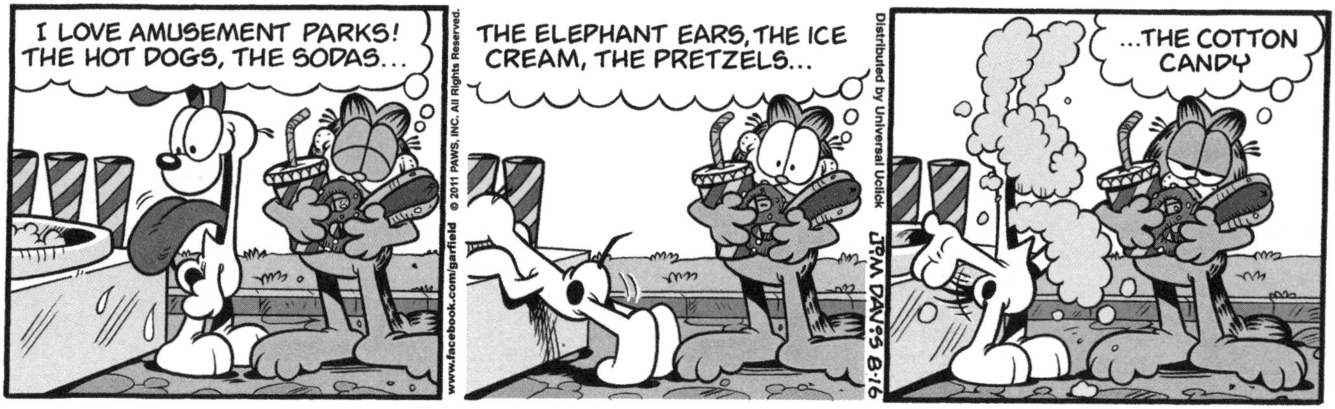
I LOVE AMUSEMENT PARKS! THE HOT DOGS, THE SODAS...
© 2011 PAWS, INC. All Rights Reserved.
www.facebook.com/garfield
THE ELEPHANT EARS, THE ICE CREAM, THE PRETZELS...
Distributed by Universal Uclick
JIM DAVIS 8·16
...THE COTTON CANDY

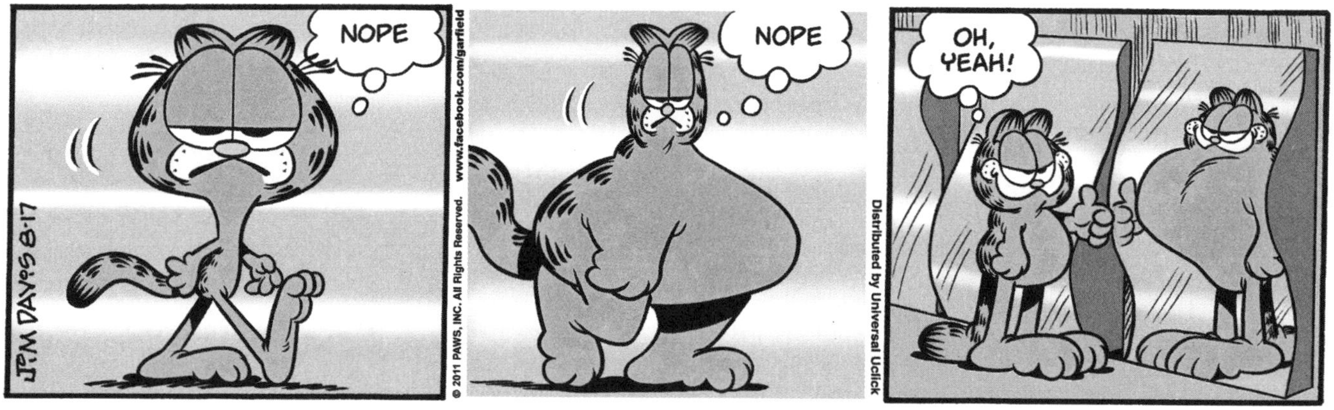
NOPE
JIM DAVIS 8·17
© 2011 PAWS, INC. All Rights Reserved.
www.facebook.com/garfield
NOPE
Distributed by Universal Uclick
OH, YEAH!

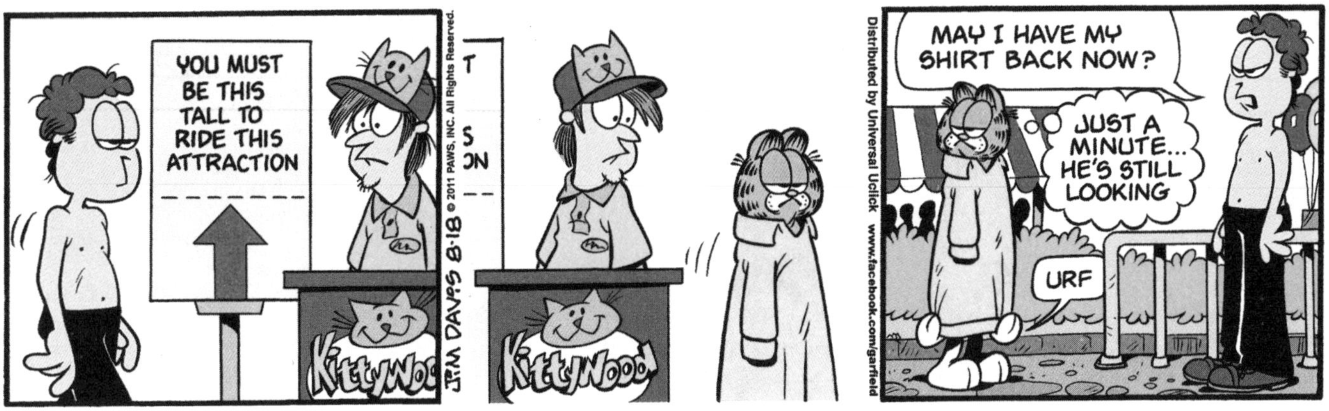
YOU MUST BE THIS TALL TO RIDE THIS ATTRACTION
KittyWood
JIM DAVIS 8-18
© 2011 PAWS, INC. All Rights Reserved.
Distributed by Universal Uclick www.facebook.com/garfield
MAY I HAVE MY SHIRT BACK NOW?
JUST A MINUTE... HE'S STILL LOOKING
URF

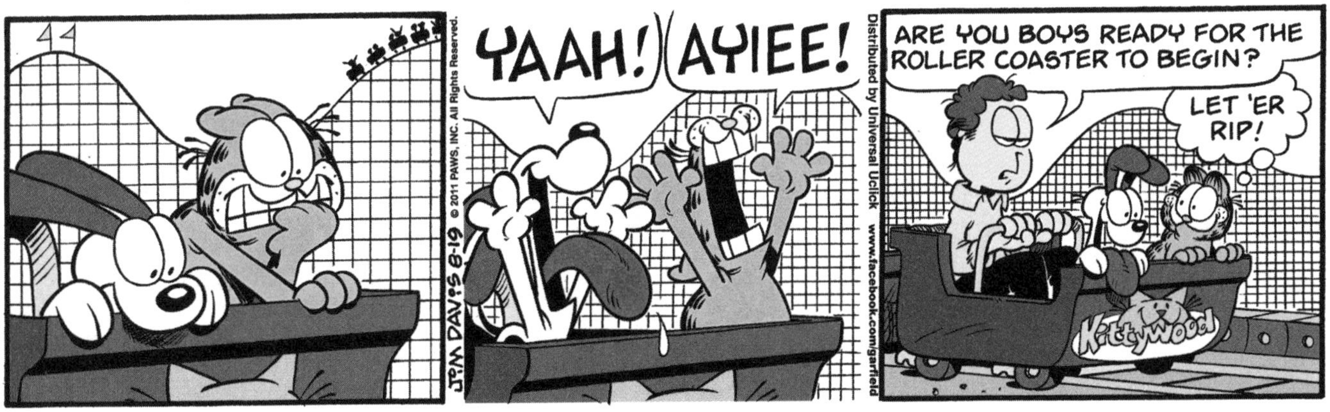
JIM DAVIS 8-19
© 2011 PAWS, INC. All Rights Reserved.
YAAH!
AYIEE!
Distributed by Universal Uclick www.facebook.com/garfield
ARE YOU BOYS READY FOR THE ROLLER COASTER TO BEGIN?
LET 'ER RIP!
Kittywood

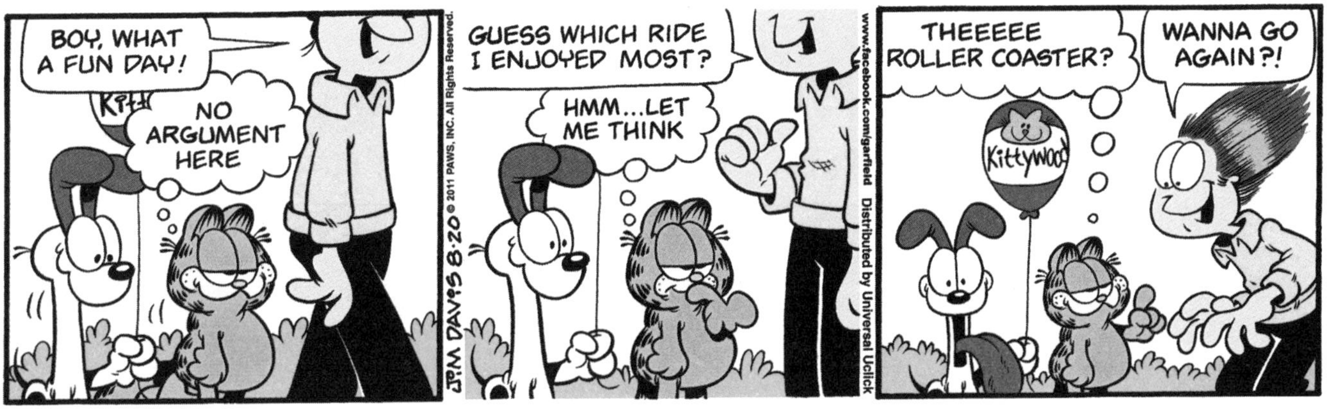
BOY, WHAT A FUN DAY!
NO ARGUMENT HERE
JIM DAVIS 8-20
© 2011 PAWS, INC. All Rights Reserved.
GUESS WHICH RIDE I ENJOYED MOST?
HMM...LET ME THINK
www.facebook.com/garfield Distributed by Universal Uclick
THEEEEE ROLLER COASTER?
WANNA GO AGAIN?!
Kittywood

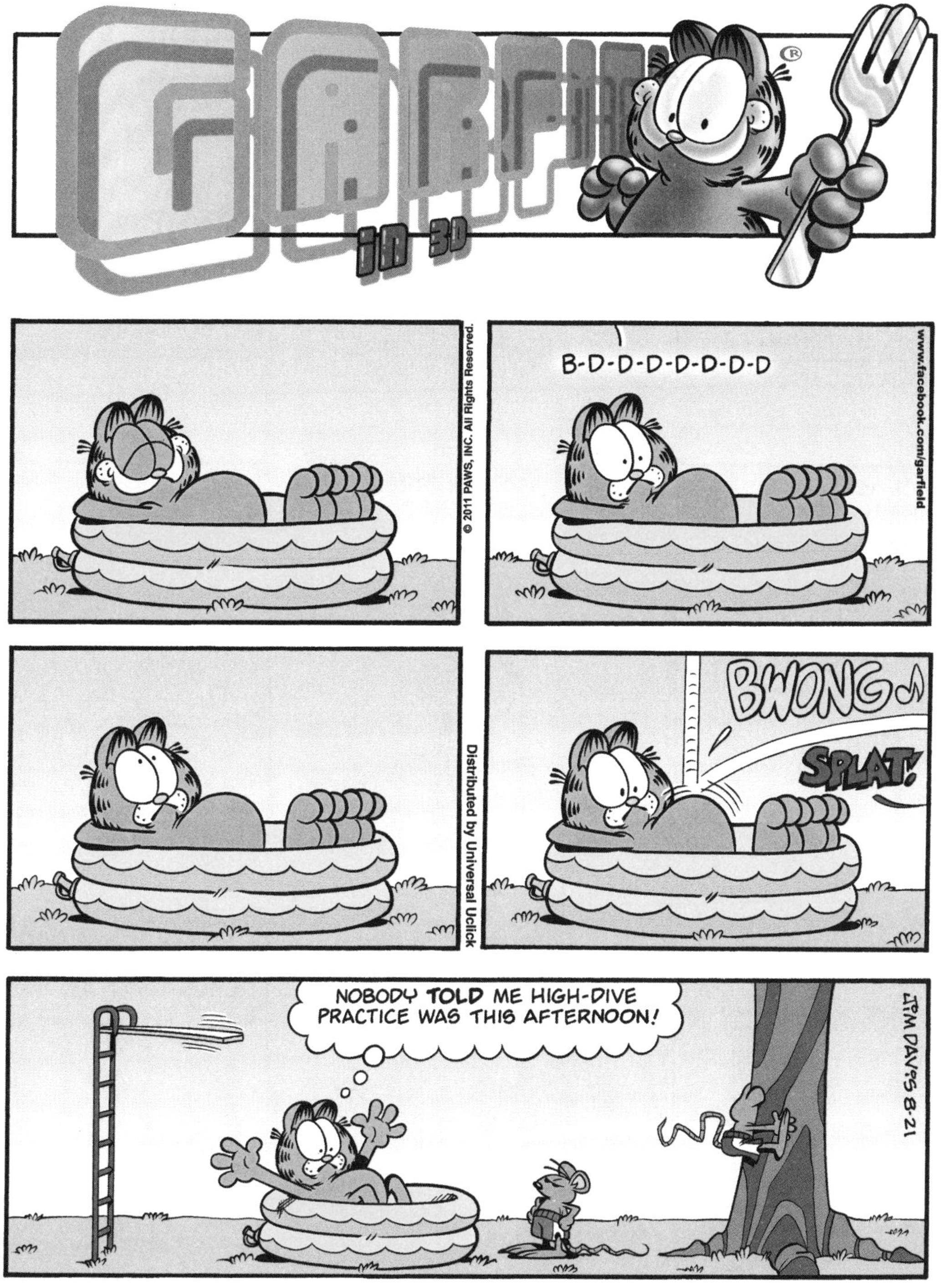
in 3D
© 2011 PAWS, INC. All Rights Reserved.
B-D-D-D-D-D-D-D-D
www.facebook.com/garfield
Distributed by Universal Uclick
BWONG
SPLAT!
NOBODY TOLD ME HIGH-DIVE PRACTICE WAS THIS AFTERNOON!
JIM DAVIS 8-21

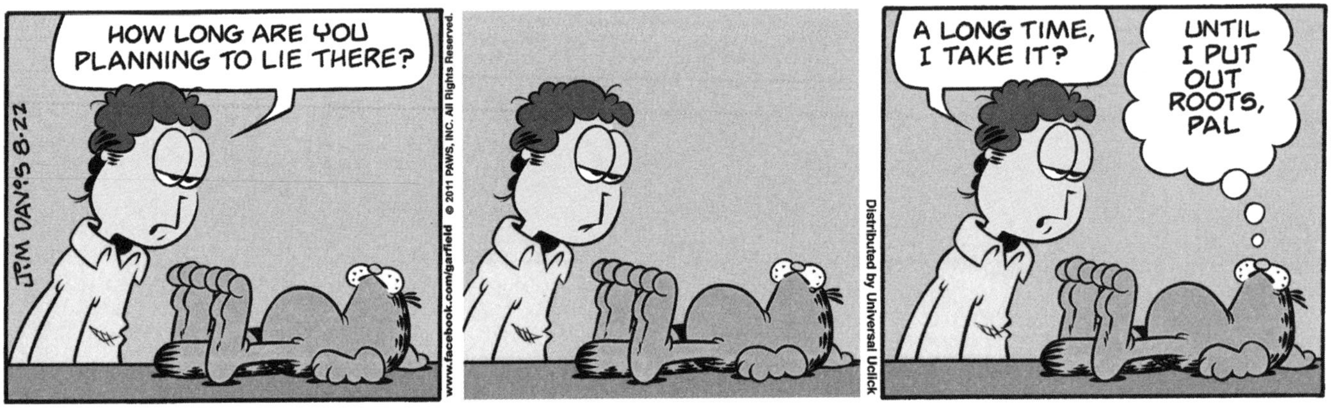
JIM DAVIS 8-22
HOW LONG ARE YOU PLANNING TO LIE THERE?
A LONG TIME, I TAKE IT?
UNTIL I PUT OUT ROOTS, PAL
© 2011 PAWS, INC. All Rights Reserved. www.facebook.com/garfield
Distributed by Universal Uclick

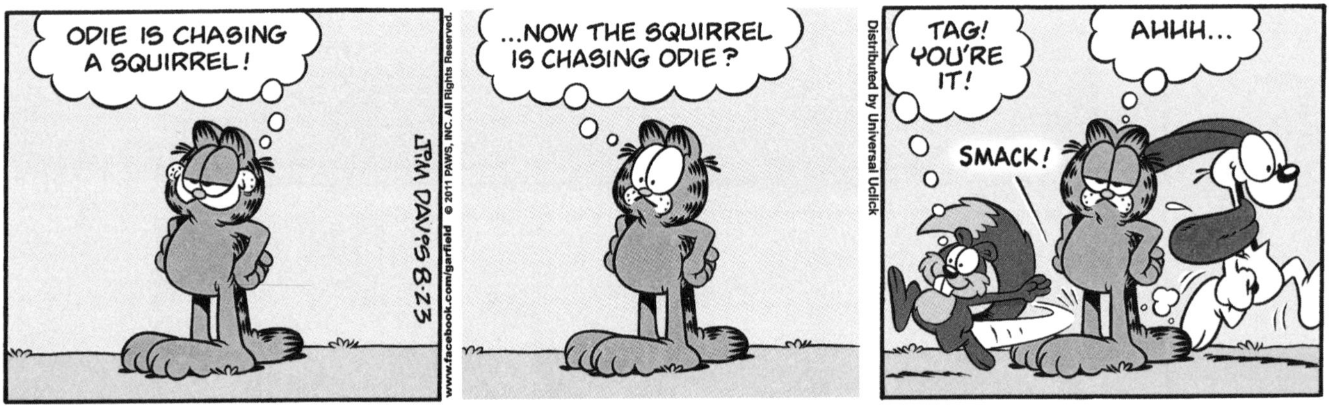
ODIE IS CHASING A SQUIRREL!
JIM DAVIS 8-23
...NOW THE SQUIRREL IS CHASING ODIE?
TAG! YOU'RE IT!
SMACK!
AHHH...
© 2011 PAWS, INC. All Rights Reserved. www.facebook.com/garfield
Distributed by Universal Uclick

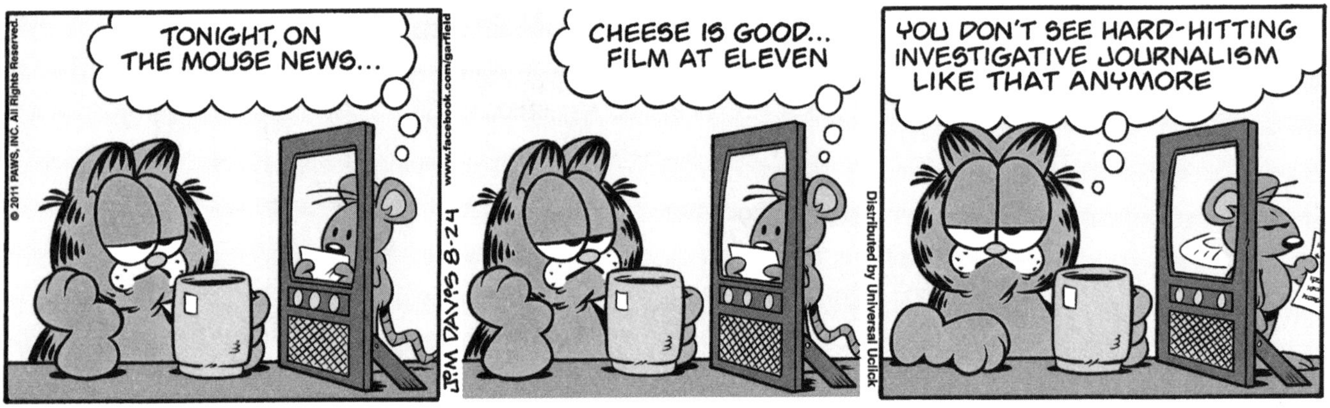
TONIGHT, ON THE MOUSE NEWS...
CHEESE IS GOOD... FILM AT ELEVEN
YOU DON'T SEE HARD-HITTING INVESTIGATIVE JOURNALISM LIKE THAT ANYMORE
JIM DAVIS 8-24
© 2011 PAWS, INC. All Rights Reserved. www.facebook.com/garfield
Distributed by Universal Uclick

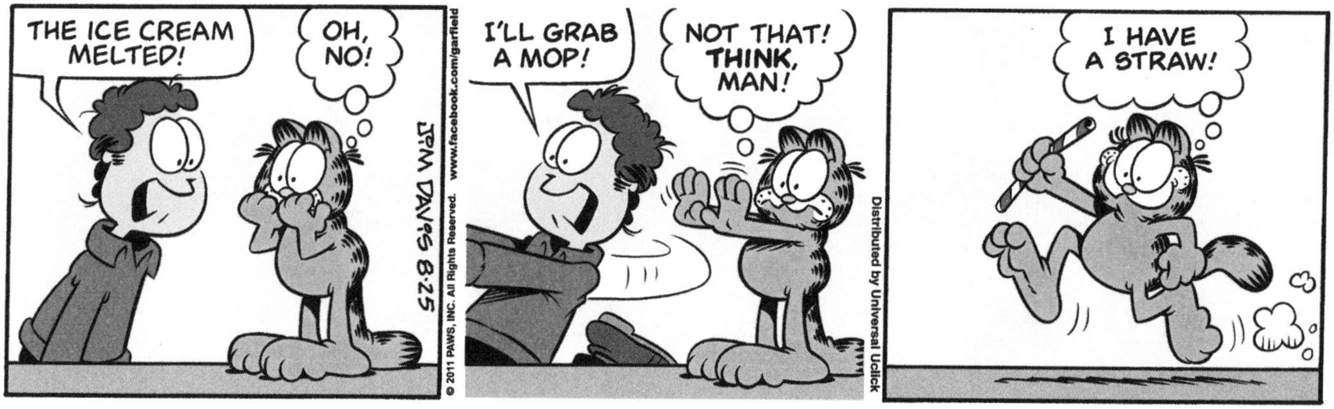
THE ICE CREAM MELTED!
OH, NO!
JIM DAVIS 8·25
© 2011 PAWS, INC. All Rights Reserved. www.facebook.com/garfield
I'LL GRAB A MOP!
NOT THAT! THINK, MAN!
Distributed by Universal Uclick
I HAVE A STRAW!

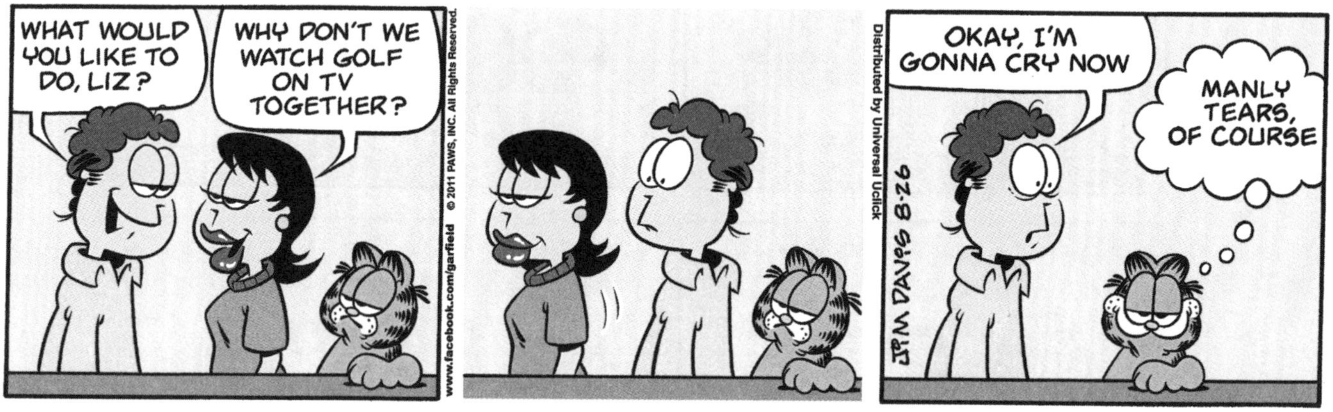
WHAT WOULD YOU LIKE TO DO, LIZ?
WHY DON'T WE WATCH GOLF ON TV TOGETHER?
www.facebook.com/garfield © 2011 PAWS, INC. All Rights Reserved.
Distributed by Universal Uclick
OKAY, I'M GONNA CRY NOW
MANLY TEARS, OF COURSE
JIM DAVIS 8·26

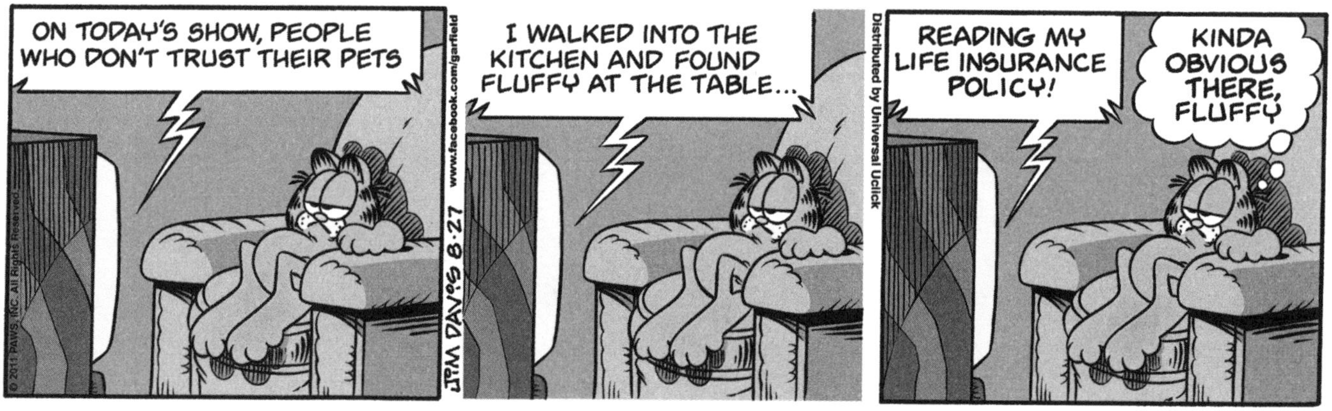
ON TODAY'S SHOW, PEOPLE WHO DON'T TRUST THEIR PETS
© 2011 PAWS, INC. All Rights Reserved.
JIM DAVIS 8·27 www.facebook.com/garfield
I WALKED INTO THE KITCHEN AND FOUND FLUFFY AT THE TABLE...
Distributed by Universal Uclick
READING MY LIFE INSURANCE POLICY!
KINDA OBVIOUS THERE, FLUFFY

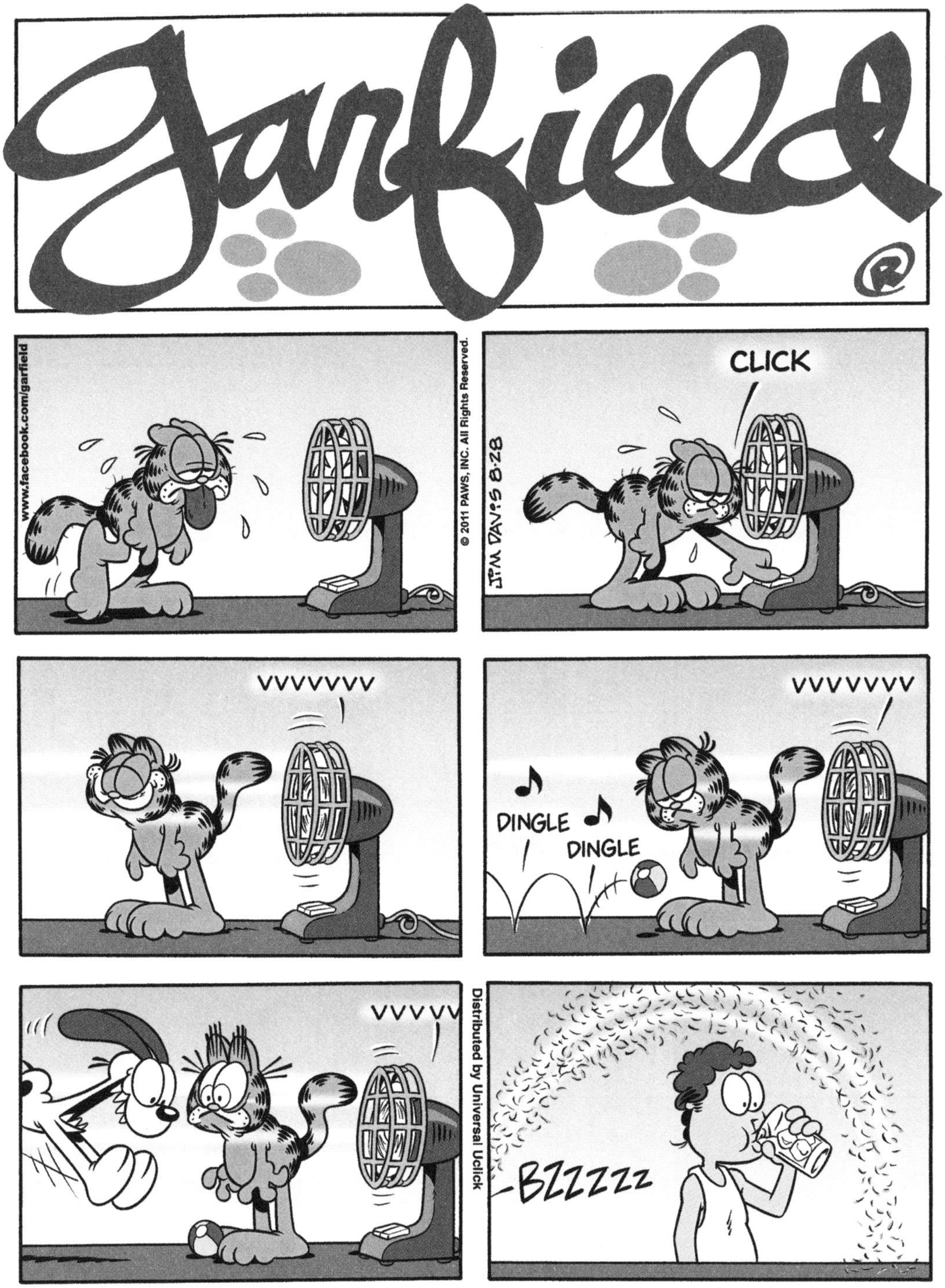
garfield
www.facebook.com/garfield
© 2011 PAWS, INC. All Rights Reserved.
JPM DAVIS 8-28
CLICK
VVVVVVV
VVVVVVV
DINGLE
DINGLE
VVVVV
Distributed by Universal Uclick
BZZZZZ

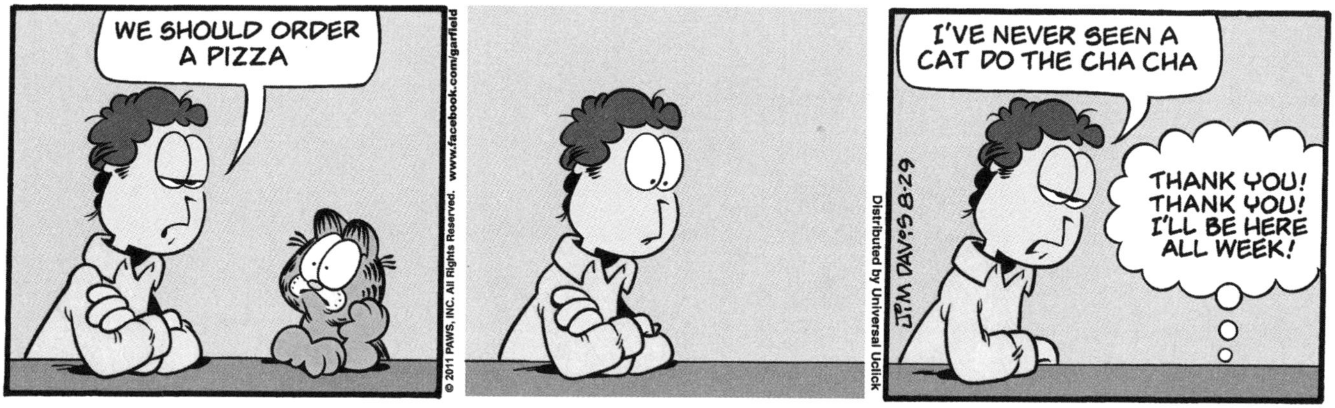
WE SHOULD ORDER A PIZZA
© 2011 PAWS, INC. All Rights Reserved. www.facebook.com/garfield
I'VE NEVER SEEN A CAT DO THE CHA CHA
THANK YOU! THANK YOU! I'LL BE HERE ALL WEEK!
JIM DAVIS 8-29
Distributed by Universal Uclick

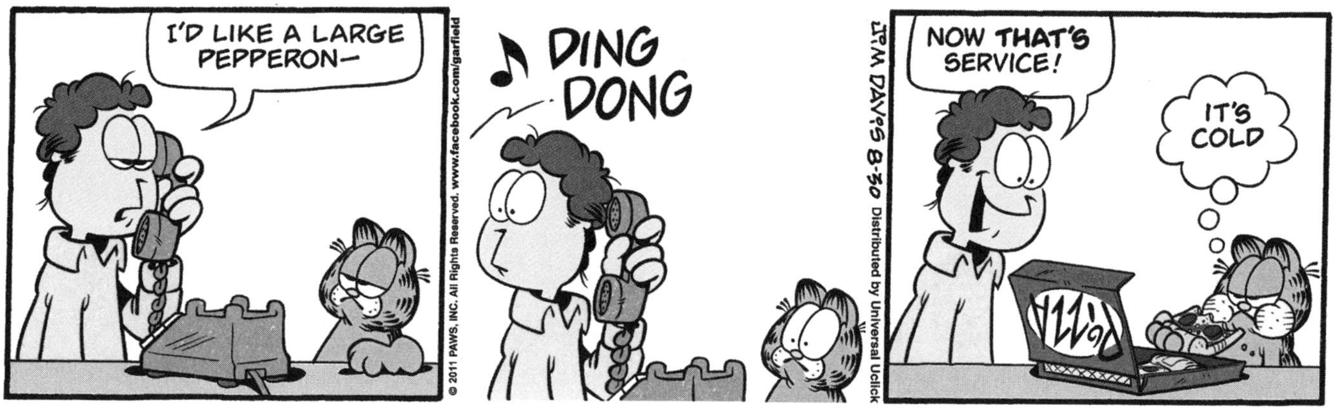
I'D LIKE A LARGE PEPPERON—
© 2011 PAWS, INC. All Rights Reserved. www.facebook.com/garfield
DING DONG
JIM DAVIS 8-30 Distributed by Universal Uclick
NOW THAT'S SERVICE!
IT'S COLD

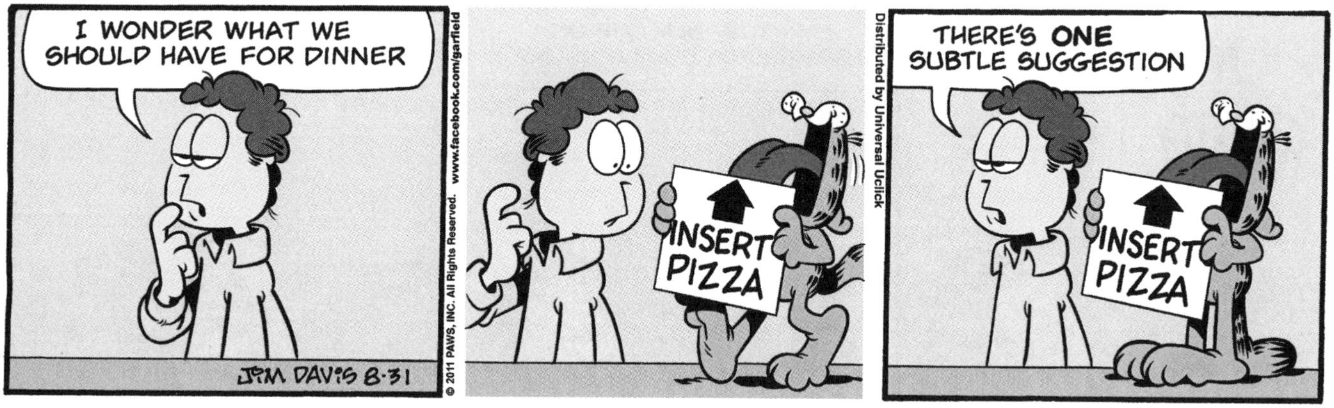
I WONDER WHAT WE SHOULD HAVE FOR DINNER
JIM DAVIS 8-31
© 2011 PAWS, INC. All Rights Reserved. www.facebook.com/garfield
INSERT PIZZA
Distributed by Universal Uclick
THERE'S ONE SUBTLE SUGGESTION
INSERT PIZZA

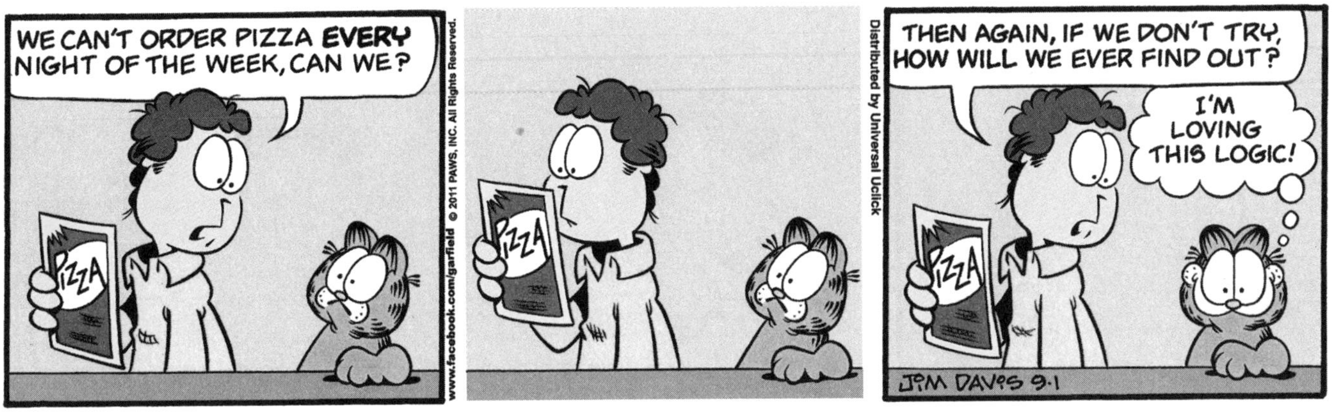
WE CAN'T ORDER PIZZA EVERY NIGHT OF THE WEEK, CAN WE?
PIZZA
www.facebook.com/garfield © 2011 PAWS, INC. All Rights Reserved.
THEN AGAIN, IF WE DON'T TRY, HOW WILL WE EVER FIND OUT?
I'M LOVING THIS LOGIC!
Distributed by Universal Uclick
JIM DAVIS 9-1

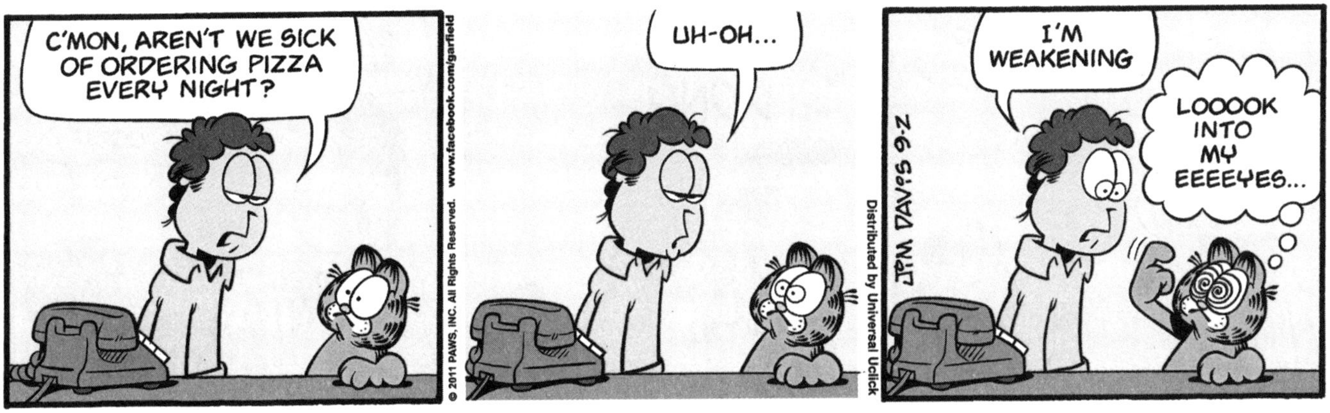
C'MON, AREN'T WE SICK OF ORDERING PIZZA EVERY NIGHT?
© 2011 PAWS, INC. All Rights Reserved. www.facebook.com/garfield
UH-OH...
JIM DAVIS 9-2
Distributed by Universal Uclick
I'M WEAKENING
LOOOOK INTO MY EEEEYES...

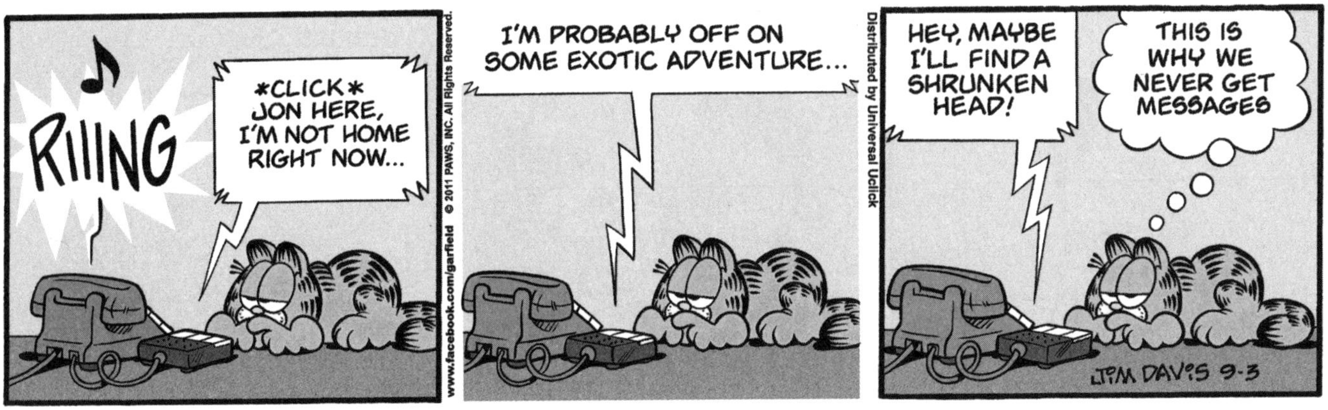
RIIING
CLICK JON HERE, I'M NOT HOME RIGHT NOW...
www.facebook.com/garfield © 2011 PAWS, INC. All Rights Reserved.
I'M PROBABLY OFF ON SOME EXOTIC ADVENTURE...
Distributed by Universal Uclick
HEY, MAYBE I'LL FIND A SHRUNKEN HEAD!
THIS IS WHY WE NEVER GET MESSAGES
JIM DAVIS 9-3

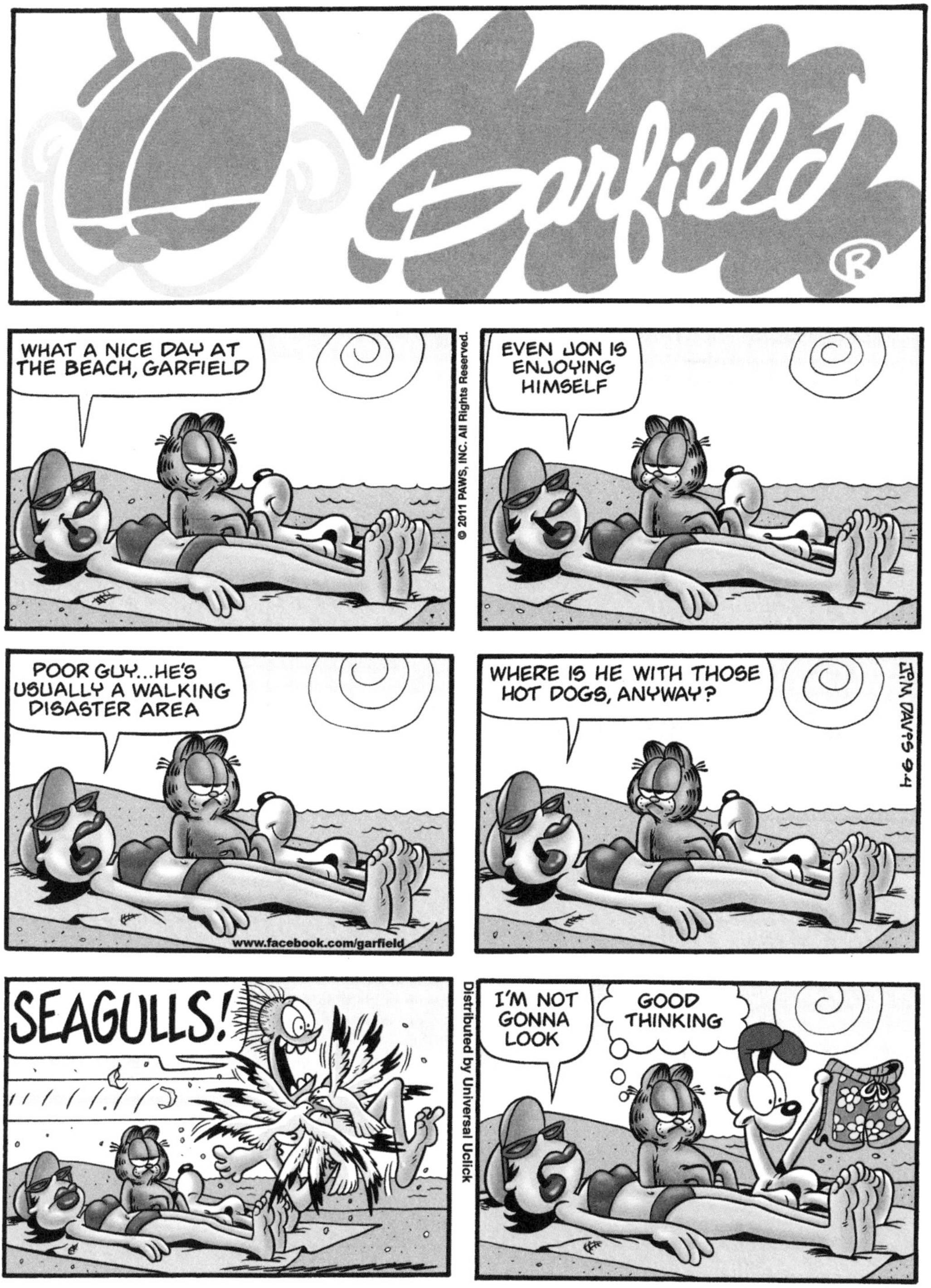
Garfield ®
WHAT A NICE DAY AT THE BEACH, GARFIELD
© 2011 PAWS, INC. All Rights Reserved.
EVEN JON IS ENJOYING HIMSELF
POOR GUY...HE'S USUALLY A WALKING DISASTER AREA
www.facebook.com/garfield
WHERE IS HE WITH THOSE HOT DOGS, ANYWAY?
JPM DAVIS 9-4
SEAGULLS!
Distributed by Universal Uclick
I'M NOT GONNA LOOK
GOOD THINKING

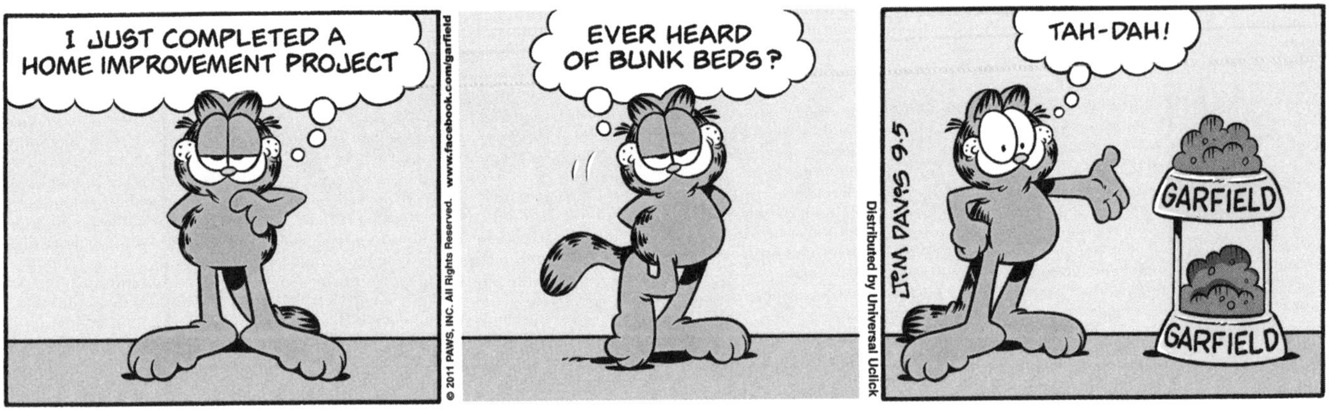
I JUST COMPLETED A HOME IMPROVEMENT PROJECT
© 2011 PAWS, INC. All Rights Reserved. www.facebook.com/garfield
EVER HEARD OF BUNK BEDS?
Distributed by Universal Uclick
TAH-DAH!
JIM DAVIS 9-5
GARFIELD
GARFIELD

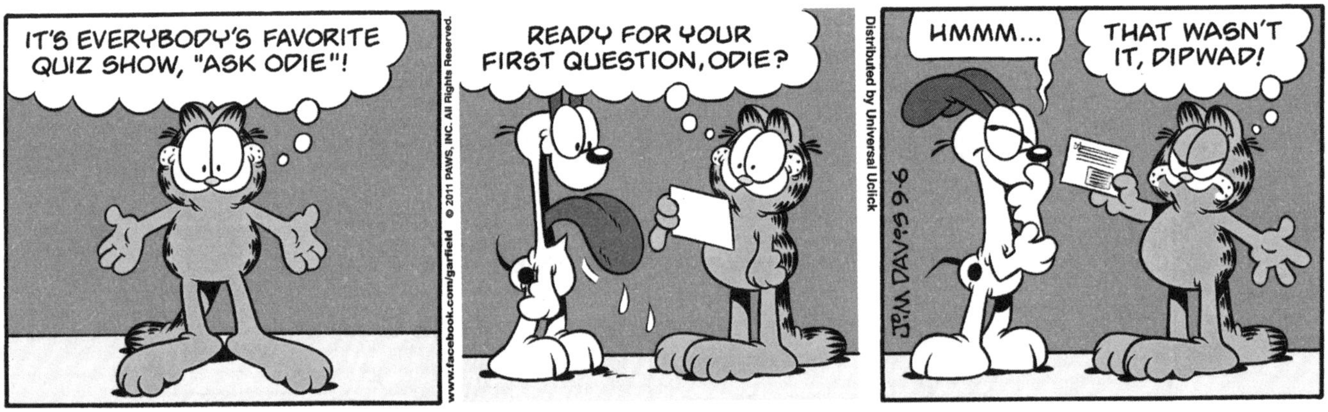
IT'S EVERYBODY'S FAVORITE QUIZ SHOW, "ASK ODIE"!
www.facebook.com/garfield © 2011 PAWS, INC. All Rights Reserved.
READY FOR YOUR FIRST QUESTION, ODIE?
Distributed by Universal Uclick
HMMM...
THAT WASN'T IT, DIPWAD!
JIM DAVIS 9-6

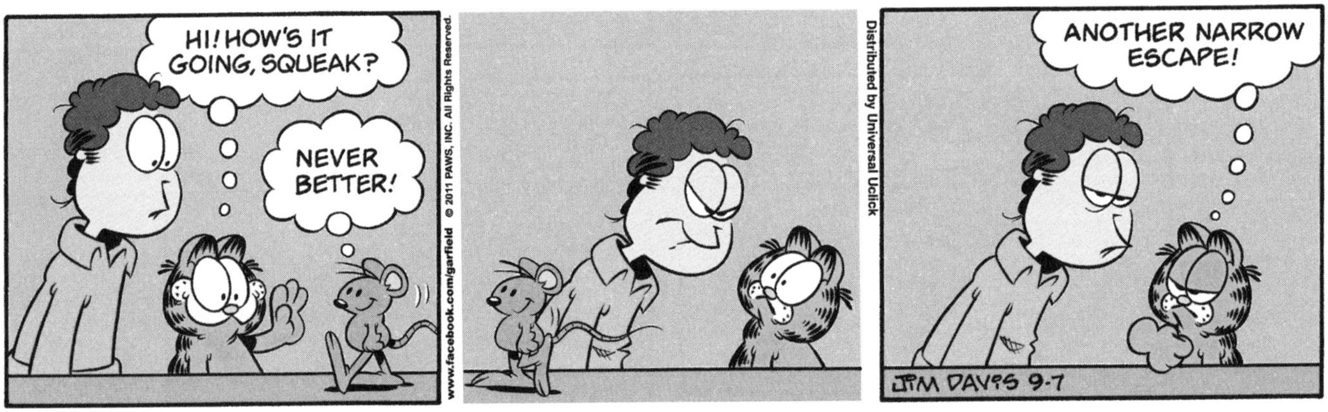
HI! HOW'S IT GOING, SQUEAK?
NEVER BETTER!
www.facebook.com/garfield © 2011 PAWS, INC. All Rights Reserved.
Distributed by Universal Uclick
ANOTHER NARROW ESCAPE!
JIM DAVIS 9-7

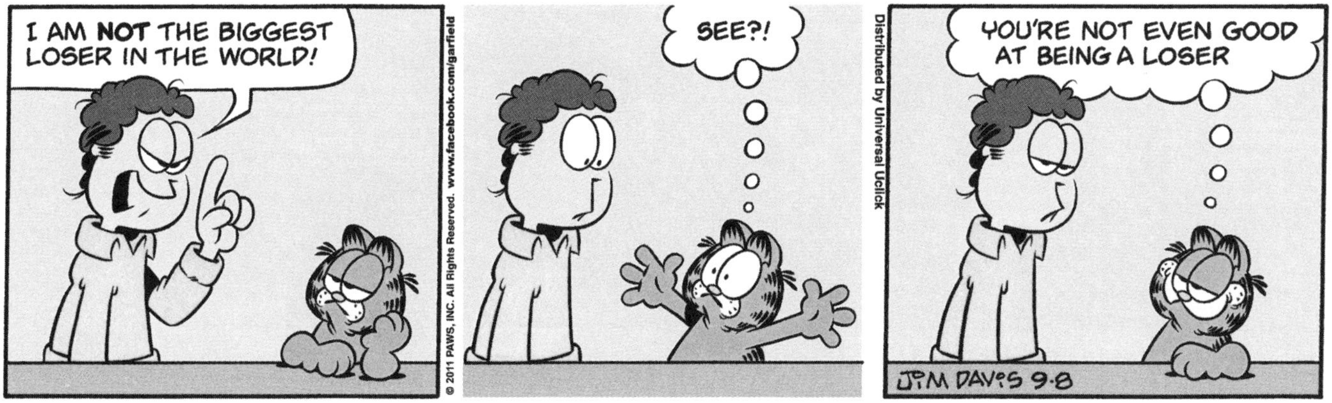
I AM **NOT** THE BIGGEST LOSER IN THE WORLD!
SEE?!
YOU'RE NOT EVEN GOOD AT BEING A LOSER
JIM DAVIS 9-8

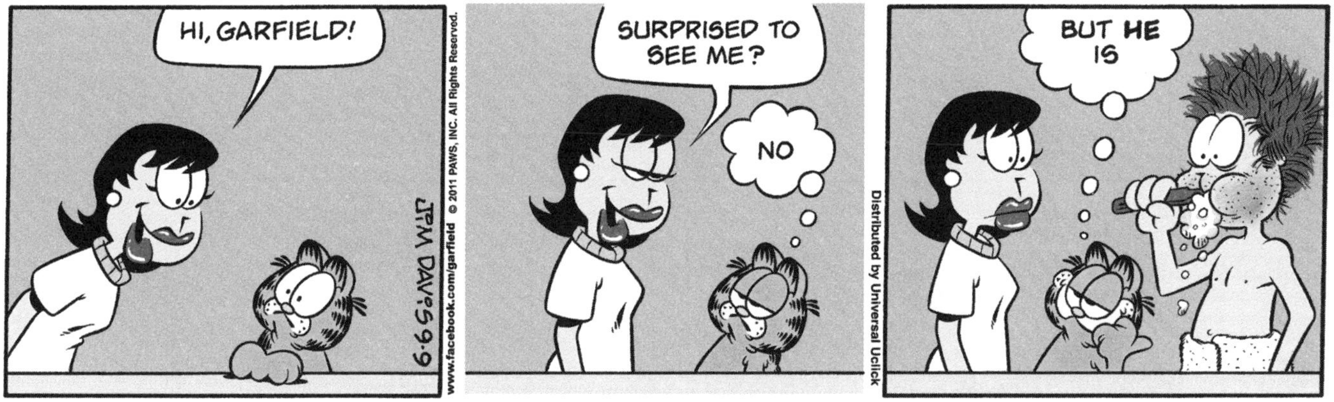
HI, GARFIELD!
JIM DAVIS 9-9
SURPRISED TO SEE ME?
NO
BUT **HE** IS

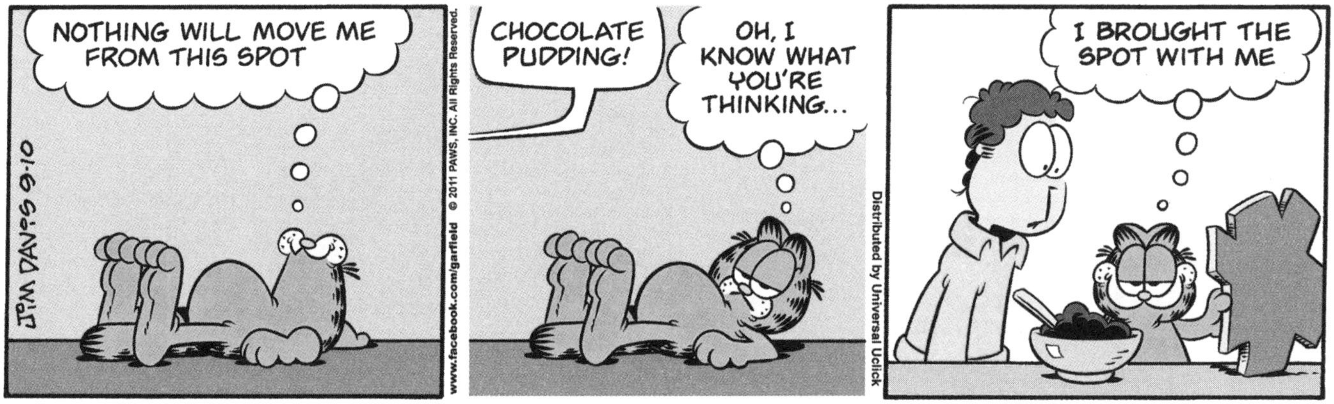
NOTHING WILL MOVE ME FROM THIS SPOT
JIM DAVIS 9-10
CHOCOLATE PUDDING!
OH, I KNOW WHAT YOU'RE THINKING...
I BROUGHT THE SPOT WITH ME

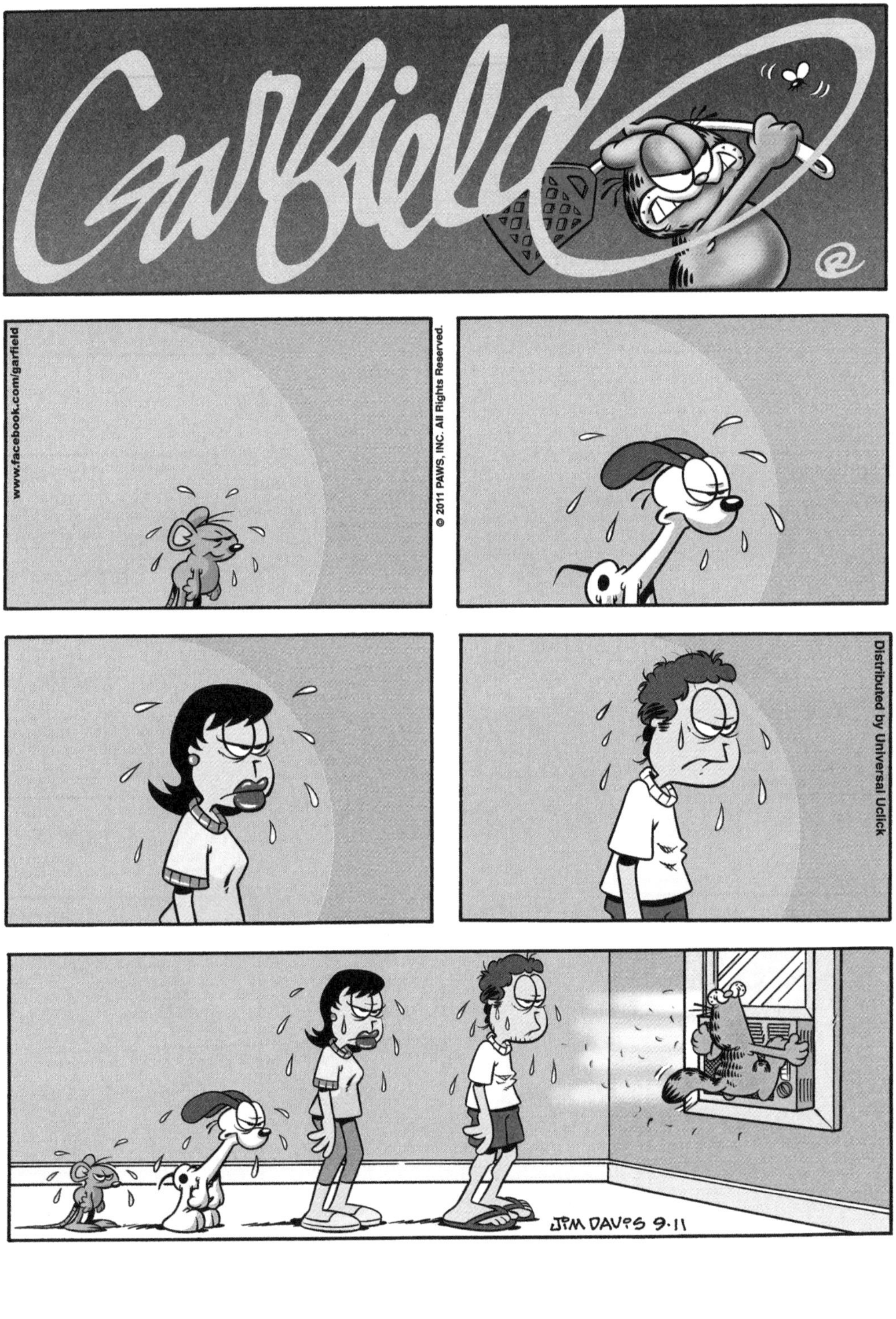
Garfield
www.facebook.com/garfield
© 2011 PAWS, INC. All Rights Reserved.
Distributed by Universal Uclick
JIM DAVIS 9-11

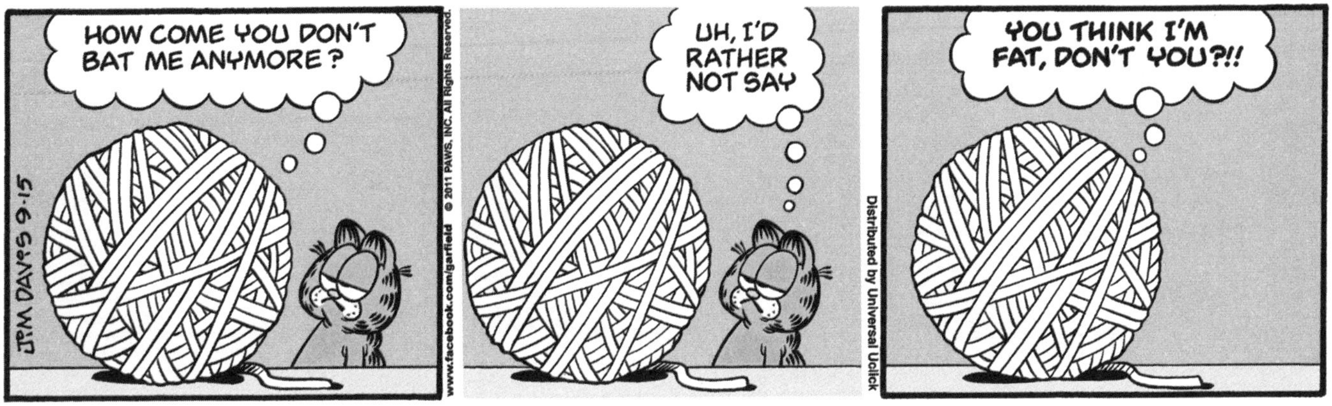
HOW COME YOU DON'T BAT ME ANYMORE?
UH, I'D RATHER NOT SAY
YOU THINK I'M FAT, DON'T YOU?!!
© 2011 PAWS, INC. All Rights Reserved. www.facebook.com/garfield
Distributed by Universal Uclick

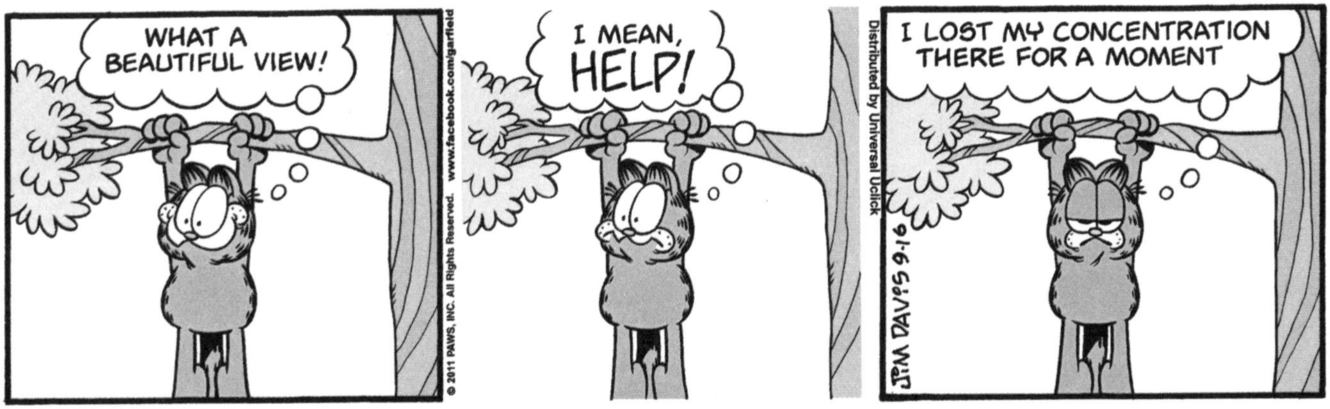
WHAT A BEAUTIFUL VIEW!
I MEAN, HELP!
I LOST MY CONCENTRATION THERE FOR A MOMENT
© 2011 PAWS, INC. All Rights Reserved. www.facebook.com/garfield
Distributed by Universal Uclick

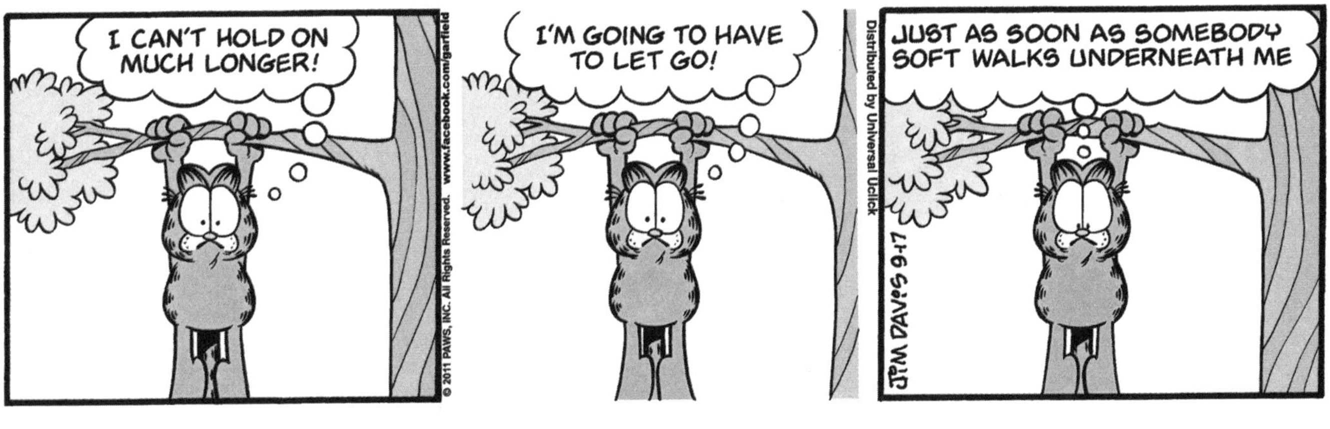
I CAN'T HOLD ON MUCH LONGER!
I'M GOING TO HAVE TO LET GO!
JUST AS SOON AS SOMEBODY SOFT WALKS UNDERNEATH ME
© 2011 PAWS, INC. All Rights Reserved. www.facebook.com/garfield
Distributed by Universal Uclick

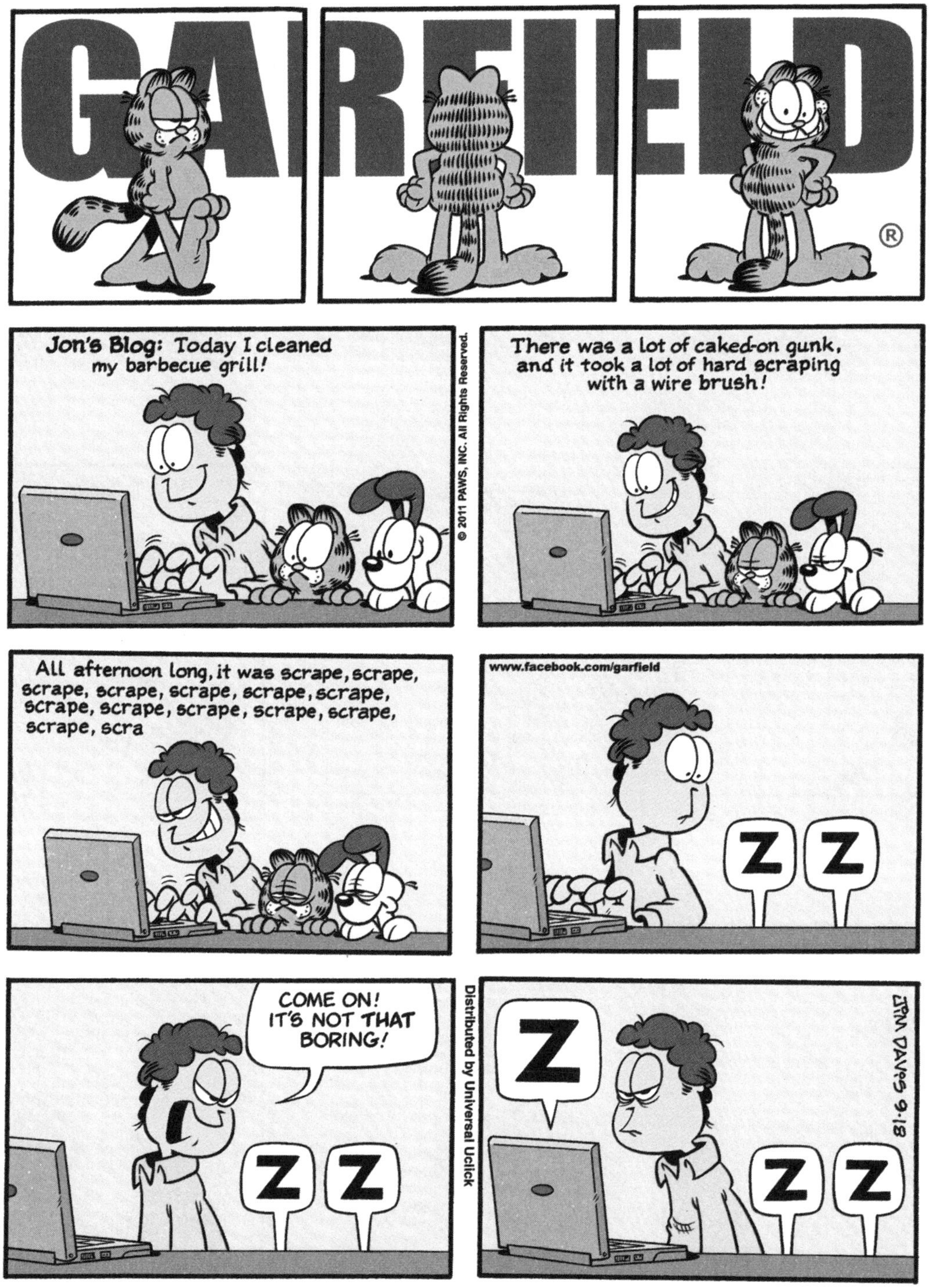
GARFIELD
®
Jon's Blog: Today I cleaned my barbecue grill!
© 2011 PAWS, INC. All Rights Reserved.
There was a lot of caked-on gunk, and it took a lot of hard scraping with a wire brush!
All afternoon long, it was scrape, scrape, scrape, scrape, scrape, scrape, scrape, scrape, scrape, scrape, scrape, scrape, scrape, scra
www.facebook.com/garfield
Z Z
Distributed by Universal Uclick
COME ON! IT'S NOT THAT BORING!
Z Z
Z
Z Z
JPM DAVIS 9-18

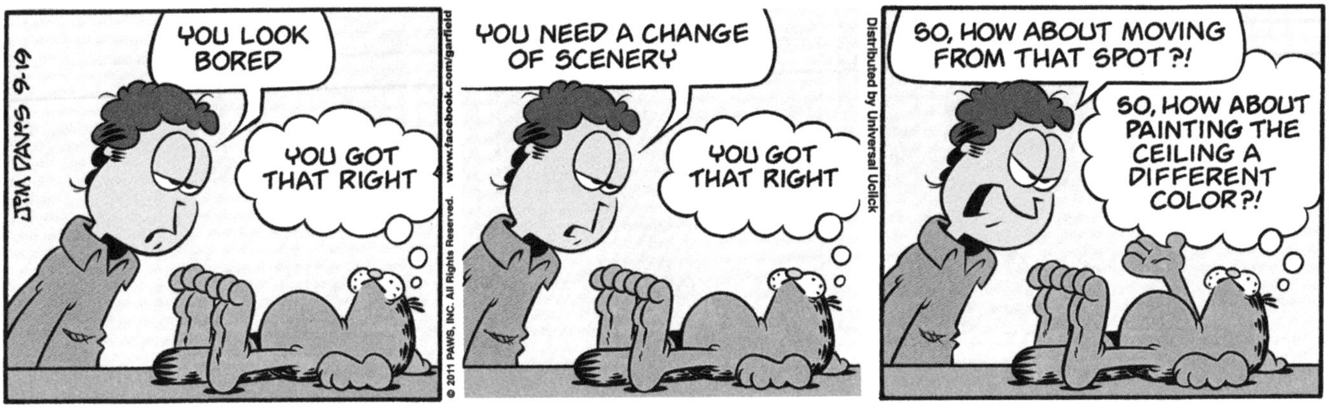
JIM DAVIS 9-19
YOU LOOK BORED
YOU GOT THAT RIGHT
© 2011 PAWS, INC. All Rights Reserved. www.facebook.com/garfield
YOU NEED A CHANGE OF SCENERY
YOU GOT THAT RIGHT
Distributed by Universal Uclick
SO, HOW ABOUT MOVING FROM THAT SPOT?!
SO, HOW ABOUT PAINTING THE CEILING A DIFFERENT COLOR?!

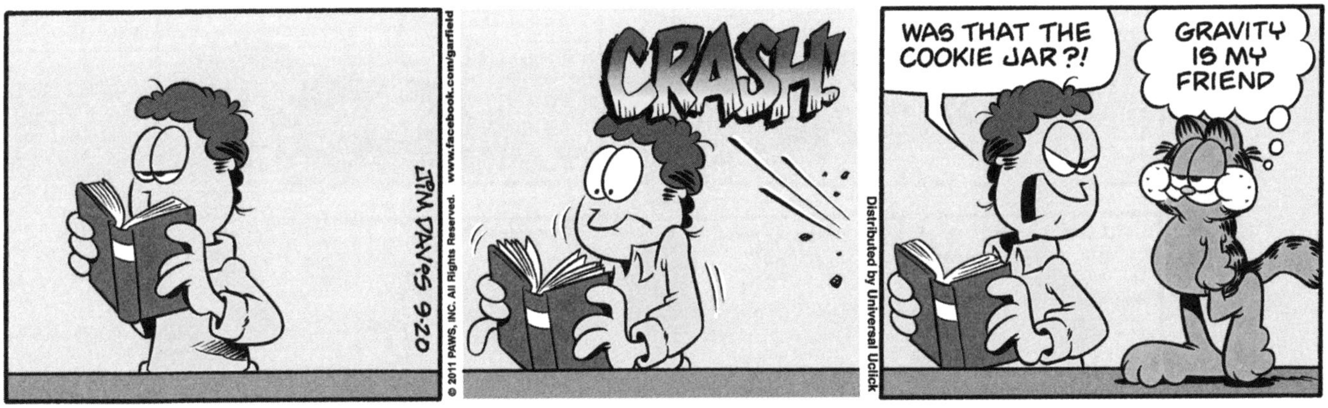
JIM DAVIS 9-20
© 2011 PAWS, INC. All Rights Reserved. www.facebook.com/garfield
CRASH!
Distributed by Universal Uclick
WAS THAT THE COOKIE JAR?!
GRAVITY IS MY FRIEND

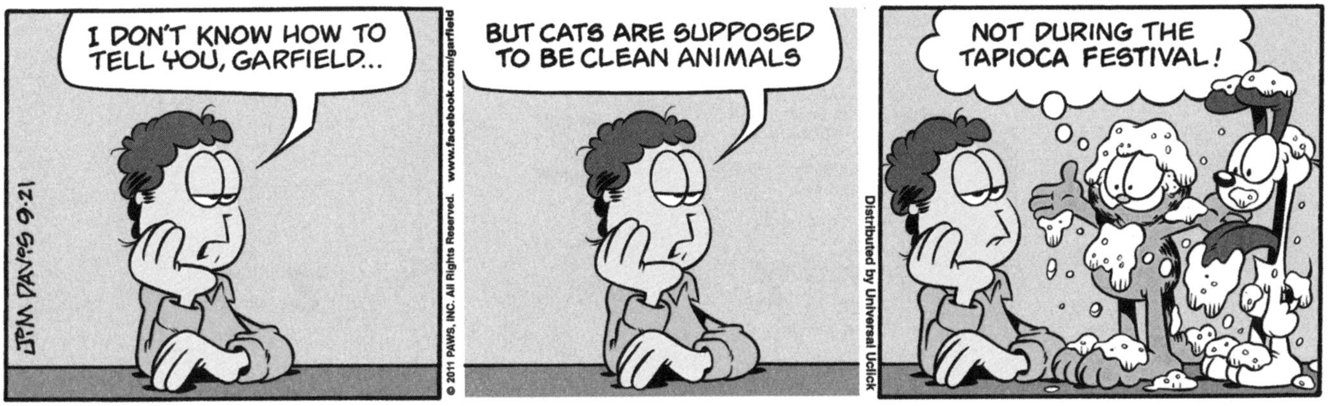
JIM DAVIS 9-21
I DON'T KNOW HOW TO TELL YOU, GARFIELD...
© 2011 PAWS, INC. All Rights Reserved. www.facebook.com/garfield
BUT CATS ARE SUPPOSED TO BE CLEAN ANIMALS
Distributed by Universal Uclick
NOT DURING THE TAPIOCA FESTIVAL!

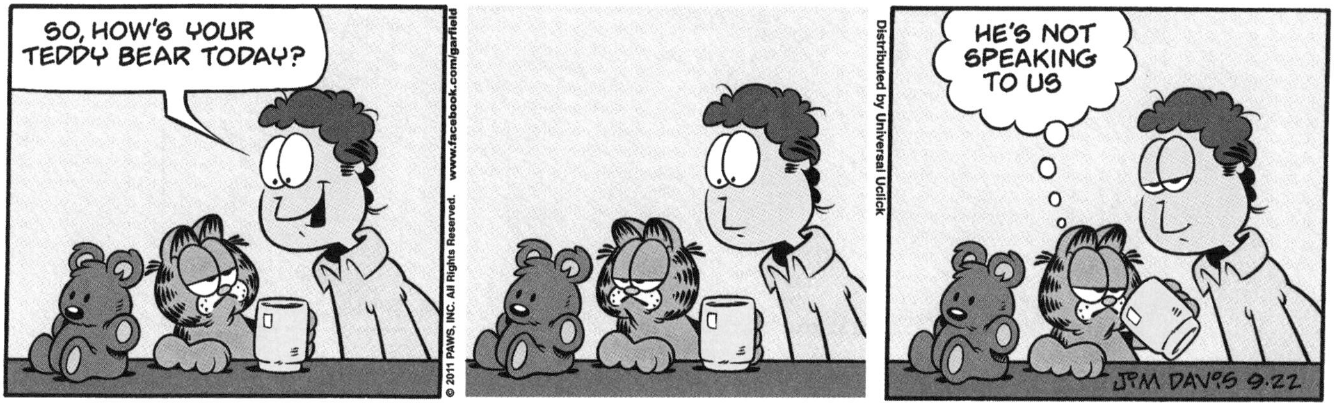
SO, HOW'S YOUR TEDDY BEAR TODAY?
HE'S NOT SPEAKING TO US
JIM DAVIS 9·22
© 2011 PAWS, INC. All Rights Reserved. www.facebook.com/garfield
Distributed by Universal Uclick

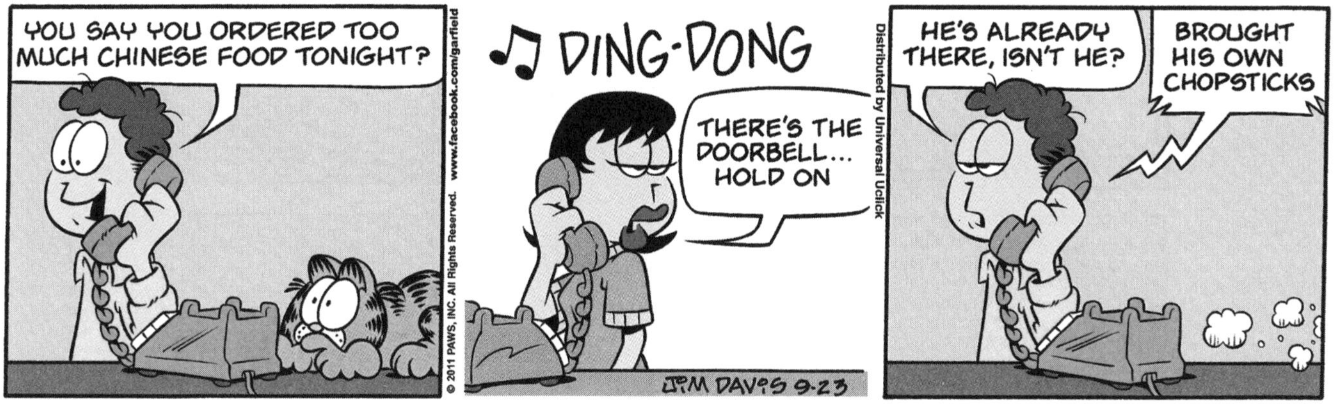
YOU SAY YOU ORDERED TOO MUCH CHINESE FOOD TONIGHT?
DING-DONG
THERE'S THE DOORBELL... HOLD ON
JIM DAVIS 9·23
HE'S ALREADY THERE, ISN'T HE?
BROUGHT HIS OWN CHOPSTICKS
© 2011 PAWS, INC. All Rights Reserved. www.facebook.com/garfield
Distributed by Universal Uclick

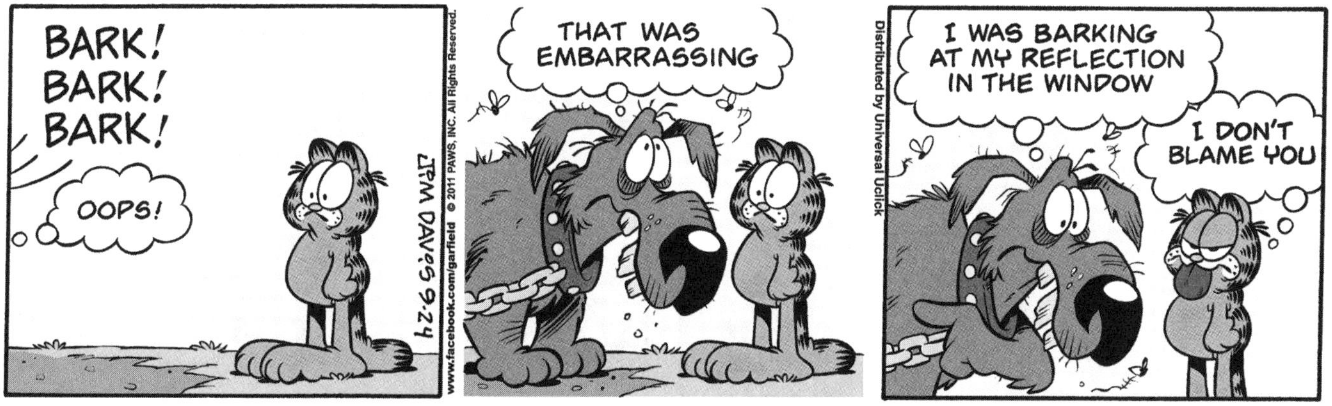
BARK! BARK! BARK!
OOPS!
JIM DAVIS 9·24
THAT WAS EMBARRASSING
I WAS BARKING AT MY REFLECTION IN THE WINDOW
I DON'T BLAME YOU
© 2011 PAWS, INC. All Rights Reserved. www.facebook.com/garfield
Distributed by Universal Uclick

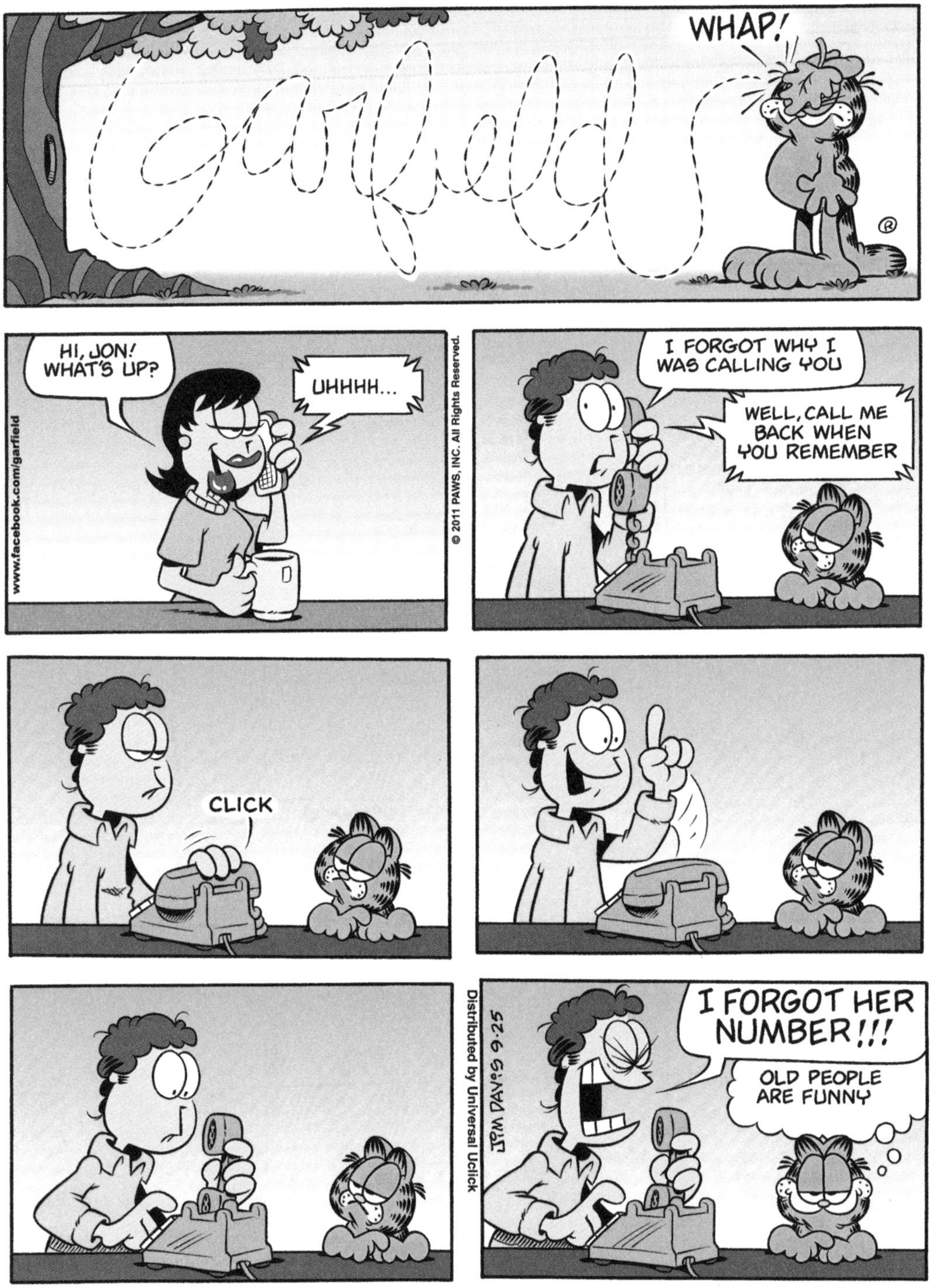
garfield
WHAP!
®
www.facebook.com/garfield
HI, JON! WHAT'S UP?
UHHHH...
© 2011 PAWS, INC. All Rights Reserved.
I FORGOT WHY I WAS CALLING YOU
WELL, CALL ME BACK WHEN YOU REMEMBER
CLICK
JPM DAVIS 9·25
Distributed by Universal Uclick
I FORGOT HER NUMBER!!!
OLD PEOPLE ARE FUNNY

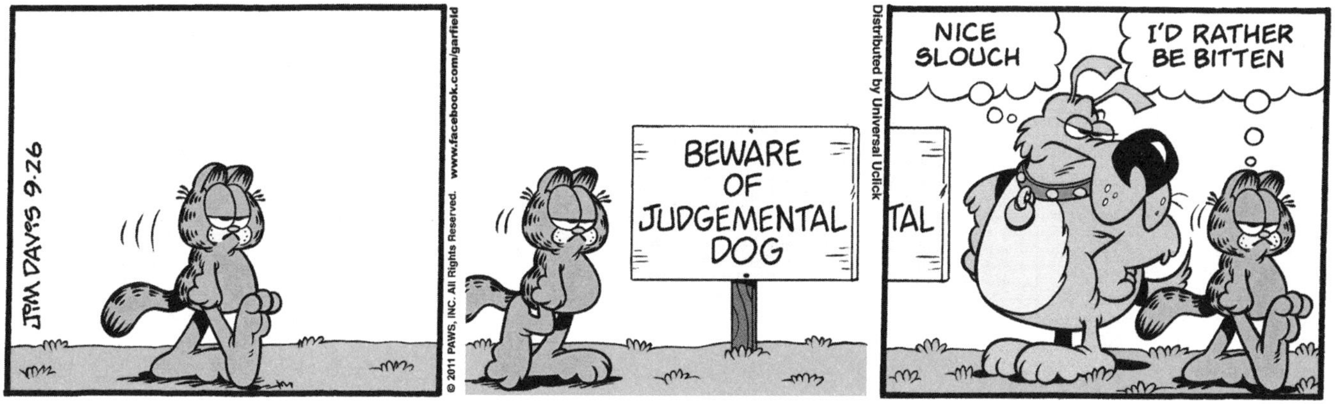
JIM DAVIS 9-26
© 2011 PAWS, INC. All Rights Reserved. www.facebook.com/garfield
BEWARE OF JUDGEMENTAL DOG
Distributed by Universal Uclick
TAL
NICE SLOUCH
I'D RATHER BE BITTEN

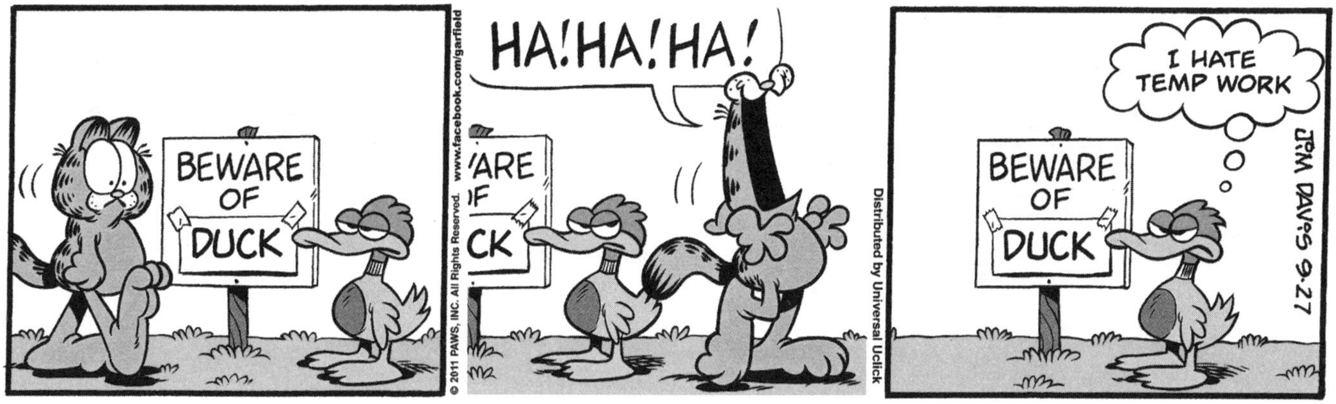
BEWARE OF DUCK
© 2011 PAWS, INC. All Rights Reserved. www.facebook.com/garfield
HA!HA!HA!
Distributed by Universal Uclick
I HATE TEMP WORK
BEWARE OF DUCK
JIM DAVIS 9-27

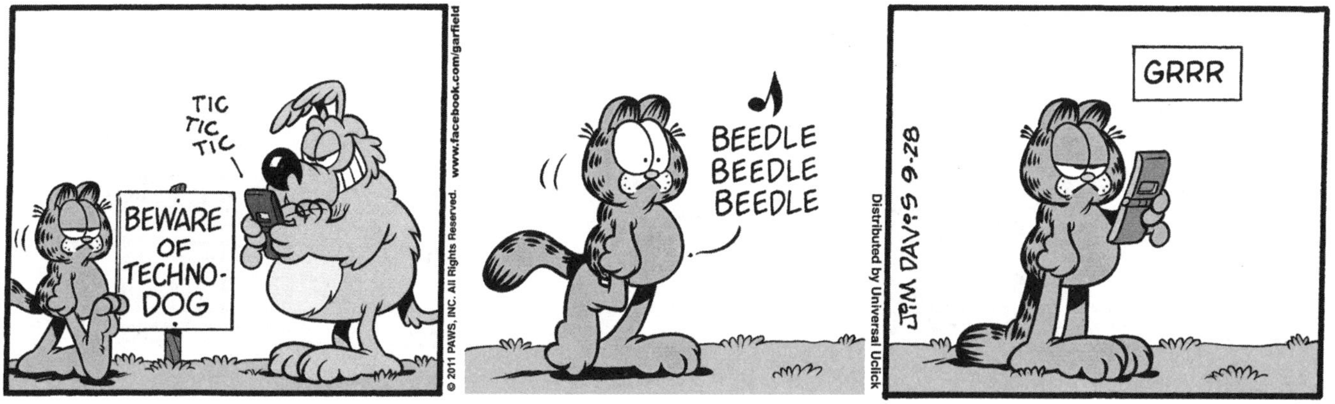
TIC TIC TIC
BEWARE OF TECHNO-DOG
© 2011 PAWS, INC. All Rights Reserved. www.facebook.com/garfield
BEEDLE BEEDLE BEEDLE
JIM DAVIS 9-28
Distributed by Universal Uclick
GRRR

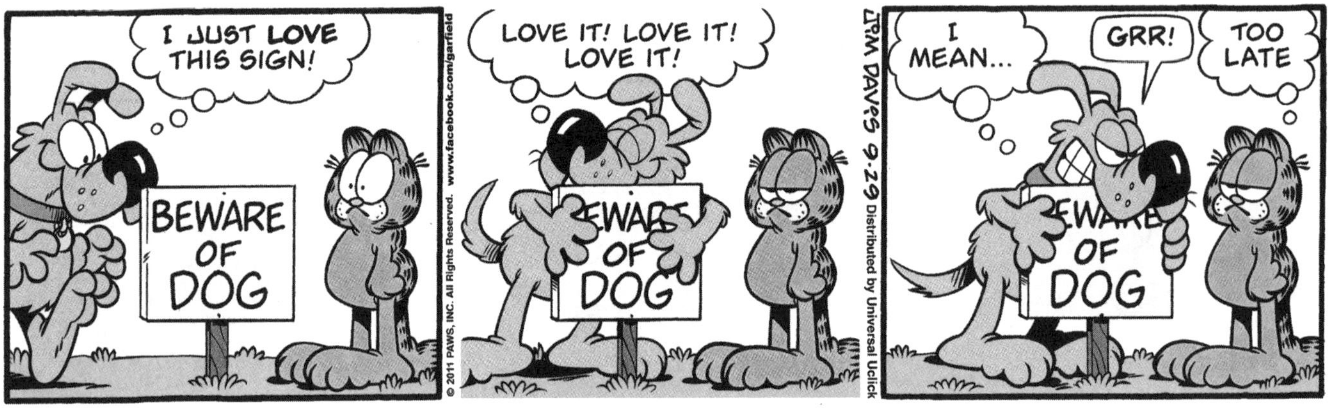
I JUST LOVE THIS SIGN!
BEWARE OF DOG
© 2011 PAWS, INC. All Rights Reserved. www.facebook.com/garfield
LOVE IT! LOVE IT! LOVE IT!
JIM DAVIS 9-29 Distributed by Universal Uclick
I MEAN...
GRR!
TOO LATE

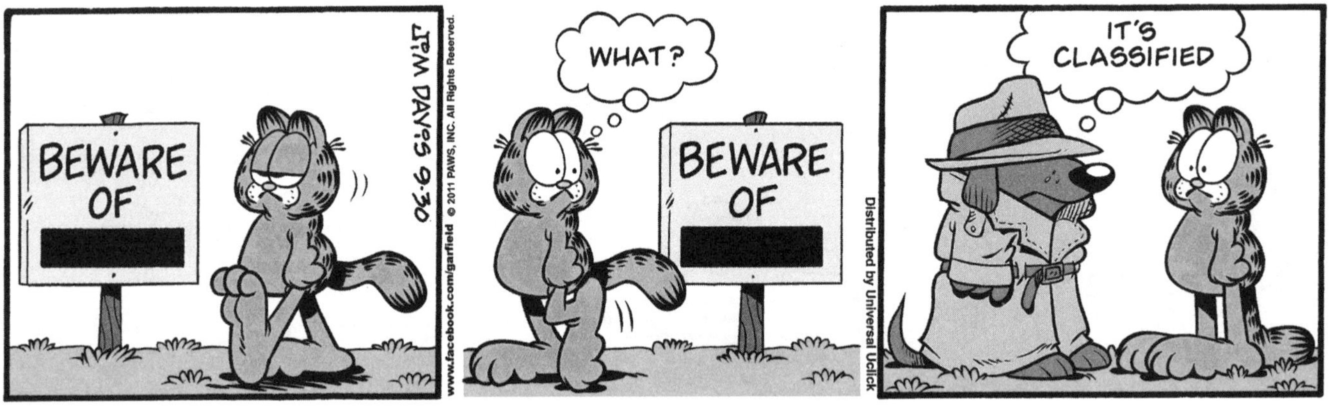
BEWARE OF
JIM DAVIS 9-30 www.facebook.com/garfield © 2011 PAWS, INC. All Rights Reserved.
WHAT?
BEWARE OF
Distributed by Universal Uclick
IT'S CLASSIFIED

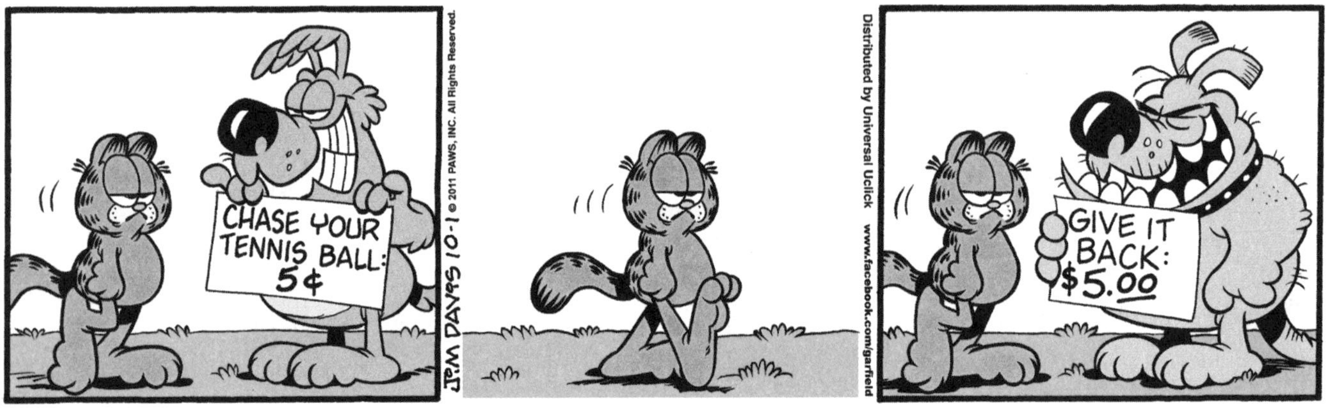
CHASE YOUR TENNIS BALL: 5¢
JIM DAVIS 10-1 © 2011 PAWS, INC. All Rights Reserved.
Distributed by Universal Uclick www.facebook.com/garfield
GIVE IT BACK: $5.00

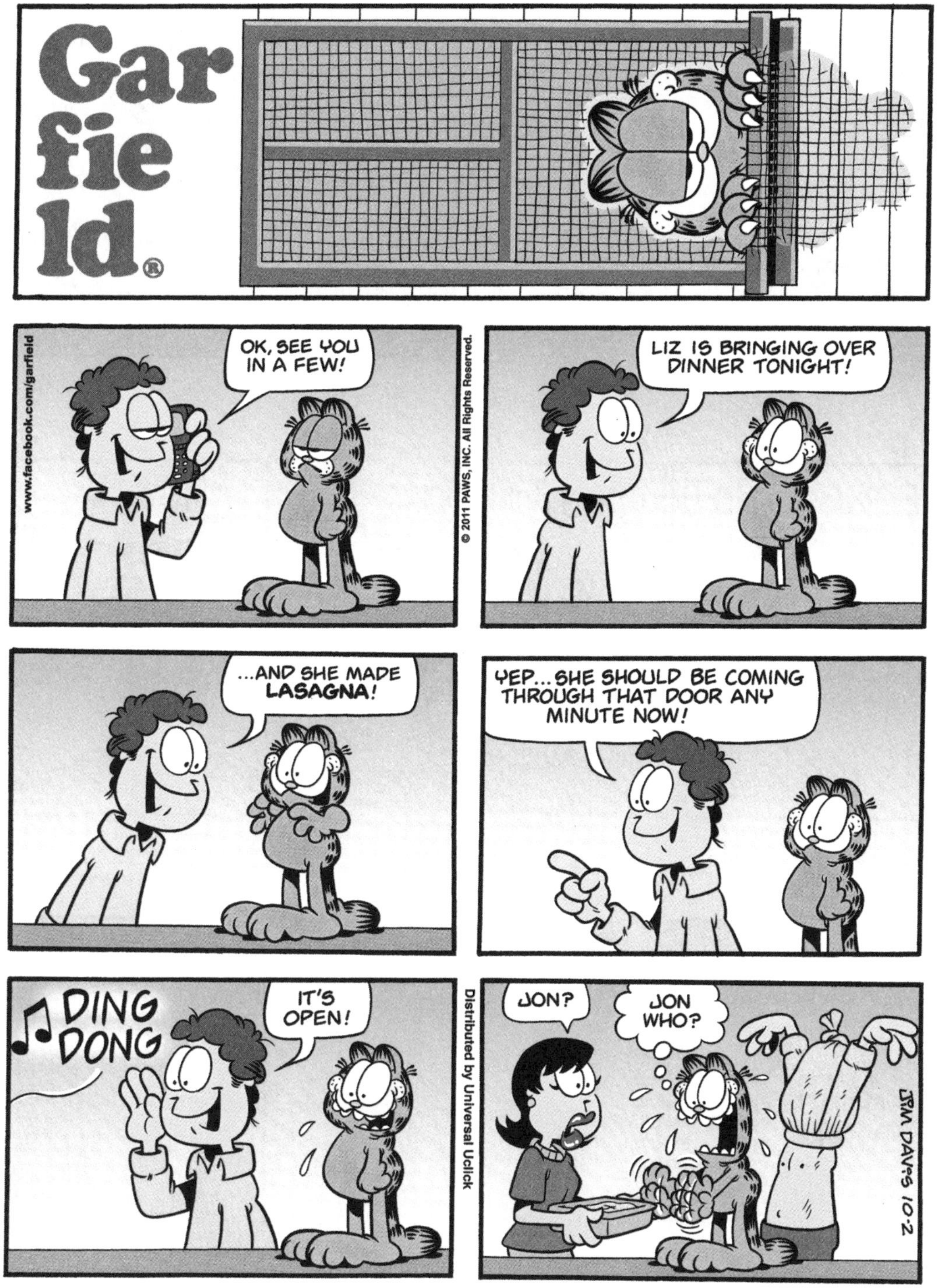
Garfield®
www.facebook.com/garfield
OK, SEE YOU IN A FEW!
© 2011 PAWS, INC. All Rights Reserved.
LIZ IS BRINGING OVER DINNER TONIGHT!
...AND SHE MADE LASAGNA!
YEP... SHE SHOULD BE COMING THROUGH THAT DOOR ANY MINUTE NOW!
DING DONG
IT'S OPEN!
Distributed by Universal Uclick
JON?
JON WHO?
JIM DAVIS 10-2

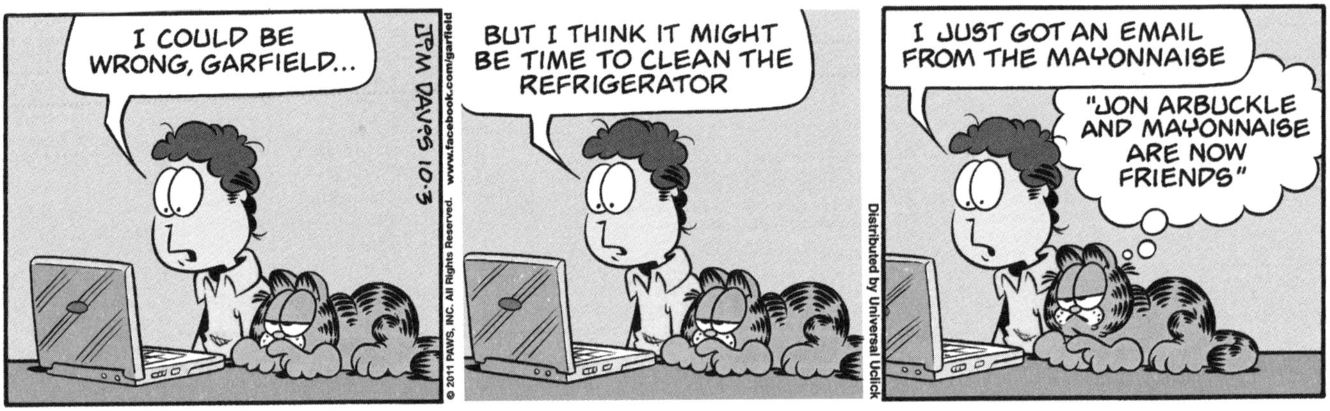
I COULD BE WRONG, GARFIELD...
JIM DAVIS 10-3
© 2011 PAWS, INC. All Rights Reserved. www.facebook.com/garfield
BUT I THINK IT MIGHT BE TIME TO CLEAN THE REFRIGERATOR
Distributed by Universal Uclick
I JUST GOT AN EMAIL FROM THE MAYONNAISE
"JON ARBUCKLE AND MAYONNAISE ARE NOW FRIENDS"

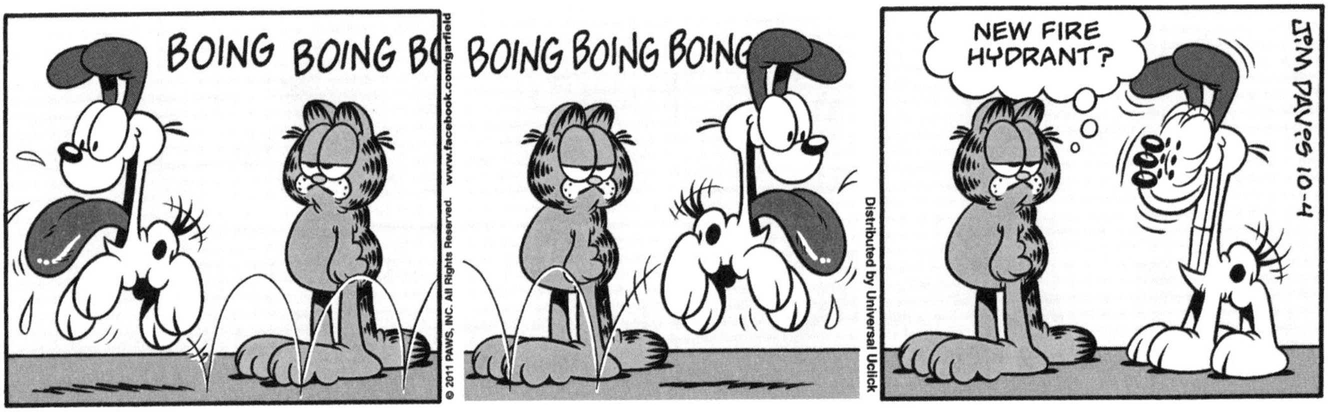
BOING BOING BO
© 2011 PAWS, INC. All Rights Reserved. www.facebook.com/garfield
BOING BOING BOING
Distributed by Universal Uclick
NEW FIRE HYDRANT?
JIM DAVIS 10-4

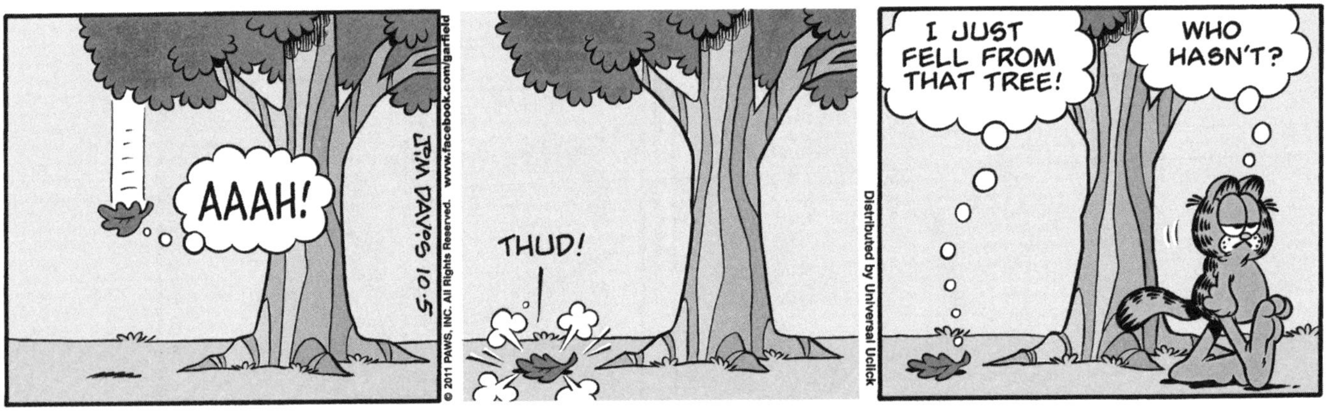
AAAH!
JIM DAVIS 10-5
© 2011 PAWS, INC. All Rights Reserved. www.facebook.com/garfield
THUD!
Distributed by Universal Uclick
I JUST FELL FROM THAT TREE!
WHO HASN'T?

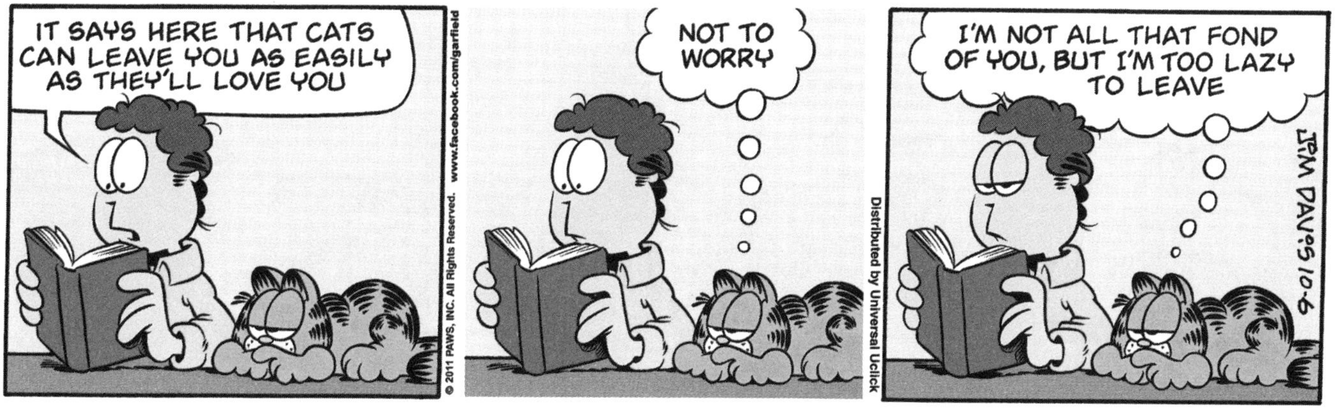
IT SAYS HERE THAT CATS CAN LEAVE YOU AS EASILY AS THEY'LL LOVE YOU
© 2011 PAWS, INC. All Rights Reserved. www.facebook.com/garfield
NOT TO WORRY
Distributed by Universal Uclick
I'M NOT ALL THAT FOND OF YOU, BUT I'M TOO LAZY TO LEAVE
JPM DAVIS 10-6

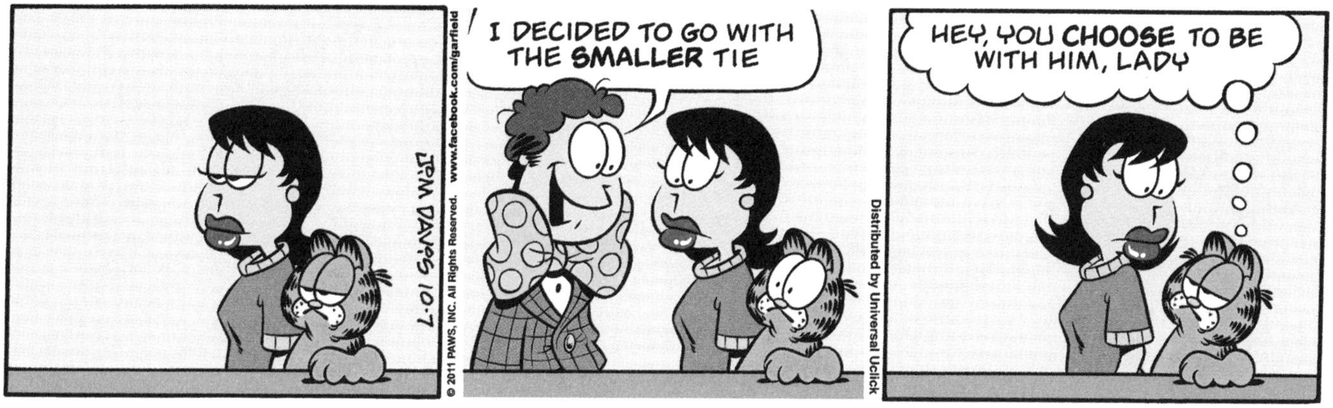
JPM DAVIS 10-7
© 2011 PAWS, INC. All Rights Reserved. www.facebook.com/garfield
I DECIDED TO GO WITH THE **SMALLER** TIE
Distributed by Universal Uclick
HEY, YOU **CHOOSE** TO BE WITH HIM, LADY

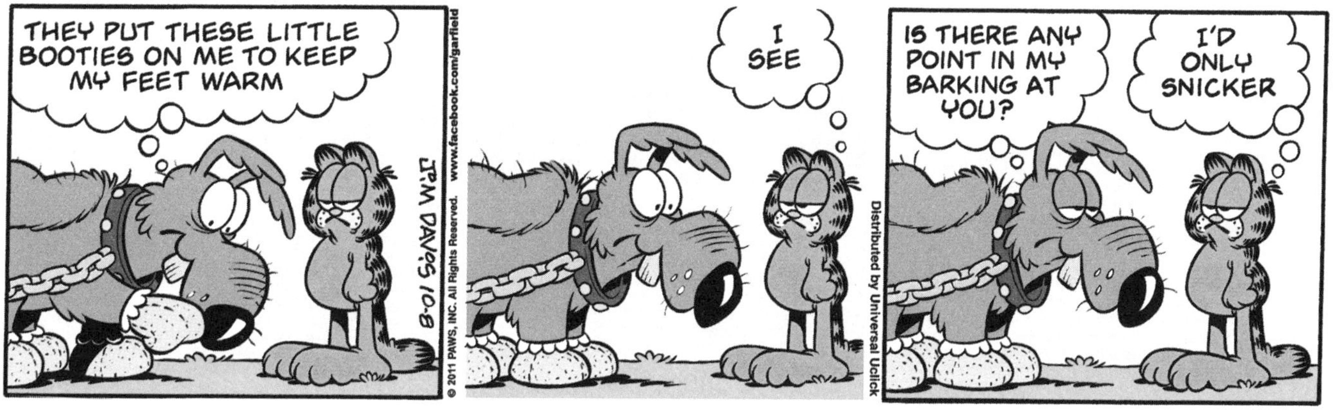
THEY PUT THESE LITTLE BOOTIES ON ME TO KEEP MY FEET WARM
JPM DAVIS 10-8
© 2011 PAWS, INC. All Rights Reserved. www.facebook.com/garfield
I SEE
Distributed by Universal Uclick
IS THERE ANY POINT IN MY BARKING AT YOU?
I'D ONLY SNICKER

VINTAGE GARFIELD

...from, like, the totally awesome '80s!

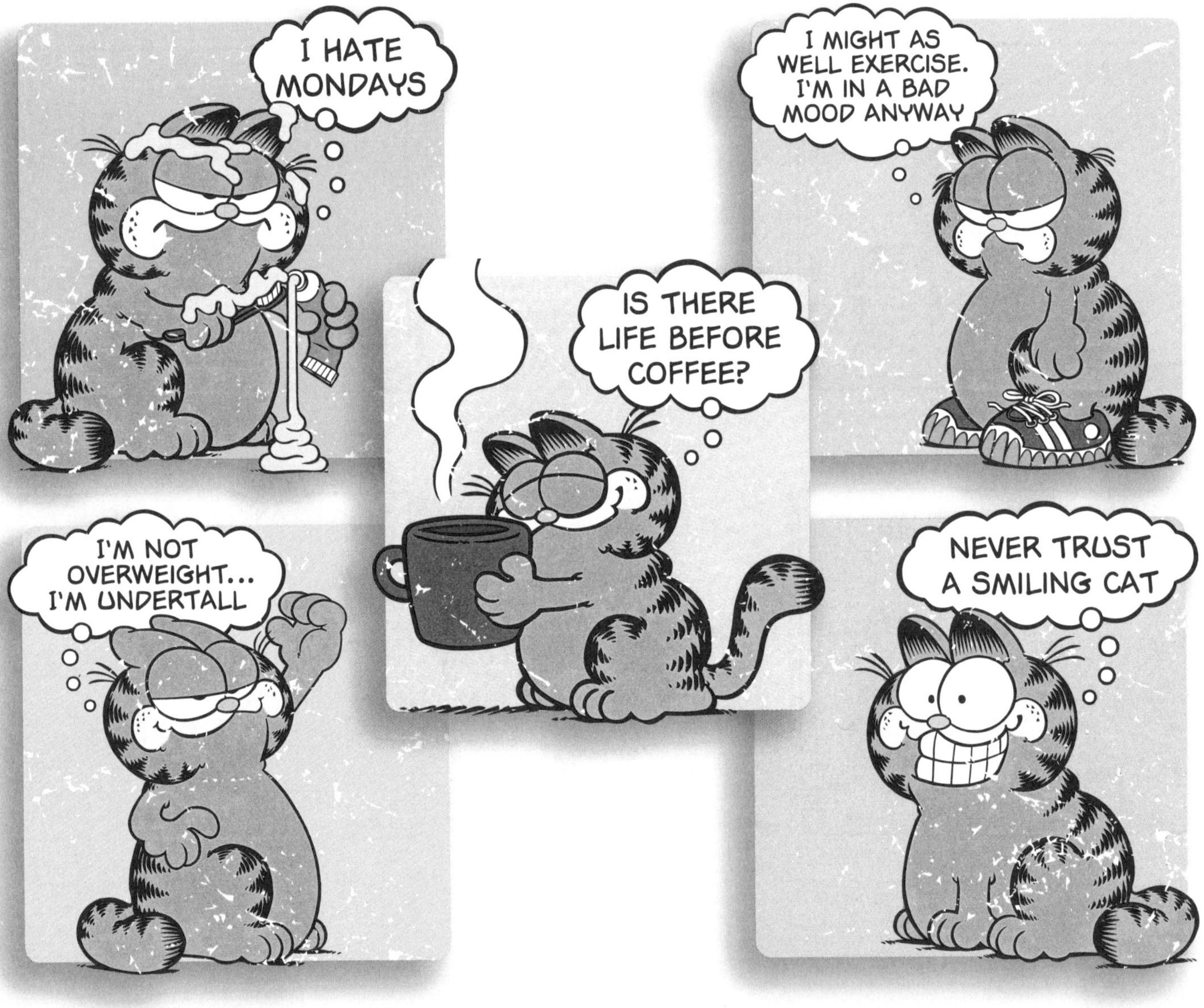
I HATE MONDAYS
I MIGHT AS WELL EXERCISE. I'M IN A BAD MOOD ANYWAY
IS THERE LIFE BEFORE COFFEE?
I'M NOT OVERWEIGHT... I'M UNDERTALL
NEVER TRUST A SMILING CAT

Watch. Read. Shop. Play.

DON'T FORGET THE SNACKS!

garfield.com

✱ *The Garfield Show*
Catch Garfield and the rest of the gang on *The Garfield Show*, now airing on Cartoon Network and Boomerang!

✱ The Comic Strip
Search & read thousands of GARFIELD® comic strips!

✱ Garfield on Facebook & Twitter
Join millions of Garfield friends on Facebook. Get your daily dose of humor and connect with other fat cat fans!

✱ Shop all the Garfield stores!
Original art & comic strips, books, apparel, personalized products, & more!

✱ Play FREE online Garfield games!
Plus, check out all of the FREE Garfield apps available for your smartphone, tablet, and other mobile devices.

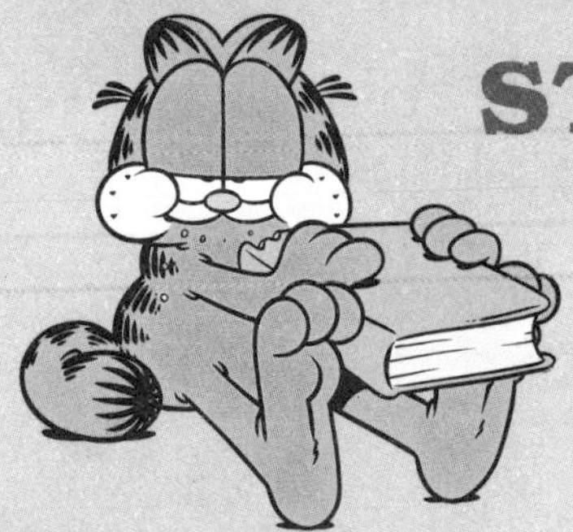

STRIPS, SPECIALS, OR BESTSELLING BOOKS . . . GARFIELD'S ON EVERYONE'S MENU.

Don't miss even one episode in the Tubby Tabby's hilarious series!

GARFIELD AT LARGE . . . . (#1) 978-0-345-44382-3
GARFIELD GAINS WEIGHT . . . . (#2) 978-0-345-44975-7
GARFIELD BIGGER THAN LIFE . . . . (#3) 978-0-345-45027-2
GARFIELD WEIGHS IN . . . . (#4) 978-0-345-45205-4
GARFIELD TAKES THE CAKE . . . . (#5) 978-0-345-44978-8
GARFIELD EATS HIS HEART OUT . . . . (#6) 978-0-345-46459-0
GARFIELD SITS AROUND THE HOUSE . . . . (#7) 978-0-345-46463-7
GARFIELD TIPS THE SCALES . . . . (#8) 978-0-345-46909-0
GARFIELD LOSES HIS FEET . . . . (#9) 978-0-345-46467-5
GARFIELD MAKES IT BIG . . . . (#10) 978-0-345-46468-2
GARFIELD ROLLS ON . . . . (#11) 978-0-345-47561-9
GARFIELD OUT TO LUNCH . . . . (#12) 978-0-345-47562-6
GARFIELD FOOD FOR THOUGHT . . . . (#13) 978-0-345-47563-3
GARFIELD SWALLOWS HIS PRIDE . . . . (#14) 978-0-345-91386-9
GARFIELD WORLDWIDE . . . . (#15) 978-0-345-91754-6
GARFIELD ROUNDS OUT . . . . (#16) 978-0-345-49169-5
GARFIELD CHEWS THE FAT . . . . (#17) 978-0-345-49170-1
GARFIELD GOES TO WAIST . . . . (#18) 978-0-345-49173-2
GARFIELD HANGS OUT . . . . (#19) 978-0-345-49174-9
GARFIELD TAKES UP SPACE . . . . (#20) 978-0-345-49178-7
GARFIELD SAYS A MOUTHFUL . . . . (#21) 978-0-345-49179-4
GARFIELD BY THE POUND . . . . (#22) 978-0-345-52558-1
GARFIELD KEEPS HIS CHINS UP . . . . (#23) 978-0-345-52559-8
GARFIELD TAKES HIS LICKS . . . . (#24) 978-0-345-52587-1
GARFIELD HITS THE BIG TIME . . . . (#25) 978-0-345-52589-5
GARFIELD PULLS HIS WEIGHT . . . . (#26) 978-0-345-52594-9
GARFIELD DISHES IT OUT . . . . (#27) 978-0-345-39287-9
GARFIELD LIFE IN THE FAT LANE . . . . (#28) 978-0-345-39776-8
GARFIELD TONS OF FUN . . . . (#29) 978-0-345-40386-5
GARFIELD BIGGER AND BETTER . . . . (#30) 978-0-345-40770-2
GARFIELD HAMS IT UP . . . . (#31) 978-0-345-41241-6
GARFIELD THINKS BIG . . . . (#32) 978-0-345-41671-1
GARFIELD THROWS HIS WEIGHT AROUND . . . . (#33) 978-0-345-42749-6
GARFIELD LIFE TO THE FULLEST . . . . (#34) 978-0-345-43239-1
GARFIELD FEEDS THE KITTY . . . . (#35) 978-0-345-43673-3
GARFIELD HOGS THE SPOTLIGHT . . . . (#36) 978-0-345-43922-2
GARFIELD BEEFS UP . . . . (#37) 978-0-345-44109-6
GARFIELD GETS COOKIN' . . . . (#38) 978-0-345-44582-7
GARFIELD EATS CROW . . . . (#39) 978-0-345-45201-6
GARFIELD SURVIVAL OF THE FATTEST . . . . (#40) 978-0-345-46458-3
GARFIELD OLDER AND WIDER . . . . (#41) 978-0-345-46462-0
GARFIELD PIGS OUT . . . . (#42) 978-0-345-46466-8
GARFIELD BLOTS OUT THE SUN . . . . (#43) 978-0-345-46615-0
GARFIELD GOES BANANAS . . . . (#44) 978-0-345-91346-3
GARFIELD LARGE & IN CHARGE . . . . (#45) 978-0-345-49172-5
GARFIELD SPILLS THE BEANS . . . . (#46) 978-0-345-49177-0
GARFIELD GETS HIS JUST DESSERTS . . . . (#47) 978-0-345-91387-6
GARFIELD WILL EAT FOR FOOD . . . . (#48) 978-0-345-49176-3
GARFIELD WEIGHS HIS OPTIONS . . . . (#49) 978-0-345-49181-7
GARFIELD POTBELLY OF GOLD . . . . (#50) 978-0-345-52244-3
GARFIELD SHOVELS IT IN . . . . (#51) 978-0-345-52419-5
GARFIELD LARD OF THE JUNGLE . . . . (#52) 978-0-345-52584-0
GARFIELD BRINGS HOME THE BACON . . . . (#53) 978-0-345-52586-4
GARFIELD GETS IN A PICKLE . . . . (#54) 978-0-345-52590-1
GARFIELD SINGS FOR HIS SUPPER . . . . (#55) 978-0-345-52593-2
GARFIELD CAUTION: WIDE LOAD . . . . (#56) 978-0-345-52596-3

DVD TIE-INS

GARFIELD AS HIMSELF 978-0-345-47805-4
GARFIELD HOLIDAY CELEBRATIONS 978-0-345-47930-3
GARFIELD TRAVEL ADVENTURES 978-0-345-48087-3

AND DON'T MISS . . .

GARFIELD AT 25: IN DOG YEARS I'D BE DEAD 978-0-345-45204-7
GARFIELD'S JOKE ZONE/INSULTS 978-0-345-46263-3
GARFIELD FAT CAT 3-PACK/ VOL. 1 978-0-345-46455-2
GARFIELD FAT CAT 3-PACK/ VOL. 2 978-0-345-46465-1
GARFIELD FAT CAT 3-PACK/ VOL. 3 978-0-345-48088-0
GARFIELD FAT CAT 3-PACK/ VOL. 4 978-0-345-49171-8
GARFIELD FAT CAT 3-PACK/ VOL. 5 978-0-345-49180-8
GARFIELD FAT CAT 3-PACK/ VOL. 6 978-0-345-52420-1
GARFIELD FAT CAT 3-PACK/ VOL. 7 978-0-345-52588-8
GARFIELD FAT CAT 3-PACK/ VOL. 13 978-0-345-46460-6
GARFIELD FAT CAT 3-PACK/ VOL. 14 978-0-345-49175-6
GARFIELD FAT CAT 3-PACK/ VOL. 15 978-0-345-52585-7
GARFIELD FAT CAT 3-PACK/ VOL. 16 978-0-345-52592-5
SEASON'S EATINGS: A VERY MERRY GARFIELD CHRISTMAS 978-0-345-47560-2
GARFIELD'S GUIDE TO EVERYTHING 978-0-345-46461-3
ODIE UNLEASHED! 978-0-345-46464-4
GARFIELD'S BOOK OF CAT NAMES 978-0-345-48516-8
THE GARFIELD JOURNAL 978-0-345-46469-9
LIGHTS, CAMERA, HAIRBALLS!: GARFIELD AT THE MOVIES 978-0-345-49134-3
30 YEARS OF LAUGHS AND LASAGNA 978-0-345-50379-4
GARFIELD MINUS GARFIELD 978-0-345-51387-8
GARFIELD FROM THE TRASH BIN 978-0-345-51881-1
GARFIELD LEFT SPEECHLESS 978-0-345-53058-5
MY LAUGHABLE LIFE WITH GARFIELD 978-0-345-52591-8
GARFIELD'S SUNDAY FINEST 978-0-345-52597-0

New larger, full-color format! (marked titles #1–#26)